TÀPIES

WITNESS OF SILENCE

T À P

Alexandre Cirici

I E S

WITNESS OF SILENCE

TUDOR PUBLISHING COMPANY
NEW YORK

SPANISH ART LIBRARY

TUDOR PUBLISHING COMPANY
NEW YORK

Lay-out: JUAN PEDRAGOSA

© Ediciones Polígrafa, S. A. - Dep. Legal: B. 1279 -1972 - Printed in Spain

Contents

TÀPIES, WITNESS OF SILENCE

FOREWORD

Like a moving net. In making an attempt to read the work of Tàpies, we must endeavour not to confuse our methodology with positivity. As Foucault says, there is an archaeological ramification in the laws governing the formation of facts which does not constitute a uniformly simultaneous net. Some of the knots are temporarily neutral, but almost all of them indicate a definite course in time.

That is why we must be particularly wary of following strictly logical schemes; nor shall we be satisfied, however, with a merely linear succession of events. We shall let ourselves be guided by warp or woof, whichever happens to be dominant, and if at the beginning the overall pattern seems rather markedly diachronic, it will only be so as a preparation for the rest of our consideration of this phenomenon.

In the final summing-up, perhaps we shall see the whole as something fixed, fixed as in a past that always tends to mummification; then, surely, we shall turn for a last look, in an attempt to synchronize, and it is there that we shall find the balance sheets of criticism.

In summing up we shall also see the personage turning into a personality. Not the man we first met at the age of twenty-five, nor yet the man we have seen approaching his fifties. A personality of oily pallor, with the pupils of his eyes dilated under their meeting brows, the hair springing straight up from his head, the muscles of his face contracted as his smile suddenly comes and goes, his body bending easily to a gentle amiability that makes his conversation a thing of softness punctuated by outbursts of irritation soon restrained and a certain expression of anguish.

A man whose eyes sometimes flash with anger, one who gives the general impression of wanting to give his whole heart without quite daring to.

From the praxis. Every work of art — or of anything else — belongs to a time, a place and a man.

When it is said that thought often takes place even behind a man's back, this reveals to us the hierarchy of this order, in which the dia-chronic, historical element is the first, the synchronic structure of the system of values of a culture the second and the specific biology of the personage the third. A man's painting is, first and foremost, the product of some given situation of society. This is brought about through the system of rites and myths with which society permits, in this situation, the necessary intercommunication. Finally, it is there that the position of any one man, on the basis of his resolution, facilitates work, sensibility and the faculty of coherence with others, to the point of being their medium.

The make-believe science of sociology, or the anthropology that takes its place, may explain the most general level. A semeiology, the second level. A personal monograph, like the one we are undertaking, the third, which has to take the other two for granted. But if we admit that all valid philosophy is born of praxis, perhaps it is only suitable that our examination of the particular case of Tàpies should help us, in the inverse sense, to sketch the structural background against which he stands and, at a greater distance, the historical situation.

The statistical bath. We give this explanation because we do not wish to mythify our personage after the fashion of Vasari. Because, like Leontiev, we believe that nobody can succeed in thinking logically or establishing a system of ideas merely through his personal experience, however rich it may be, and we agree with Wundt that the specific character of a man's activities is not to be found in the func-

tions of his brain but rather in systems of relationships provided by the development of the individual within the society in which he lives. For we know that a child does not learn to see things directly but rather to seek the reaction of the universe, the reaction the universe elicits from others, starting with its mother's look and smile. While an animal learns by sheer adaptation, a child does so by appropriation through a series of images —among them words— which he takes from his society and which make available within him a whole world of duplicate objects of his own, a world without which thought would be impossible.

This subject leads us to think of the childhood of Antoni Tàpies, and to endeavour to envisage that statistical bath of information which, in the luminous phrase of Abraham Moles, must have lapped about his childhood.

Tàpies photographed by Català
Roca, Summer, 1969.

1. Drawing on paper, 1946. Private collection, Barcelona.
2. India ink. Drawing on paper, 1945. Private collection, Barcelona.

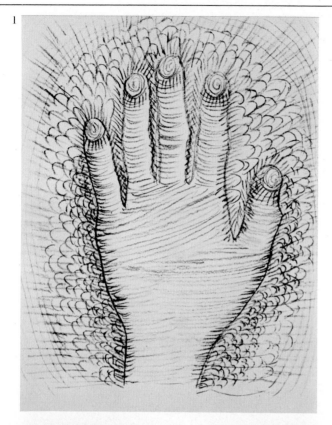

THE MAN AND HIS SURROUNDINGS

Families. It may be as well to remember that Tàpies was born into a family belonging to the more educated kind of middle class.

His maternal great-grandfather, the bookseller Eudald Puig, was born in Ripoll in 1829. At the age of eleven he moved to Barcelona, where he opened a bookshop in 1861. In an age of so few bookshops, this meant a very high level of intellectual devotion. Moreover, through his uninterrupted contacts with Ripoll, he must have lived through those heroic moments of the Catalan *Renaissance* when Elias Rogent, on the initiative of Bishop Morgades, was restoring the monastery of that town, which was the materialization of the great myth of the nascent Romanesque Catalonia, the

3. Paris pencil. Drawing on paper, 1945. Private collection, Barcelona.

4. Self-portrait. Lead-pencil drawing on paper, 1945. Private collection, Barcelona.

5. Portrait. Charcoal drawing on paper, 1944. Private collection, Barcelona.

6. Cover design for the review *Dau al Set*. Drawing on paper, 1949. Private collection, Barcelona.

7. Self-portrait. Lead-pencil drawing on paper, 1947. Private collection, Barcelona.

8. Self-portrait. Lead-pencil drawing on paper, 1946. Private collection, Barcelona.

mausoleum of the counts who had ruled Barcelona and the temple of the Christian-historical mythology of Verdaguer's poem *El canigó*, agrarian, traditional and emotive.

9. Lead-pencil drawing on paper, 1945. Private collection, Barcelona.
10. Lead-pencil drawing on paper, 1946. Private collection, Barcelona.
11. Design for the review *Dau al Set*. Drawing on paper, 1949. Private collection, Barcelona.

a) Tàpies as seen by Enric Tormo, 1949.

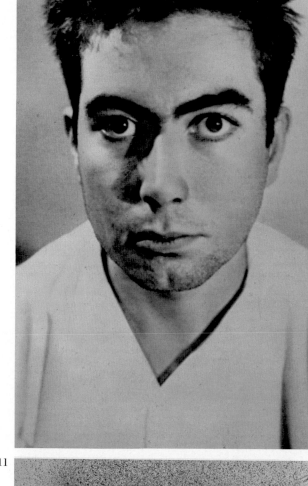

a

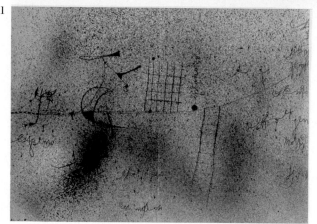

12. Lead-pencil drawing on paper, 1946. Private collection, Barcelona.
13. Lead-pencil drawing on paper. Reproduced in *Dau al Set*, 1949. Private collection, Barcelona.

He brought out various publications, among them *La Locomotora*, edited by Duran i Bas, from 1845 on, and he married an actress: Anna Alfonso. He died in 1891. The paternal grandfather, Antoni Tàpies, married to Josefa Mestres, was an ex-seminarist who trained as a teacher but never taught; instead he set up in a lamp shop, with plumbing on the side, in the street known as the Carrer de Barberà. Both he, who was probably the more liberal, and the painter's maternal grandfather, Francesc Puig i Alfonso, married to Encarnació Guerra i Pitxot —names very typical of the Empordany region in the north of Catalonia— were born around the time when the old Floral Games were restored in Catalonia, and their youth coincided with the development of urban culture in Barcelona, about the time of the Universal Exhibition of 1888, which was in fact organized during the mayoralty of Rius i Taulet, one of whose deputy

14. Crayon drawing on paper, 1946. 29×22 cm. Private collection, Barcelona.
15. India-ink drawing on paper, 1949. Private collection, Barcelona.

mayors was Eudald Puig. Both sides of the painter's family were by now living in Barcelona and they formed part of the generation which brought about the triumph of Catalanism in the elections of 1901. Francesc Puig i Alfonso took an active part in politics as a member of the *Lliga Regionalista*, the liberal-conservative party of the centre, the more leftist members of which were not to break away until 1922. Puig i Alfonso played an important role here after the party's defeat in the 1903 elections thanks to its alliance with the right wing, for he represented the new combative spirit which was to win the party the 1905 elections. At that time he formed part of the group of Duran i Ventosa, Ferran de Segarra, Pere Rahola, Ventosa i Calvell and others, whose manifesto was Duran's book *Regionalisme i Federalisme*, in his prologue to which Prat de la Riba wrote the fundamental part of his doctrine of *La Nacionali-*

14

15

tat Catalana. Puig i Alfonso and his colleagues were triumphant in the elections held on November 12th 1905, and to celebrate this they held the famous *Victory Banquet* in the Frontó Comtal, which provoked the well-known antimilitarist caricature in the *Cu-cut,* the attack on this paper among other consequences, Colonel Macià's farewell to the army and the founding of *Solidaritat Catalana,* which was to return 41 deputies out of 44 in 1907. Apart from his political activities, which led him to follow in his father's footsteps as deputy mayor of Barcelona, Francesc Puig i Alfonso was a very well-known bookseller, with his shop in the Plaça Nova, and participated in the cultural expression of the movement known as *noucentisme* (literally, "1900-ism") when he founded, with the printer Ramón Tobella, the excellent publishing firm called the *Societat Catalana d'Edicions.*

The Parents. Antoni Tàpies' father, Josep Tàpies i Mestres, son of the other Antoni, was the typical well-off Barcelona lawyer, married to Maria Puig i Guerra, the daughter of Puig i Alfonso. In his professional career he inherited the practice of Lluhí i Rissech, together with Lluhí i Ballescà and Pere Comes i Calvet. Among his closer relatives there was one very well-known figure, his first cousin Jaume Mestres i Fossas, an architect who represented, long before the creation of the G.A.T.C.P.A.C.*, the progressive tendency in Catalonia towards the new ideas expressed in reinforced concrete and cubistic forms, as conceived by Auguste and Gustave Perret. Mestres was a typical representative of the leftwing bourgeoisie; he designed the *Mutua Escolar Blanquerna* and later became the first architect to the Catalan Government, for which he designed the Departments of Health and Finance.

* "Group of Catalan Artists and Technicians for the Progress of Contemporary Architecture".

a) Campins. Photograph by Joaquim Gomis.

b, c, d, e, f) The house and the studio at Campins. Photographs by Català Roca and Joaquim Gomis.

Josep Tàpies, though married to a deeply religious woman, was a Catalan nationalist, a materialist and an atheist, carrying this last credo to the unusual lengths, for that time, of never attending even a First Communion. The painter's mother, despite a family background that made her more faithful to tradition, had a marked propensity to innovation, as may be seen in her fondness for moving house, from the old part of Barcelona to the *Eixampla* (the quadricular extension planned by Ildefons Cerdà), from the Eixampla to the newly developed upper part of the town; she also had a weakness for constantly changing the rooms around, buying new furniture and selling the old pieces to the rag-and-bone man. Josep, though he had no sensibility in plastic art, was nevertheless a great lover of poetry and music, being a fervent Wagnerian. He also had an extensive library and wrote not a few books himself, which have remained unpublished: poetry, short stories, novels, essays and translations. All his writing is pervaded by a taste for mystery and the extraordinary.

Josep Tàpies and Maria Puig had four children: Maria Josepa, the elder daughter, who is married and has also become a painter in later life, Antoni, the painter, Enric and Maria dels Angels, who has also painted, signing her works "Angels T.". She is now a widow and lives in Italy with her three children.

Josep Tàpies practised mainly as a juridical adviser in Barcelona. The family at first spent the summer months in Puigcerdà, but later in Tona, on account of the reputed healing properties of the malodorous waters of the place.

When Antoni Tàpies i Puig was born, in 1923, the year of the Dictatorship of Primo de Rivera, his parents were living in the Carrer de la Canuda, but soon afterwards they moved, significantly enough to the 4th District, the quarter of the well-to-do bourgeoisie; their new address was in the Gran Via, near the Carrer del Bruc, and there they stayed throughout the Dictatorship. When this ended and the Republic was proclaimed, they lived for a short time in the Carrer d'Aragó, between the Rambla de Catalunya and the Carrer de Balmes. Shortly afterwards, however, the family moved to the upper part of

Barcelona, to number 97 in the newly laid out Travessera de Gràcia, just beside the Carrer de Regàs. Quite near them at that time were the Europa football club and the great pine wood of Laforja. But when the football field was built over they moved again, this time to number 207 in the Carrer de Balmes, which is where we first knew them.

In 1926, at the age of three, Antoni had been sent to school at the Loreto convent in the former palace of the Simon family, on the corner of Claris and Mallorca, but his father soon managed to send him to the German School in the Carrer de Moià, in order to get him away from clerical influences. Later on, in 1931, his mother's ideas and Antoni's own dislike of this school caused him to be sent to the Col·legi Balmes, which was run by the Piarist Fathers right in front of his house, and there he began his secondary studies in 1934.

During the Spanish Civil War Josep Tàpies became a civil servant in the Catalan Government, in the department run by his friend Closas, father of the famous actor, Albert Closas. Antoni continued his studies at the Liceu Pràctic, in the Rambla del Prat, and finished them after 1939, first at the Institut Menéndez y Pelayo and later returning to the Col·legi Balmes. In one of the air raids on the city some very heavy bombing completely destroyed his grandfather Puig i Alfonso's bookshop in the Plaça Nova.

At the end of his life Josep Tàpies went through a religious crisis. He died in 1958.

Houses and Schools. Antoni Tàpies has no memories of the house in the Carrer de la Canuda where he was born. But he does remember the other four, in the Gran Via, in the Carrer d'Aragó, in the Travessera de Gràcia and in the Carrer de Balmes. As to the houses in

a) The studio at Campins. Photograph: Català Roca.
b) Teresa and Antoni Tàpies as seen by Eduard Torras, 1964.

a

b

themselves, he remembers nothing
particularly outstanding, except
that the furniture, objects and pictures were more often than not
in bad taste. Of the schools he attended he retains a rather negative
impression. The Loreto nuns, for
instance, terrified him. They used
to make the children walk in line
by threatening them with an instrument called the *xasca*, which
sounded like a spectacle case and

a, b, c)   The house at Campins, by Català Roca.

b

c

gave you the feeling that you were going to be pinched. Everything was done by terror. Even to preach virtue to their charges, the nuns had a red velvet cushion in the shape of a heart; this represented the Sacred Heart of Jesus and was stuck all over with pins representing sins. The children had to walk past it in procession and each of them had to take out one of the pins, as a symbol of a good action. This was a cause of great fear and distress to the little Antoni, not yet three years old.

In his obsession with this practice, when he got home he used to play at pushing pins into the little velvet pincushions on his mother's sewing table and pulling them out again, with all the excitement of a child's sadic-masochistic game. The years he later spent at the German School left a deep mark on him. There can be no doubt that this school, in its strictness, in the very way things were done there,

frightened him, and he was very happy when his mother had him removed. And yet in this very fear there was something of admiration. The idea that the Germans were the finest people in the world, in a romantic admiration both for their physical constitution and for their culture and music. A handful of *lieders* have stayed with him among his happiest childhood memories. Through the influence of his father, moreover, from a very early age he connected the romantic vision of an ideal Germany with the strength, the violence and the obscure inner life of Wagner's music.

The spirit that presided over this sensitization was connected with some of the books that Tàpies found in his home during his childhood and adolescence, books that belonged rather to the cultural generation of his grandparents than to that of his parents. I can understand this very well because they are the same books I found at home my-

a) Lluís M. Riera, Arnald Puig, Tàpies and Joan Brossa during one of the stays made at Riera's house at Fuirosos, Montnegre, 1949.

b) Tàpies, Pere Portabella, Josep-Lluís Sert, Joan Prats and Joan Brossa at Campins, Summer, 1967.

by Dostoievsky, Ibsen and Oscar Wilde.

All of this means, among other things, a mixture of naturalism and symbolism; of an interest in the profound, instinctive forms of life and in the right to freedom; of a taste for passionate enthusiasm, for purification achieved through a *Descensus Averni*, but also for the cynical intelligence that overleaps taboos and guarantees the independence of superior beings.

Tàpies' father, in common with many of his contemporaries, combined his love of Wagner with admiration for Maragall. Not, of course, for the bourgeois Maragall, but for the pantheist who seeks *to savour the secrets of the mysterious earth*, the one who, like Haidé, liberates love from human laws, in his *L'Excelsior* preaches the abandonment of ports and beaches and with his theory of the living word places the spontaneity of expression before thought itself.

self, where all the books were from my mother's early youth, the Art Nouveau period. Tàpies, then, nine years younger than I, read the Russian novelists at a very early age —he was very much impressed

c) Tàpies during a visit to Picasso at Notre-Dame-de-Vie, 1967. Photograph
by Jacint Reventós.

a) With Joan Miró at Son Abrines, 1958.

a

The Spanish Civil War.

Tàpies was twelve years old when the Civil War broke out. On July 19th of 1936 he was spending his summer holidays in Puigcerdà with his family. For a month they were separated from his father, who had remained in Barcelona, where they dared not go at first. Later on they came down to the city on a train of the International Brigade.

His memories of the war are terrible. One raid came very close to where he was working, in his father's office at the *Generalitat* (the seat of the Catalan Government); the marks can still be seen on the walls of the church of Saint Philip Neri and in the Carrer del Bisbe. On other occasions bombs destroyed his grandfather Puig i Alfonso's bookshop in the Plaça Nova, the painter's birthplace in the Carrer de la Canuda and his grandfather's flat in the Carrer dels Arcs. When this last bomb fell, his grandfather and his aunts came to his house for shelter, arriving covered in blood from the wounds caused by the broken glass. But his most poignant memory of all is that of having seen his mother crying with hunger. One Sunday she had spent the whole afternoon making doughnuts

a) The painter Antonio Saura, Tàpies, Rodolph Stadler and the Japanese
   painter Domoto, at the Venice Biennale in 1958.
b) Cover of a number of the Japanese art review «Mizue» dedicated to Tàpies.

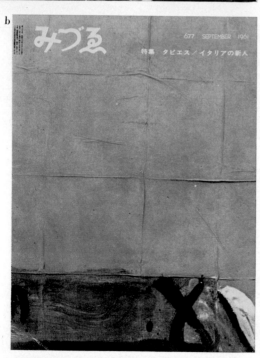

oster by Tàpies in Paris, advertising an exhibition at the Galerie Maeght.
Stills from Clovis Prevost's film about Tàpies, 1969.

g) Still from Rolph Wohlin's film about Tàpies, 1967.
h) Preparatory work for *El pa a la barca*, in the studio at Campins.

32

a to l) Tàpies at work, photographed by Ralph Hermann, 1967.

m) Tàpies as seen by the American photographer Arnold Newman, in the Barcelona studio in 1965.

m

a, b, c) Working on a lithographic stone at St. Gallen (Photographs by Ruedi Mettler).

a, b, c) Working on a lithographic stone at St. Gallen (Photographs by Ruedi Mettler).

with a little maize, which was all she had left in the house. Round the table that evening everybody started eating them so quickly that there were none left for her, and she burst into tears.

Tàpies was fifteen years old when the war ended.

Sickness and crisis. It is difficult now to re-create the feeling of the immediate postwar years, so much do they belong to a strange world. The atmosphere was pervaded by irrationality. Just after the Civil War, when he was finishing his secondary studies, Tàpies had a heart attack, which produced se-

d) Working on the mural for the library of the University of St. Gallen, 1962 (Architect: Walter Förderer).

e) Fixing of the mural of the University of St. Gallen.

Works in the Barcelona studio, photographed by Català Roca.

d

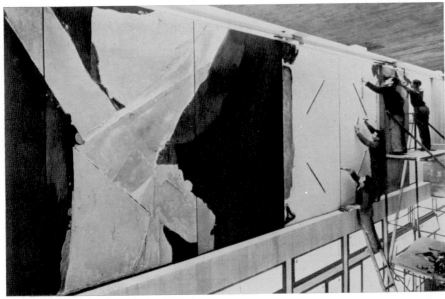

e

vere shock and left him with breathing difficulties which upset him very much. These difficulties lasted for years, but instead of pulling him down they stimulated him. Through some strange phenomenon, moreover, they gave him a peculiar clairvoyance, something he compares to the result of certain breathing exercises of Yoga. Later he caught a tubercular infection, which prevented him from taking the State examination for university entrance until he was well again. Jacint Raventós made him a pneumothorax and he had to wear it for four years.

He was sent first to the sanatorium of Puig d'Olena, where, incidentally, he met Carles Riba, in hiding there after his return from exile. Later he was in Puigcerdà for a year, except for the two coldest months, which he spent at La Garriga.

During his sickness he abandoned his religion entirely. From an

a

b

c

The Tàpies exhibition at the Guggenheim Museum of New York, 1962.

a

a) Tàpies as seen by the photographer Leopold Pomés, 1964.

b) Lithographic stone and proofs at the Im Erker workshops, Switzerland.

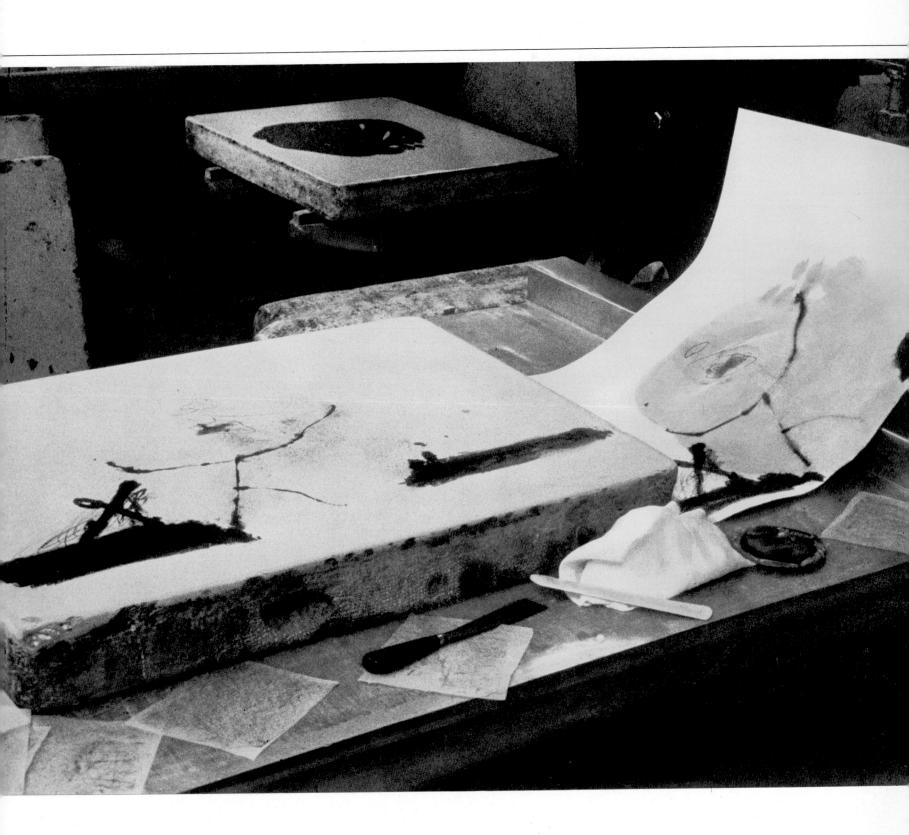

early age, under the influence of his father, he had not felt the phenomenon of religion with any intensity, though thanks to this mother's vigilance he practised it. Then came his readings of oriental writers, the natural result of a desire to go deeper into the subjects of the symbolist sensitization of his childhood. The adolescent Tàpies began to read Schopenhauer and Nietzsche, and from there went on to an interest in Yoga, the Vedas and Zen Buddhism, like many other Catalans who read the Catalan translation of Okakura Kazuzo's *Book of Tea*, basically a Zen work. Through Zen he penetrated into a spirit of comprehension of the void, of the asymmetric, of the art of seeing the stars at midday or the sun by night, through the earth. (The book had had considerable impact and had created in the University, shortly before the Civil War, such a great interest in Japanese poetry that we all learnt by heart a book of poems of geishas that Joan Teixidor had.)

The mystery of Zen suited Tàpies' mentality, which, without the emotive basis of his childhood religiousness, soon made him feel what he calls naturalistic mysticism, a vocation for mystery and for a mysterious communication with things, without any need to believe in supernatural factors.

To please his father, he began his legal studies and attended the University from 1943 to 1946. He was of the same year as Reventós, Carner, Josep Maria Castellet, Manuel Sacristán, Jordi Cots, Alfons Costafreda, Carles Barral and Jaume Ferran, but he did not make many friends among his fellow-students. He had a feeling that he was merely drifting there, like an extraneous body, a feeling that inhibited him, at that time, even with the few friends from childhood: Albert Jacas, whom he had met at the Col·legi Balmes, and the Samaranch bro-

Tàpies photographed by Català Roca, 1969.

thers, classmates from the German School.

In 1946 he abandoned his studies to devote himself to painting.

Impacts of childhood. Tàpies' artistic activity made itself felt from early childhood, in the form of an aptitude for and interest in things, on the one hand, and on the other, a certain acquaintance with art through the magazine *D'aci d'allà*, especially in the beautiful coloured covers, reproducing works by contemporary Catalan artists. A special place in this acquaintance belonged to the 1934 number, brought out by Joan Prats and Josep Lluís Sert and dealing with the Avant-garde, which he did not understand at the time.

His father, seeing the boy's interest, used to suggest subjects for composition. A family gathering, for instance, with his parents manipulating puppets and the children watching and laughing.

He was also fond of doing portraits and was beginning to be intrigued by modern art, but his parents treated this as something unimportant. It could hardly be otherwise, indeed, for the citizens of an autarchic country, cut off from the outside world and dominated by a general condemnation of what was called *degenerate art*.

Incommunication. Tàpies' artistic vocation first appeared to him when he was finishing his secondary studies. He has never forgotten that day in 1936 when the poet Cruzet, one of his teachers at the Col·legi Balmes, reproved him sharply for not expressing himself correctly, saying in emphatic Spanish: «*Usted no sabe hablar*» ("You do not know how to speak"). This made him think for the first time that perhaps he might be better able to express himself through painting.

The long convalescence after his illness gave him plenty of time for practising his drawing. He made some experiments in Expressionism with pastels and charcoal. In 1943, at the age of twenty, he had his first studio, in the Carrer de Jaume I, before beginning his legal studies, and in 1944 he attended classes for a few months at a drawing school in the Carrer de Jonqueres run by Nolasc Valls, the uncle of Manuel and Xavier Valls, but he soon left this school. All he did there was draw plaster casts and study the History of Art.

He went to an exhibition of works by Rogent, Fin and Vilató, which attracted his attention, as did an exhibition by Gabino at the Galería Syra, with works of deformed, slightly post-cubist realism, in which he seemed to find something new, in comparison with anything else that could then be seen in this country.

Another world. In 1947 Gabino, who frequently met Tàpies at the gatherings in the tavern called *La Campana* in the Carrer de Sant Eusebi, introduced him to the group of young artists known as the *Blaus*, from their connection with the hiking club of that name in Sarrià. In this club a company of restless young men foregathered as though in a catacomb. There Tàpies first met Joan Ponç, August Puig and Tort, painters enthusiastically patronized by the poet J. V. Foix, also from Sarrià, who had been so closely connected with the surrealists of the thirties and who saw these venturesome young men as the possible continuers of the old avant-garde, after the great eclipse of the postwar years. Joan Ponç, through contact with the poetry of Foix, became the fabulous visionary of violence, of disgust, of diabolical magic; Puig, after winning the first of the French scholarships awarded to Catalan artists, was to become one of the very first informalists; Tort was later

to emigrate to Brazil, where his work took an esoteric turn. At the club in Sarrià there was also a surprising young poet, Joan Brossa, who had been led by Foix's influence to abandon the old traditional verse in the style of Verdaguer for a new poetry, in which phrases taken from everyday language and placed in unusual juxtaposition produced a kind of juggling effect that was full of ambiguously polyvalent meanings, like a demythified mystery and an irony of emotion. It was also among these artists that Tàpies first met Arnald Puig.

Considering Tàpies' bourgeois background and the fact, at that time (1944-1946), that he was a university student, the artisan milieu of the *Blaus* must have come as a shock to him. But it must also have served him as a weapon in his struggle against his own conditioning.

He at once became very friendly with Joan Brossa, drawn to him by their common enthusiasm for the music of Wagner and Brahms. As Tàpies was the only one whose family possessed either books or a gramophone, they would all meet at his house in the Carrer de Balmes, to listen to music, to read or simply to look at things.

His neighbour Ramón Julià, who at a time when it was practically impossible to leave the country was one of the privileged few who could travel abroad, brought the group books published outside Spain on Impressionism, Picasso and Van Gogh, of whose works Tàpies used to make copies.

Entrance to the underground. The ambience of the group weakened Tàpies' connection with his original background and helped him to find his way out of what he calls today the physical, mental and sexual disorder of his earlier years. His vocation of expression had not yet taken definite shape, and at the same time as he worked at his drawing he also wrote poems and essays and kept an intimate literary diary. Obsessed by the idea of connecting with the old prewar avant-garde, he longed to know Joan Miró, and it was Joan Prats who gave him the chance of visiting Miró at his studio in the Passatge del Crèdit. We need hardly say what a discovery this visit meant to him; Tàpies confesses that his friend-ship with Prats was an enormous help to him. It was Prats who gave him access to a lot of reviews and other material published before the war, and it was also he who introduced him to Joaquim Gomis and his magnificent collection of documentary photographs. He made a special study of the Skira review *Minotaure* and of the works of Miró and Klee, which he found in *Cahiers d'Art*. All of this was of decisive importance for Tàpies and his friends, who were beginning to think of themselves as Surrealists, *poètes maudits* in relation to the rest of society. Thus came the moment when Tàpies took part in the 1948 *Saló d'Octubre*, where his work was seen in public for the first time, and where he sold his first picture to Xavier Vidal de Llobatera, for 500 pesetas. In September of 1948, too, Tàpies and his other painter friends, under the leadership of the graphic promoter and producer Joan Josep Tharrats, the young would-be existentialist philosopher Arnald Puig and the poet Brossa, began the publication of the review *Dau al Set*, which was to have so great an impact. Later on, about 1950, Tàpies' contact with Joao Cabral de Melo, a Brazilian living in Barcelona, and his own sojourn in Paris, with a scholarship from the French government, helped to develop in him a way of considering problems that was influenced by Marx, with greater projection outwards than that of the personal conflict that had dominated him till then.

He went through a stage of interest in everyday *fait-divers* during 1951, the year when he was discovered and invited to take part in the international exhibition at the Carnegie Institute in Pittsburgh, and shortly after that there was a short period when he indulged a propensity for the monumental treatment of subjects that evoked social and historical problems.

The twilight of the Dau al Set. In France meanwhile, where he spent ten months, he visited Picasso, who received him with great cordiality, and travelled through Belgium and Holland. In the autumn of 1951 he took part in the *Dau al Set* retrospective exhibition at the Sala Caralt in the Rambla dels Ocells, which was then run by Luis Sánchez Poveda. The exhibition ran from the 6th to the 19th of October 1951.

The text of the catalogue spoke of plastic and poetic conquests and emphasized the group's superiority to all the others that had appeared in Catalonia in the last ten years.

This exhibition was the *Dau al Set's* swan song. It was closed by the police because no heed was taken of their demand that the name *Dau al Set* be withdrawn, since it was, in fact, the name of a clandestine publication in Catalan, circulating without permission and ignoring the censorship regulations. After this the members of the group no longer kept in very close touch with one another and the *Dau al Set* became a collection published by Tharrats on his own sole responsibility.

In 1952 Enrique Lafuente Ferrari, who knew the painter's work through the exhibitions called the *Salones de los Once*, organized by Eugeni d'Ors, took the initiative of including Tàpies among the painters chosen to represent Spain at the Venice Biennale. This inclusion and the resumption of relations with the Carnegie Institute, which invited him to exhibit there again, were great incentives for Tàpies to go on working and free himself from those peculiar characteristics that were largely a result of the international isolation entailed in the United Nations' condemnation and the closed frontiers.

The Switchmen. After seeing Tàpies' 1952 exhibition at the Galeries Laietanes in Barcelona, the representatives of the Marshall Field Art Gallery in Chicago invited him to hold his first one-man show in the United States. The exhibition was a failure, but Josep Maria Gudiol, knowing that Tàpies was anxious to obtain some material assistance to enable him to continue (which he had not yet found either in Barcelona or in Paris), had recommended him to Gordon B. Washburn, of the Carnegie Institute, who had met Tàpies at his first exhibition in the Galeries Laietanes, and Washburn sent Martha Jackson to see the Chicago show.

She had just opened her first gallery in New York and she immediately offered Tàpies a contract. It was then that Washburn wrote of Tàpies that he was the great white hope of the younger generation of Catalans.

Tàpies made the trip to New York and had his first exhibition there, with works of different periods, 1949, 1950 and 1951. The text of the catalogue was written by Washburn.

Tàpies also sent some works to the São Paulo Biennale, where he won a prize. Through Martha Jackson his work came to the notice of the critic Tapié, director of a Right Bank gallery in Paris, who later recommended him to Stadler.

In 1954 Martha Jackson made arrangements for him to take part in a number of exhibitions around the United States: the Wadsworth Athenaeum, in Hartford, Connecticut, the Nebraska Art Association of Lincoln, the Milwaukee Art Institute, the Walker Art Center of Minneapolis, etc. He also showed once more at the Carnegie Foundation. In Europe, thanks to the initiative of the Marqués de Lozoya, who also knew his work from the *Salones de los Once*, he took part in the 27th Venice Biennale. At the *Saló del Jazz* in Barcelona, organized by the Hot Club and the Club 49, he was awarded the first prize for art related to jazz. At the Galeries Laietanes he showed a large part of the work done in 1953, his exhibition being presented by a text of my own, *Tàpies o la Trans-*

verberació, which was published in *Dau al Set.*

This was the time of his marriage, in Barcelona, to Teresa Barba i Fàbregas, and his setting up house in the Carrer de Sant Elias. The married state has been a very happy one for Tàpies, and one of the most important factors in the stability of his life. His wife, a sensible, lucid and constant woman, has been a great support. With the termination of a period of confusion in the painter's life, in which he might well have lost himself, she has acted as a kind of constant compass for her husband.

In 1955 Michel Tapié introduced Tàpies to Rodolphe Stadler, who began to exhibit works of his when he opened the new Stadler Gallery. In the same year Tàpies exhibited in Stockholm, along with the painter Tharrats and the sculptor Isern (now an important figure in the art world of Norway), with a preface by Salvador Dalí. He also ex-

hibited in Paris and in Barcelona; in the latter city the show was held under the aegis of the Club 49, in the underground room of the Sala Gaspar. He took an important part, too, in the 3rd Hispano-American Biennale, which was held in Barcelona that year and at which he won the prize of the Republic of Colombia, one of the most important awards. For the Catalan public in general, this was the year of his launching as an important artist. Edouard Jaquer then invited him to take part in the *Pha-*

c

ses de l'Art Contemporain exhibition at the Creuze Gallery in Paris.

The arrival.   The year 1956 marked the triumph of Tàpies in Paris. The Stadler Gallery opened his first one-man show there and the critic Tapié published his book *Tàpies et l'œuvre complète*, which was brought out by *Dau al Set*. In Barcelona this was the time of those gatherings at the house of Leopold Pomés, who was just beginning his ambitious career as a photographer, and these were sometimes attended by Tàpies. Apart from him, the people were always the same: Pomés himself, Brossa, Francesc Vicens, Jacas, Pere Portabella, the young photographer Riera, René Métras, the psychiatrist Segimon and myself, with one or two women as well.

We talked about anything and everything. We listened to music by the hour: lots of old music-hall numbers, songs of Raquel Meller, Leo Ferré, Georges Brassens, Piaf...

Frequently, very frequently indeed, the party became a kind of "happening" composed of personal acts: Brossa would entertain us with his own brand of elliptical juggling, Pomés would do imitations of bashful peasants or small-town mayors from Aragon, the girl we called Mitty would do her best to offer us erotic dances. Pere Portabella did marvellous dances, in which he writhed on the floor, in a love scene played with a bottle of wine, to the accompaniment of *Ebb tide;* or else he would give impressions of the *Folies Bergères*, to the music of *Paris canaille*, or variations of negro dances. Tàpies rarely performed. When he did, his favourite role was that of an idiot, in which he sometimes made a very strong impression on us. His inarticulate cries were really harrowing.

At about the same time Tàpies often came to *Zen*, in the Plaça Urquinaona, where Francesc Granados and I had started an advertising agency. There he used to spend the time chatting, or taking part in talks —practically lectures— on all sorts of interesting subjects, especially a series of them directed by Manuel Sacristán.

The year 1956 saw the birth of his first son, Antoni. His children have been of great importance in Tàpies' life. Two years later, in 1958, his daughter Clara was born and two years after that, in 1960, his second son, Miquel. He has a great feeling of *veneration* for children (and that is the word he uses in speaking of it). In observing them, he finds that they are both imaginative and at the same time extraordinarily logical, and they often give him a great feeling of sadness, when he thinks of the evils that life may be holding in store for them.

In 1957 he won the Lissone prize in Milan, which gave him the chance to travel in Italy, and in 1958 a separate room was asigned to his work at the 29th Venice Biennale, at which he won the UNESCO and David Bright Foundation prizes; at almost the same time he won the painting prize of the Carnegie Institute of Pittsburgh, awarded by a jury which included J. J. Sweeney, Marcel Duchamp, Lionello Venturi, F. J. Kiesler, Mary Callery, Raoul Ubac and Vincent Price, and shortly afterwards the prize at the Tokyo International Engraving Biennale of 1960. All these circumstances emphasized Tàpies' new position in the very first rank, with respect to the whole optic of success which is the measuring instrument proper to the avant-garde phenomenon.

More milestones along Tàpies' road to success are to be found in the growing number of works published about him, among them *Tàpies* by Michel Tapié, published in 1959 by Editorial R. M. of Barcelona, *Tàpies* by Cirlot, published in 1960 by Editorial Omega, the text written by Sweeney for the catalogue of his paintings published in America in 1961 and that of Giulio Carlo Argan, written in the same year for Tàpies' one-man show at the Tella Institute of Buenos Aires, which was directed by Romero Brest. A kind of anthology of the critiques then appeared, on the initiative of the writer Camilo José Cela, forming a special monographic issue of his review *Papeles de Son Armadans*, with texts by Argan, Aguilera-Cerni, Umbro Apollonio, Bayl, Cirici, Cirlot, Jacques Dupin, Chueca, Udo Kultermann, Guy Habasque, Gaya-Nuño, Herbert Read, Pierre Restany, Santos Torroella and Joan Teixidor. On his second visit to the United States, in 1959, Tàpies became friendly with Hoffman, Kline, de Kooning and Motherwell. In 1961 he made his third trip there.

It was at this time, as a result of the prizes and the critical success, that commissions began to come in. Some of them of a rather obliga-tory kind, as when, in 1959, he received a commission for three large paintings for the Town Hall of Barcelona. It was a commission typical of the official dichotomy of the period. A Town Hall that could contentedly commission a monstrous chapel from the conventional sculptor Monjo, with all the *kitsch* of which the age was capable, trembled at the thought of putting the important works of Tàpies in a place of honour and finally hung them, badly placed and half hidden, in the bar, as if they were mere frivolities.

The Gothic house. The purchase in 1960 of an old Gothic farmhouse just outside Campins, on the upper slopes of the Montseny near the town of Sant Celoni, a district which he had known in his childhood, meant the materialization of a sort of security and stability, in which his marriage, the birth of his children, his world-wide critical success and the high esteem now enjoyed by his work all converged. In an ensemble formed by an ancient building, very typical of the mountainous part of the Vallès district, and the "squire's house" nearby, the architect Antoni Coderch was Tàpies' adviser for the alterations, which produced a result of great charm. The main motif developed in it is one closely linked to that taste for intimacy so characteristic of Tàpies: the idea of the little glassed-over spaces, rather like holes in the roof, which form a sort of patio for the rooms on the upper floor.

Tàpies furnished his house with antique furniture and objects, not from the antique shops, but of that kind of furniture and objects that really exist in the peasants' houses, full of human significance and, especially, sentimental and nostalgic beauty; and this furnishing he completed with Art Nouveau pieces. This choice of furniture is in consonance with Tàpies' well-known aversion to so-called "modern" things. He told me one day that he dislikes the excessive attention paid nowadays to design and designers. The polemic he waged with Xavier Rubert in 1969, in the article entitled *«L'acadèmia d'allò social i allò implicat»*, developed logically as a result of this spontaneous inclination, so firmly rooted in the deepest part of his formation.

In a conversation we had in 1963, he revealed other parallel points of view: his lack of interest, for instance, in the purely utilitarian and technical architecture to which people attempt to attribute artistic pretensions.

He finds that poor architecture, on the other hand, is often more authentic and alive. As far as industrial objects are concerned, he does not simply feel a lack of interest in them as aesthetic works, but very frequently an absolute horror of the efforts made to consider them as art. Just the sight of a refrigerator or a sofa is enough to make him turn up his nose.

If he likes the fin-de-siècle objects with which he has furnished the house at Campins, he says it is because they are a kind of reaction against the creations of technology, because they are sensitive, delicate and very human, even in their weakness, and because he thinks that very often, besides their utilitarian sense, they have a spiritual content.

From this house of his, where he spends a great deal of his time, he can «live» the landscape with intensity. He says that he really loves the landscape; the mountains rather than the coast, and the more Nordic the mountain the better. Not the humanized, Romanized little hills behind the Barcelona coast, but wilder mountains, with their gloomy woods. All plants leave an impression on him, not only the little ones, the herbs and flowers, but especially the great trees and the dense forest... he becomes enthusiastic when he talks about it and adds: "*And the storms I love, too, you can imagine, and the mists, the lakes...*".

Irradiation.   In the sixties Tàpies was finally able to visit the nearest to hand of the countries of his dreams, Germany, England, Switzerland. In Germany, in 1962, Werner Schmalenbach organized an anthological exhibition of his work at the Kestner Gallery in Hanover, which was later presented at the Kunsthaus in Zurich, with an introductory text by Eduard Hüttinger. In the autumn of the same year, when he was commissioned to paint some murals for the Handels-Hochschule of St. Gallen, Tàpies took his family to live near this Swiss city on the shores of Lake Constance. Meanwhile, Thomas M. Messer was organizing his anthological exhibition at the Guggenheim Museum in New York, which was presented by Lawrence Alloway in 1962. This latter critic was to include Tàpies among the candidates for the Guggenheim Foundation prizes, with the result that one of these prizes was awarded to him in 1964, by a jury consisting of Hoffman, Haftmann and Rüdlinger. In 1963 he had already won the prize awarded by the Art Club of Providence, Rhode Island.

Also in 1963, Tàpies exhibited works on paper and cardboard at the Berggruen Gallery in Paris; these were subsequently shown at the Tartaruga Gallery in Rome, in 1964. He had a room to himself at the Documenta III exhibition in Kassel, exhibited at the Sala Gaspar in Barcelona and had a retrospective show at the *London Institute of Contemporary Arts* in 1965, presented by Roland Penrose. In 1966 he participated in the 6th Biennale of Menton, at which he was awarded the *Grand Prix du Président de la République*, and in the same year he took part in the exhibition organized by the *Convegno Internazionale di Artisti, Critici e Studiosi d'Arte* in Rimini, Verucchio and San Marino. Then, in November of 1967, he had a retrospective exhibition at the Vienna *Museum des 20 Jahrhunderts* and a show in Paris which marked the beginning of a new period in his exhibitions there, since it was not held at the Stadler Gallery, where he had shown for the last time in June and July of the previous year, but at the Maeght Gallery, where he has continued to exhibit ever since.

The foregoing does not pretend to be an exhaustive list of his exhibitions. There were many more at the same time: Düsseldorf, Milan, Venice, Washington, Berne, Bilbao, Buenos Aires, Stockholm, Essen, Zurich, Caracas, Rome, Turin, Cologne, Toronto, Montreal, Solothurn, Manresa, Toulouse and Cannes.

The bibliography was also growing. In 1962 the Barcelona firm of Seix i Barral published Cirlot's *Significación de la pintura de Tàpies*; in 1963 Jacques Dupin's *A. Tàpies, papiers et cartons*, published by Berggruen, appeared, and in 1964 Joan Teixidor's *Antoni Tàpies, papers, cartons, fustes i collages*, published by the Sala Gaspar. In the same year La Polígrafa of Barcelona published Blai Bonet's *Tàpies*, while 1967 saw the apparition of Giuseppe Gatt's *Antoni Tàpies*, with a prologue by Argan, published by Cappelli of Bologna, and of *Antoni Tàpies o l'escarnidor de diadèmes*, with a "fotoscop" by Joaquim Gomis and Joan Prats, the original text of Joan Brossa's *Oracle* and a very lucid essay by Francesc Vicens.

The new house. In 1963 Tàpies became even more definitely settled, with the building of his new house, designed by Antoni Coderch, in the Carrer de Saragossa in Barcelona.

The site was narrow and deep, as is often the case with houses in the Sant Gervasi district. This part of the city was originally built up in the eighteen-sixties, on a basis of long leases, as a kind of summer resort for the citizens of Barcelona, who were then still confined, a couple of kilometres away, within the 14th-century city walls. This particular site belonged to Tàpies' wife's family, who owned a little house there where the painter at one time had his studio. After pulling down the old house, and in planning the new one, Coderch worked with great understanding of his client's needs, not only physical but also psychological. The lack of space was the reason for the curiously vertical treatment of different levels. The studio is in the basement and the garage occupies the ground floor; living and dining space is on the first floor, the bedrooms on the next and still higher up is the library, which is devoted to reading, thinking and listening to music; all of these areas are connected by a lift, which makes circulation easier.

On the outside the house is shut in behind a façade consisting entirely of adjustable wooden louvres, which ensure a cloistered privacy. The roomy studio receives sufficient vertical illumination without losing its subterranean character.

The living room is a great, shady space, with the side walls left uncovered, independent of the iron supporting structure and perfectly external and visible, with a glass wall separating it from the patio, where some sculptures by Fontana (rather like big, half-opened nuts of grey material) co-exist with the luxuriant hothouse vegetation. Coderch's iron chimney, a fine Picasso, a Miró nocturne, a Charles Eames armchair (a concession to humanized design) and some simple peasant furniture for meals, some archaeological pieces and Melanesian

paintings: these are the elements of the living space. The view from it over the terrace is limited. You cannot see the sky, for the terrace is roofed over by a great horizontal louvre that limits visibility so as to preserve the intimate character of the whole space.

Nor is there any view from the library, at the very top of the house. It has a very high window, but veiled by curtains. There are books in plenty, many of them works of philosophy. There are a great many records and some Tibetan pictures on one wall. It is here that Tàpies still foregathers every week with Joan Brossa and a very few other intimate friends, to listen to music and to talk. It is here that he listens to music all alone or reads, nearly every day, in that half of his day that he devotes to meditation or writing.

When a certain stability seemed to favour the idea of a Tàpies "style", as something fixed in an historical

16. Zoom. Paint and whiting on canvas, 1946. 92×73 cm. K. H. Müller Collection, Düsseldorf.

TÀPIES BEFORE TÀPIES

moment, his 1969 exhibition at the Maeght Gallery in Paris made many critics realize that Tàpies should not be considered as a witness to a departing moment, but rather as the prophet of the new poor art (Arte Povera), which was arriving in Paris at the same time from Berlin, from Berne, from Frankfurt, from Naples, by way of a visual translation of the deeply dissentient movement of the young.

Shortly afterwards, when Tàpies exhibited his *graffiti* on sexual themes at the Sala Gaspar in Barcelona, at the end of 1969, he reaffirmed in very characteristic fashion the confluence between the natural and the historical approaches to the problems of mankind.

The imprint-mosaic. Of Tàpies' works previous to 1945, we have seen those done at the art school of Nolasc Valls, which are of no particular interest, portraits of his mother, of his sister Maria Angels, of a little girl —with aspirations to purity of line— in the style of Ingres, and by way of contrast the self-portraits, a theme that was to fascinate him for a long time; some of them represent him painting, making us think at the same time of Gimeno and of the portraits of the Fayum; in them we can already see some of the obsessive themes: the forehead bent low over the eyebrows, which meet like a sign, the hypnotist's eyes, the mouth full of little radial folds, the face

shaded over by the hairs of the beard, the pensive hand supporting the chin.

Manifestation of the frontal icon. The year 1945 is the real starting-point for Tàpies' painting, in an extraordinarily thick and densely mixed material, which ranges from the texture of a Van Gogh almost to the quality of a Visigothic bevelled bas-relief. On the whole, his work was still indecisive. It still contained the highly-worked, Ingres-like drawing, rather reminiscent of Picasso's portrait of Stravinsky, in the area most faithful to the traditional canons. There was the expressive graphism of Van Gogh, a somewhat fauve-like arabesque and a deforming of the hands that brought to mind both the twisted fingers painted by Picasso and the inflated ones of Miró. But the most personal element was in the exaggeratedly frontal icons, in which we can detect the fascina-

tion of the self-portrait, for this front that hypnotizes us is either the image in a looking-glass or the *mandala*, the transcendental icon. The mysticism of Tàpies leaves no room for surrealism. Some densely impastoed works remind one of the hostages of Fautrier or Dubuffet's *hautes pâtes*, but in a more barbaric fashion, with the staring, distracted eyes of the Ashburnham Pentateuch. Others, with great hands and a swirling at the breast, take on movement and phosphorescence, in an operation that makes evident a certain irradiation of the bodies, a certain communication, instinctive and direct.

Some, in their strength of structure, remind us of negro sculpture. Others, with a rather mannered arabesque in the pupils of the eyes, recall the drawings done by schizophrenics. The heads, uncovered or with the faces hidden by the hands, take on a Biblical resonance; the one of the face with

17. Scraping on cardboard, 1947. Henry Lazard Collection, Paris.

17

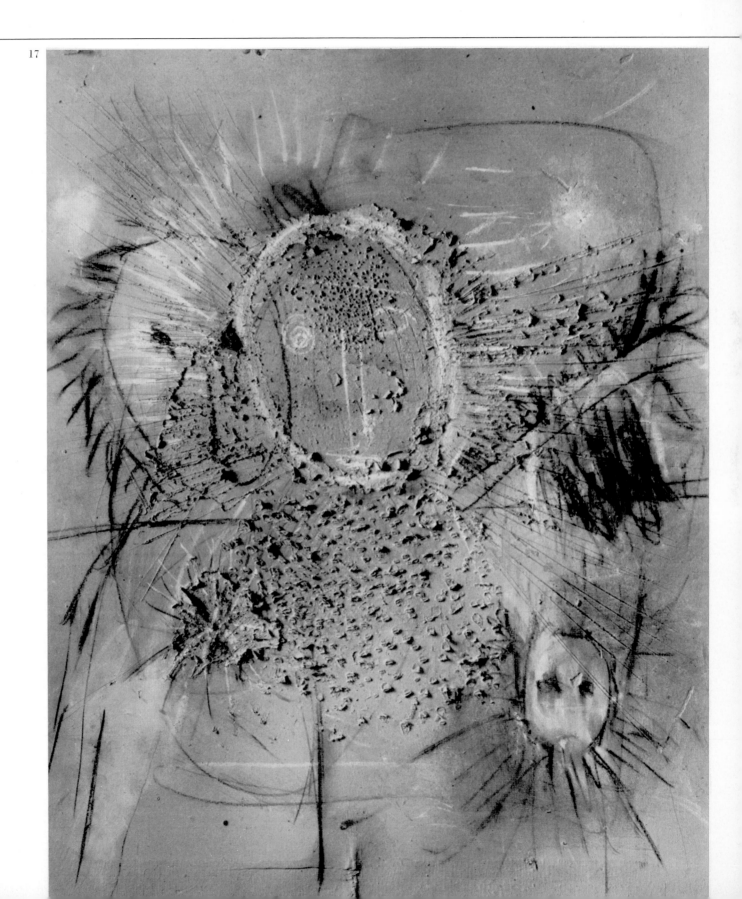

18. Personage. Paint and marble-worker's sand on canvas, 1946. 65 × 54 cm.
    Private collection, Barcelona.

18

two profiles is trinitarian. A figure seen from behind, with arms upraised and the sun in front, is the naturistic, pantheistic hymn of a brutal, elemental and deeply material age.

Structure at the first level. The atmosphere that unites all of these works suggests, directly, the name of Munch. The structural correspondence is a very complete one, because the community between these first works of Tàpies and those of Munch includes not only the stylistic relationships, the spontaneous execution, the brutality, the frontalism, the parallel lines, the paste-thick sinuosity, the presence of the effects of material and those of clarity and the calligraphy used as a means of expression, but also the system of values implicit in these stylistic characters.

The value of what arises out of natural life, as against artificial values, the decision to fight against civilized subtleties and conventions; an attitude of veneration for the energy of nature as a way of communicating with it; a rejection of *trompe l'œil* (on account of the deceit implied in its very name), rejection of the chaste and cerebral concept of the straight line, and rejection of disgust (when taken to mean a repugnance for certain aspects of what is natural); classification of material reality as a tactile fact (which admits no intermediaries) and of a spiritual reality expressed in terms of (intangible) light; and calligraphic automatism as a form of sincerity.

Matter as a self-portrait. Wagner, Nietzsche, Ibsen can all be glimpsed in a sort of filigree that runs through this system of values, both for Tàpies and for his Nordic predecessor, at that time surely unknown to him. But in this deep-level reading, as Chomsky would call it, we discover that there are some

19. Composition with figures. Paint on canvas, 1945. 61×50 cm. Private collection, Barcelona.

20. Collage of the rice and strings. Paint and sizing on cardboard, 1947. Henry Lazard Collection, Paris.

19

20

21. Figure on burnt wood. Paint, pastel and fire, 1947. 77×64 cm. Private collection, Barcelona.

22. Composition on cardboard, 1946. 42.5×35.5 cm. Private collection, Barcelona.

23. Figure. Paint on canvas, 1945. Josep M. Gudiol Collection, Barcelona.

24. Figure. Paint on canvas, 1945. Private collection, Barcelona.

1   22   23   24

implicit facts which already separate Tàpies radically both from these names and from Munch. There is the historical fact of the shifting situation of a Germany which had been transformed by two almost consecutive wars from the marvellous country of his dreams into the country of inhumanity, cruelty, arrogance and bad taste. Tàpies was to preserve a system of values which was that of Nordic irrationalism, but he was incapable of giving it the rhetorical, monumental, ascensional sense, the mystical optimism, of the "Avenue of Splendour". In the face of the scandal of triumphalism become a crime, he could not embody these values in their external, cosmogonical or political manifestation, but only in an internal, biological or psychological representation.

This brought him close to Dostoievsky and to the search for the truth at the bottom of the deepest wells.

As with the intemperance of his former disordered life, he saw in this a purification, a catharsis, a *Descensus Averni* as defined by Jung. There is a desire to penetrate

25. Two personages on cardboard. Paint, scraping and sizing, 1947. 76 × 64.5 cm. Private collection, Barcelona.
26. Box of strings, 1946. 48 × 40 cm. Private collection, Barcelona.
27. Figure of newspaper and threads. Sizing and paint on cardboard, 1946-1947. 45 × 37 cm. Private collection, Barcelona.

25

into matter, to seek out in the obscure intimacy of the lowest, most vulgar, most despised matter the strongest and most authentic life, and to identify this matter, felt within and confined, with the ego. Matter is the chief character of his work, but a form of matter that is somewhat like his self-portrait, voluntarily toned down.

At about this time he would often pick up things thrown away in the street, pieces of torn paper, bootlaces that were usually frayed, poor things; but with them he did not create a marvellous, romantic, transformation-scene assembly, as Schwitters did, but preferred rather to incorporate the whole with the intention of not magnifying it, remaining faithful to the identification between the vicissitudes of material objects and those of human destiny.

The failure of the icons. The year 1946 marks the period when the

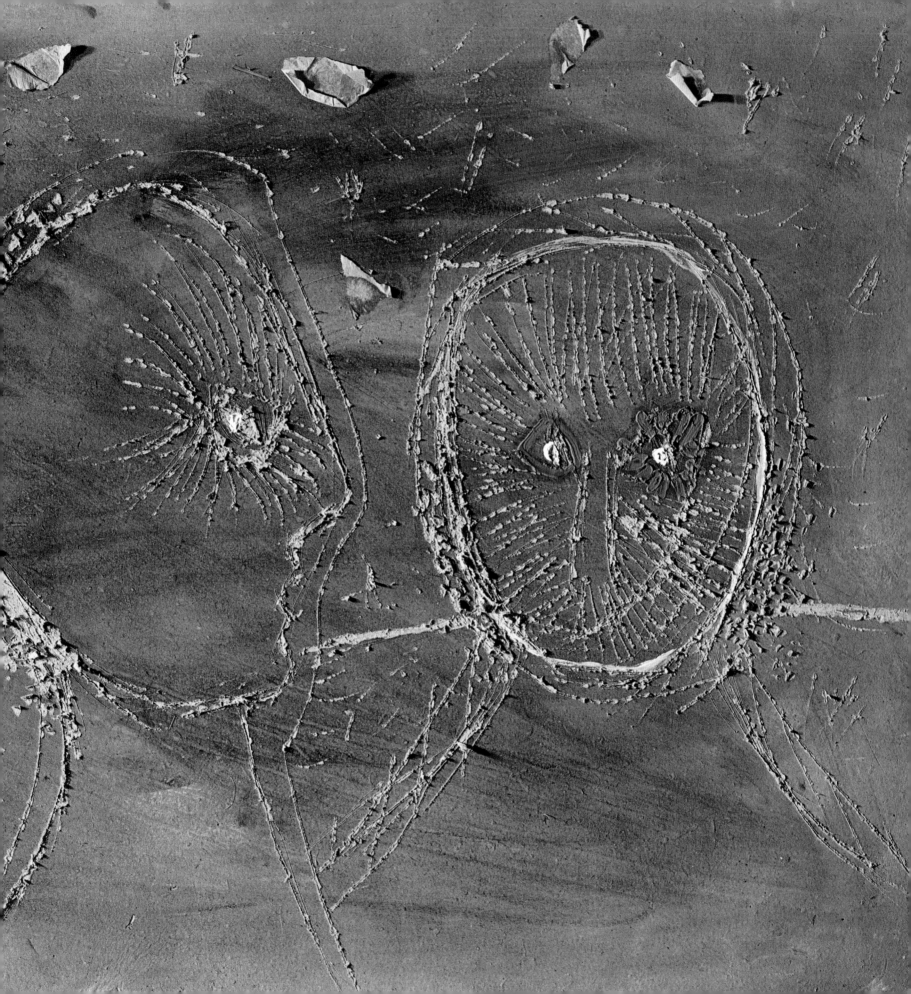

message of existentialism took its place in Tàpies' culture. Its roots in certain irrational concepts, in the absurd and in direct experience, its sense of destiny and of the man who lives to die, all of these factors corresponded at many points with the chiaroscuro vision that Tàpies had taken from his Germanic sources. But every time a man widens his vision of the world he finds himself for the moment unable to classify it in accordance with the concepts available to him, which in fact block his comprehension of the new reality he has begun to experience.

Tàpies, therefore, welcomed the ideas of existentialism, so much in accord with his cultural and emotive formation and so closely connected with the backlash of the historical experience of World War II, of the extermination of the Jews and of the bombing of Hiroshima and Nagasaki. But it was difficult for him to see at once the structure translated into plastic form. He therefore continued with the icons, though the icons of this period often seem to crumble, to lose their way, to fall flat; that is, he continued with the unknown.

Terrible masks, turned upside down, arms upraised as if imploring help or simply attempting to say that they can no longer find anything to cling to, hands that seem to be mere imprints, marks left by vanished hands: these are the elements in this period of the failing icons.

Some of the paintings are no more than survivors of the failure, though still iconic. Heartless faces which have become masks, obsessive eyes and nipples, like pieces of life converted into mere traces. Just as the imprints of the hands replaced the palpitating hands themselves with their memory, now it is a whole world of graffiti that is established. No longer the icon of man, but the face of man. Man no longer is, no longer remains, but passes, has passed, passes altogether. So we have the child's scribble and the graffiti of the soldier or the hooligan, like an archaeological vision of man from his own death.

Now and then a funereal way of expressing himself helps us to see it, as in that picture, completely smooth, in which a bootlace holds a medallion, with a little photographic portrait stuck on to it. The memory of one who is no longer there, on the medal of one who is no longer there either. A sort of evocation of death, in the second degree.

But where we really seem to find the sense of the anguish of living in its greatest purity is in the collages, in which the curtain rings (a theme from Kafka), the amulet cross or the little portrait possess very much the character of memory within destruction, and in which, above all, the compositions with bootlaces on different planes,

frayed, faded, confused, shut up in a glass cage, are a materialization of nausea.

Pact with the avant-garde. The works with which Tàpies made his first appearance, in 1948, had been done in 1947, by which time he had already definitely abandoned the study of the law in order to devote himself to painting. His father, incidentally, who already feared that this would happen, had tried to prepare something of reputation for his son by calling the attention of Sebastià Gasch to his work; Gasch was then the only critic that survived of the old avant-garde and he wrote an article about Tàpies in *Destino* which appeared on March 29th 1947.

1947 was the year in which Tàpies became friendly with Brossa and visited Miró. This direct acquaintance with certain aspects of the old avant-garde prepared a diastole for his evolution. The hazard

28. Threads on cardboard. Sizing and paint, 1946. 39×47 cm. Private collection, Barcelona.
29. Composition. Paint on canvas, 1947. 38×46 cm. Vidal de Llobatera Collection, Barcelona.

28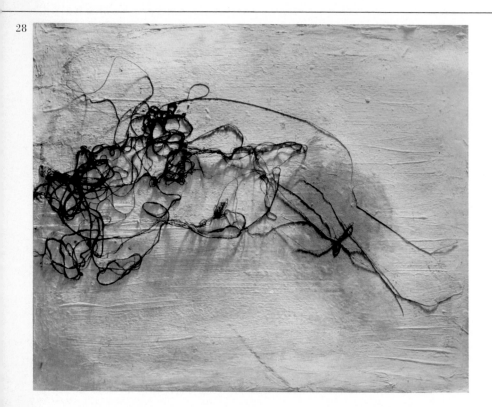

29

of various impacts had dispelled this before he was twenty-two; inner meditation had concentrated it later on.

Now, at the age of twentyfour, his encounter with a new horizon dispelled it once again, but gave him a decisive idea: that of the need to integrate himself within the history of painting and contribute something new, following the example of Miró.

30. Composition. Paint on canvas, 1945. 46×38 cm. Private collection, Barcelona.
31. Head on blue background. Paint and photograph stuck to cardboard, 1946. 39.5×31.5 cm. Private collection, Barcelona.

32. Collage. Paint and sizing on cardboard, 1946. 105×75 cm. Fragment. Private collection, Barcelona.

30

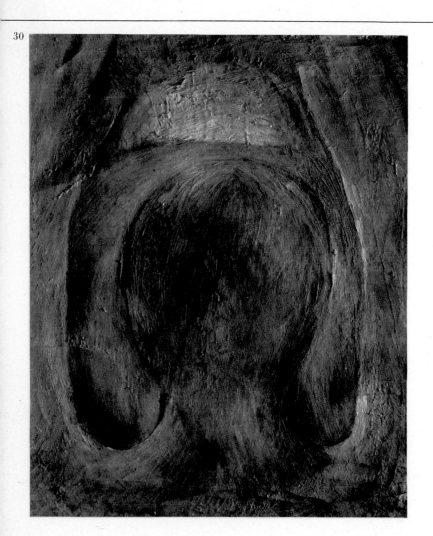

31   32

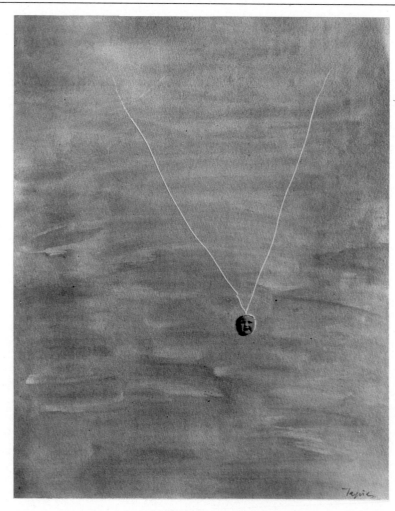

This was the same idea as that of the avant-garde, as defined by Sanguinetti: the social and economic integration of the artist through the only system possible for a bourgeois society. When there can no longer be the personal relationship of the old peasant craftsman, nor the relationship that obtained with the Church, the feudal lords or the courtiers during the Middle Ages, in the Classical period or in the age of Baroque, *the only thing to do is to work for a great unknown public, for what is called the market, and there is nothing for it but to have recourse to systems that resemble, and are to a certain extent parallel to,*

33. Threads and curtain ring. Paint and sizing on cardboard, 1946. 53 × 75 cm.
Private collection, Barcelona.

those of an economy of production in an open market: novelty and the trust. It becomes necessary to establish protectionist barriers, set up by galleries, critics and art dealers, and there must be art museums and biennales to serve as exchanges for price quotations; and the whole will be justified by the measuring-stick of diffusion and imprint on the market, i. e., success.

If there are any moralistic scruples to be felt with regard to this situation, which may at times be inhuman insomuch as it can be discriminatory or an instrument of alienation, it would be absurd to address them either to the artists or to the dealers, who have to work within the inevitable context of the capitalist system. Any accusation should be directed against the system itself.

The fact that Tàpies' direct contact with the avant-garde came to him through Joan Brossa helps to explain the fact that the origin of his decision to join this movement coincided with the beginning of the previously mentioned influence of Brossa's poetry on the painter's work.

Brossa, who is a nimble and expert conjurer, an enthusiast of quick-change acts, theatrical magic, dicing and mechanical toys, is a poet and playwright whose purpose is to use as his materials, like so many objects, people's ways of speaking, which he captures with complete fidelity, forming them into ensembles in which the hare leaps when you least expect it. A marvellous world, without any transcendental pretensions, but on the other hand, which is his great triumph, absolutely drenched in a human emotion which is all the stronger for the very reason that it catches us unawares and defenceless, just when we are most distracted by the entertainment.

In Tàpies' works of 1947 we can still see that painting of matter as a self-portrait, born of certain imperatives inherent in the painter's personal situation; but beside them, or mingled with them, there are already signs of magic painting.

Apparition of the signs and symbols. In the self-portraits of matter there are some key works, with thick paste on wood, applied directly from the tube, in counterpoint to the significant violence of the poker-work, that technique of surface decoration which was such a favourite with young ladies of the leisured classes before the wars, but which he transforms into a burning, wounding instrument, with tragic overtones.

But side by side with these works there is the apparition of signs, symbols and semanticized icons which announce the imminence of the magic period.

The sign —an element which refers to something immediate and, in fact, designates— and the symbol

—which corresponds unequivocally to things that are absent and lack any relation to it but the conventional— are mingled together in a dynamic that is still indecisive.

The signs, naturally, accompany the icons and to a certain extent constitute prescriptions for using them; they materialize the rites, the ceremonial of what has to be done with icons, that ceremonial which is the incorporation into life of the viewer and, in short, the whole value. The pure symbols, on the other hand, are, as they should be, self-sufficient.

The most outstanding element of the iconology comes from the self-portrait. I mean the eyes, eyes which belong to a head with its brow bent forward and which, in consequence, are usually seen flanged, oblique, as is the case with the figurative self-portraits of the artist himself. As an enlargement of the eyes there is the whole head, furiously frontal.

Mandala and oneirism. The eye is what stands out from the face, with a hierarchically exaggerated format, because the eye —the eye that looks at itself in the looking-glass— is a dominant element of suggestion, of hypnotism. Its *mandala* character is common to the other iconic elements, such as the strongly centered and obsessive graphisms of the crosses and the irradiant stars.

We should remark that Tàpies' eyebrows, joined together by a bridge of hair over the upper part of his nose, underline —or rather, over-line— the eyes of his iconology with a strong, double-arched line, like a pair of horns or a yoke, in a fashion that helps to make one sole image of the double theme of the eyes and accentuates, therefore, their *mandala* character. This theme is frequently confused with the moon.

There are also mouths, beaks, sexes and disquieting objects like

34. Newspaper cross. Paint and sizing on cardboard, 1946-1947. 40×31 cm. Private collection, Barcelona.

weathercocks, which seem to move by themselves.

In the syntax of this iconology of obsession-creating objects appears the oneirical theme of flight. Flying characters, as in the work of Chagall or in the best work of Kokoschka. The oneirism, in effect, accentuates their character of symbols of something unknown, which is, in short, the character assumed by the icons.

Symbol icons. Some of the icons are very complex, using the self-portrait of matter as a process. Thus the head with the great oblique eyes, with the beard made of cords and with real rice stuck to the face. A pointed hat, mitre of some unknown cult, completes the character of mystery. There is also the androgynous figure, a sort of Mesopotamian priest, still more blatantly prophetic.

Around these icons the signs and the symbols make room for each other. There are signs to indicate the trajectories of the flying personage, to the lines of force that show themselves near the eyes, the beaks, the sexes or the mouths, to the pointing arrows.

There are symbols as attributes of the icons. The cross, the star, the moon, themes that coincide with historical symbologies; the cobweb, more a loser, but which also has historical existence in the allegories: they appear, in effect, as complements, associated with the forms of the self-portrait, as if they were defining advocations of it. Sometimes they act as transformations of the same theme, as is the case in the painting that was purchased by Vidal de Llobatera, in which the paste, the matter source that Gatt describes as caressed in accordance with parallel movements, is violated by signs which are scratches, cuts, abrasions and deep incisions, like those of a scalpel, where the sensitization of the

35. Painting. Oil on canvas, 1948. 92×73 cm. Charles Zadok Collection, New York.

36. Triptych. Paint on canvas (central panel), 1948. 97×130 cm. Private collection, Barcelona.

matter leads to the *transfert* that identifies it with the human flesh. These scratches here evoke the frontal face, which has become the astral centre of irradiation, a phenomenon of which the arms or the legs are but partial aspects. Thus the *transfert* is effected at one and the same time in the field of the picture's own construction, as an object, and in that of its reflex nature, as a representation. But of the two fields undoubtedly the more powerful, the one that introduced something with all the force of a new meaning that bestowed new life on the meaning, was still the first, which made the painting of Tàpies a painting of matter.

37. Collage of the crosses. Paint and sizing on cardboard, 1947. 53 × 75 cm.
   Henry Lazard Collection, Paris.

38. Harlequin and cat. Paint on canvas, 1948. Enric Tormo Collection, Barcelona.

39. Greens on dark brown. Paint on canvas, 1948. 89 × 116 cm. Museum of Modern Art Collection, Barcelona.

40. Charcoal and ink. Drawing on paper, 1948. 43 × 44 cm. Private collection, Barcelona.

41. The eyes. Paint on canvas, 1948. 73 × 60 cm. Private collection, Barcelona.

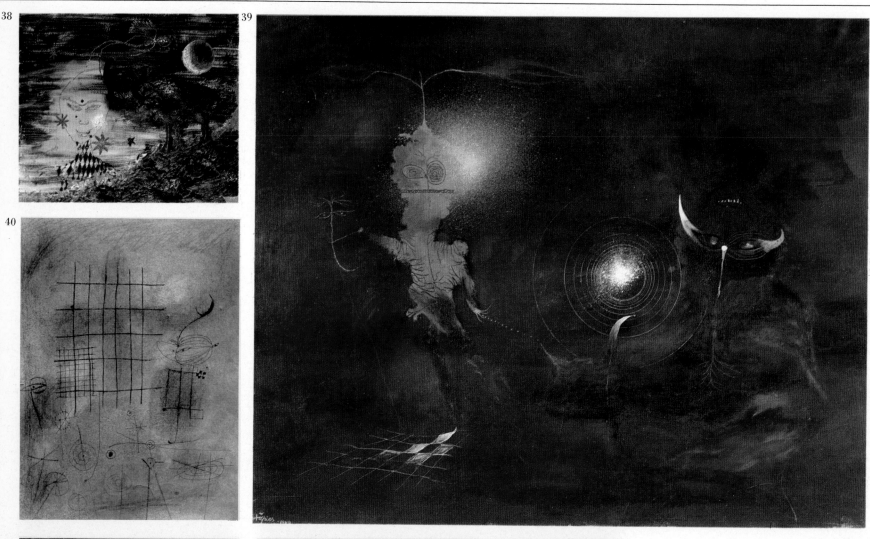

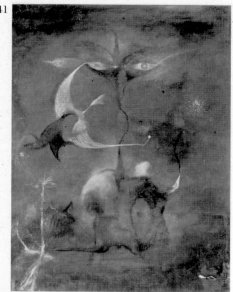

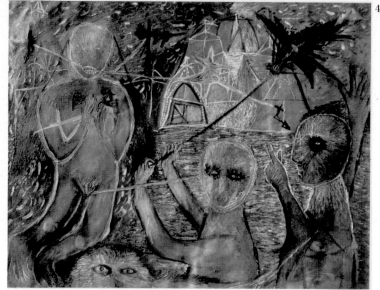

42. Composition with figures. Paint on canvas, 1947-1948. 89×116 cm. Private collection, Barcelona.

43. Charcoal and ink. Drawing on paper, 1948. 24.5×31.5 cm. Private collection, Barcelona.

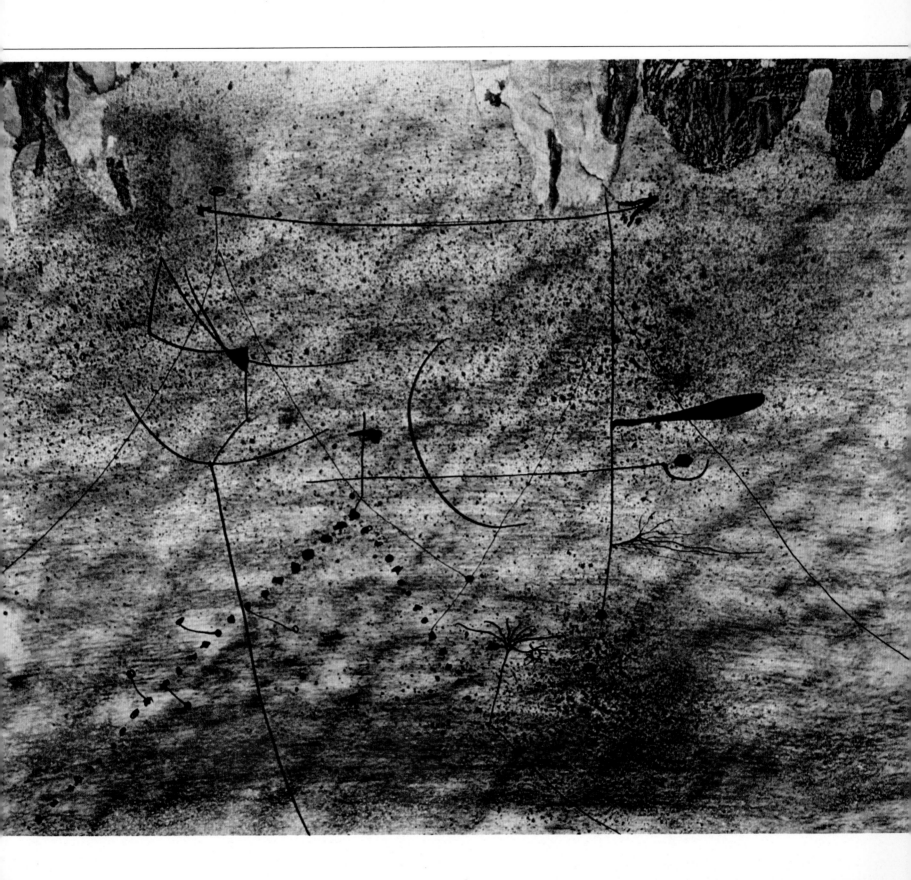

THE MAGIC PERIOD

Dialogue with Brossa and Surrealism. The shock produced by the contact with Surrealism was intense. Here Prats played a part, as did the information patiently assimilated from the few sources Tàpies could reach, such as the above-mentioned special number of *D'Ací i d'Allà*, which he practically learnt by heart (including the poems of Hans Arp), the catalogue of the exhibition of Surrealism in the year 1947, at the Galerie Maeght, and the book of the *Ismos* by Gómez de la Serna, in which he discovered Breton, Péret, Eluard, etc. There was also Joan Brossa, who not only impressed him with his own poetry but also with that of others to whose work he introduced him, such as Salvat-Papasseit, Mallarmé, the Surrealists and Vivekananda.

The influences were reciprocal. Brossa also told Tàpies one day, when the latter confessed that his friend's work stimulated him greatly, that he experienced the same phenomenon.

The poetry of Joan Brossa entered Tàpies' life like a tumultuous river, or rather, like a great flood. When the waters finally went back to their usual course, the matter painting of 1946 and 1947 was to appear once more, but in it would remain for ever traces of the submersion he had gone through.

Brossa had started out from an unexpected confluence. From a very early age, when he wrote war poems, he interpreted poetry as an epic and rhetorical inspiration, which had its roots in Jacint Verdaguer, and confined to the realm of amusement his participation in the world of gambling, of the theatre, of conjuring and the harmless magic of the funfair. When his contact with Foix and, through him, with Surrealism made it possible for him to use the world of his former amusement as an instrument of poetry, the confluence was like a spring which projected him towards a new and dizzying fecundity. As Cabral de Melo says, he explored all the varieties of formalism and all the corners of the magician's box of tricks, from the meticulously orchestrated babblings of the *Sonets de Caruixa* to the threepenny opera of *Dragolí*, alternating these with prose and theatre of systematic hallucination, in which he sought a fifth leg for every cat, a seventh face for each of the dice. Brossa, convinced of this method of research, invented on his own account other mechanisms equivalent to those of the conjurer, with the added virtue that he did not make of them a transcendental, escapist faith, as some of the post-surrealists might try to do, but a technical medium for a new approach to reality, one that was more alive, purer, completely new, with all the force of surprise.

Inevitably Tàpies, who had really, on account of the social position of his family and possibly also because of his long sickness and convalescence, lived a rather too well-guarded life, was enormously tempted by this methodology, which afforded him an opportunity of approaching the reality from which he was separated by so much padding.

44. Two figures. Paint on canvas, 1947. 59×80 cm. Josep M. Gudiol Collection, Barcelona.
45. Drawing on paper, 1948. 32×48 cm. Private collection, Barcelona.

44

45

The year 1948 was extraordinary on account of this leap forward, and it was in fact the year that saw the real emergence of Tàpies, who now published, exhibited and came into the limelight generally for the first time.

Dau al Set. The most important event of this period was the founding of the review *Dau al Set* (the title, chosen by Joan Brossa, can be approximately translated as "Seven-faced dice"), organized by a group of friends and produced by the young Joan Josep Tharrats, born in 1918, the son of a rather conventional poet from Girona, who was an amateur of graphic arts and had a little Boston press on which he could personally print a review; a review which, simply because it was written in Catalan, at that time was necessarily clandestine.

A predecessor of the *Dau al Set* was the review *Algol*, the first one that had had any creative intention since the Spanish Civil War. There had been another called *Ariel*, which attempted to preserve what it could of prewar culture; *Algol*, however, had no nostalgia, but rather a radical desire to break away which led it to give itself the subtitle of "diabolical review". Its artistic contributors included Jordi Mercadé, Boadella and, above all, the most dissentient of the lot, Joan Ponç, whose negative and magic art was like that of a kind of Brossa overflowing with poison and without the lyric vein.

Algol, only one number of which was published, was the immediate predecessor of *Dau al Set,* which began publication in September of 1948 and continued to appear in successive phases. Until 1951 it was very homogeneous, but from that moment on, the differences between Tharrats and Brossa having caused the latter to leave the review, *Dau al Set* opened its pages to all kinds of different people, from Aulèstia to Cocteau and from Surós to Aleu, in a final burst of eclecticism. After 1953 it could no longer be considered a review. The name of *Dau al Set* was used indifferently by scattered publications brought out separately by the different members of the group now dissolved.

In the first numbers of the *Dau al Set,* Brossa published texts that he had written since 1945, in which he wrote that *there will be so few roses on the surface of the water that we shall split the canes to prevent even one from blooming;* he also said that *experience is the least illuminating of theories,* and that *the tongue prevents us from ruminating;* and he responded to the disenchantment of recalling that he had *sought a heart for years and years* with *and why should I not invite her to dance?*

These were texts that expressed a disenchantment with his experience of life, the ascertainment of a certain smirching, but also a great obstinacy and a creative vitality that had no need of hope or belief to make it act. He saw quite clearly the cardboard façade and the snares. A man is *little more than the trunk of a tree that is hollow within,* a man and a woman mere *broomsticks dressed up.* He said: "*I cannot escape* the fire", but also: "*if you blow hard, a dense smoke comes out*", and somewhere else: "*If chance is the servant of fire, we shall sow stones*". He was conscious of an historical moment that he was able to define when he said: "*the cracks are filling up with weeds*". But he was always ready to attempt something positive, even when it seemed impossible. In the wager implied in the very name of the review *Dau al Set*, for instance. Here he said: "*Let us carve at lip-level this magnetized die*". He preferred to forget the plaintiveness of the old songs. *When the ring is lost, or the watch, or any other jewel, and those whose hearts are pierced have turned out the lights, it is better to leave off strewing the earth with flowers.* He felt that he had nothing to lose by the wager. *Miracles do not kill on these days of foul weather.* Rather should we *seek for treasures around the corpse* and weep no more. *To go into mourning twice for the same*

person is too much. His programme aspired to include everything, though without any sureness of success. But he was open to great things. It was, in fact, of some drawings by Tàpies that he wrote, in 1945, a text that read in part: *Silence is enough to conceal, by dint of presents, a rendezvous by night. Whether we shall be cured respectively or discover treasure, I will not speak of it. I can only say that the greatest loves never have their beginning in the pleasure of music.*

In the *Dau al Set*, as in *Algol*, we find the existentialist position; its advocate is Arnald Puig, some of whose aspects are directly related to what the painting of Tàpies and the poetry of Brossa have most in common at first, as when he says that *philosophic knowledge today is concerned with any manifestation of life, from the purest —that of thought— to the most vulgar and everyday;* and he quotes as an example the action of Sartre, who

46. Oil chest. Paint on canvas, 1949. 70×100 cm. Joan Gaspar Collection, Barcelona.

47. Composition in reds. Paint on canvas, 1949. Private collection, Barcelona.

chooses as the principal theme of his research the most simple and vulgar acts of everyday life and, facing up to them, takes from them all their possible transcendency.

As against the formalism that some attribute to the *Dau al Set*, we should not forget the historical conscience to be found in the fundamental text of Brossa and in the very fact that the review indicated certain loyalties: to Gaudí, to Catalan Romanesque painting, to jazz, to Georges Melies, to the immediate precedent of J. V. Foix. There is also an explicit social intention when Romanesque art is claimed as an art of service, the antithesis of an aesthetic art, while Foix is claimed as someone who expresses the *dialogue between the mind and what it has in common with other men.*

The "Saló d'Octubre". One month after the apparition of the *Dau al Set*, Barcelona witnessed the historic event of the first *Saló d'Oc-*

48. Parafaragamus. Paint on canvas, 1949. 89×116 cm. Private collection,
     Barcelona.

49. The scoffer at diamonds. Paint on canvas, 1949. 92×73 cm. Juan Perucho Collection, Barcelona.

48   49

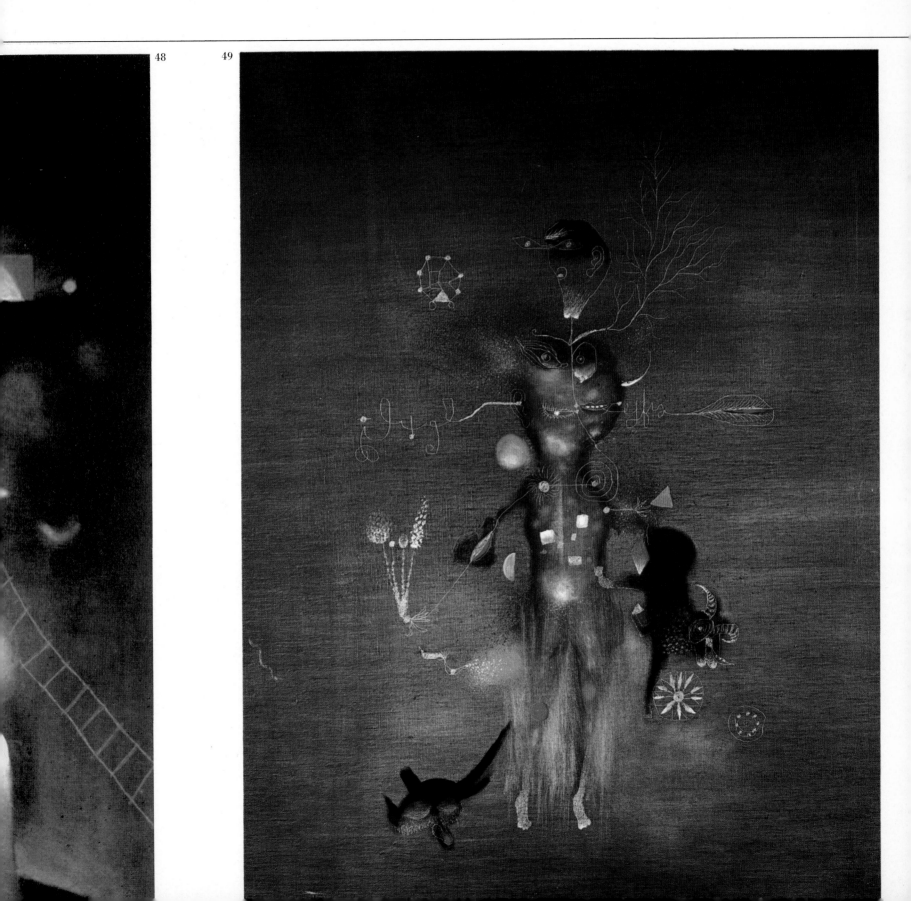

50. Sofar. Paint on canvas, 1949. 50×61 cm. Private collection, Barcelona.

51. Hindu London. Paint on canvas, 1949.

52. Inks and paint on opaque paper, 1949. 46×33 cm. Galería René Métras, Barcelona.

53. Mudre. Paint on canvas, 1949. 92×73 cm. Josep-Lluís Samaranch Collection. Barcelona.

50

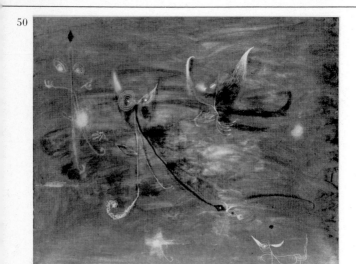

51

52

53

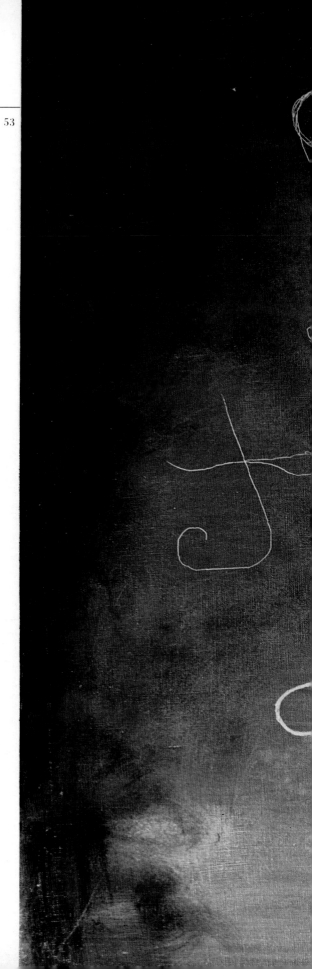

54. The bouquet in eclipse. Paint on canvas, 1949. 89×116 cm. Sala Gaspar, Barcelona.

54

55. Lunar disconsolation. Paint on canvas, 1949. 81×100 cm. Pere Casadevall Collection, Barcelona.

tubre. After a long silence of nine years of fat postwar profiteers and their *pompier* painters, with avant-garde art totally condemned, came the tempestuous apparition of a group of young men —for the most significant among them were only twenty-five years old— who showed that the dirges being sung for the death of living art were a sham.

In this combative position, which gave rise to violent reprisals on the part of the *Sindicato Español Universitario* (the official Students' Union), the young men of every kind of renewing tendency stood together, however contrary to one another these tendencies were: post-cubists, expressionists, surrealists and even one or two abstract artists.

The *Saló* was fostered by a group of enthusiasts, which included Victor M. d'Ymbert as its great promoter and men like Xavier Vidal de Llobatera, of the old art-lovers' society known as A.D.L.A.N. (Friends of the New Art), and Josep

Maria de Sucre, of the new Cercle Maillol, which, from the French Institute of Barcelona, represented an exiguous breathing-outlet to the outer world. Tàpies has told us that, in spite of the historical avant-garde intention defended by Gasch in his introductory text, and the evocation by Sucre of Josep Dalmau and Picasso (a valiant stand to take in those days), the organizers of the exhibition were alarmed when Tàpies presented himself with such dissentient works as the *Painting* we have already described, which was bought by Vidal de Llobatera, or the *Encolat* with the cemetery crosses and the lavatory paper, now in the Lazard Collection. When we look today at the catalogue of this first *Saló d'Octubre*, which was opened in the Galeries Laietanes on October 2nd of 1948, we can see at once that the whole of the avant-garde that was being reborn in this show played a very submissive role beside the mordant work, the spitting in the public face, of Tàpies. It was then that we first met him and began to believe in him.

Cosmic images. It should not be forgotten that 1947 was the year in which, together with Brossa and J. V. Foix, Tàpies made the acquaintance of Joan Miró and Joan Prats and through them gained access to information regarding the avant-garde all over the world. In 1948 we began to realize the impact of this new atmosphere on his work:

The icons, the signs and the symbols accentuated their magic character, a character that was accredited by the theme of the self-portrait, with the cross on the head, the balloon and the kite. But generally speaking the works took on a breadth of subject matter that transformed them into little works for the theatre. Here we have the figure of his grandfather Puig i Alfonso, his beard giving him the air of a character from some mythology of Barcelona, against the background of Gaudí's Church of the Holy Family and with the staff and sash of a city councillor; the allegory of Death, the tryptich with a corpse in the centre, beside the woman with her arms cut off and the bust on a column that rises out of a lake peopled with monsters; the Mesopotamian queen, with her crested tiara, beside the gallows victims and the palm trees; the standing man with the zodiac head, close to the volcano; the quadruped weeping between the star and the moon; the flying creatures, the petrified landscapes and the extraordinary cock upside down, done in dialogue with Brossa.

In these works there also appeared some graphisms related to those of Klee and Miró and like the game of chess, sometimes in enormous perspectives across the sky or over the water of unreal landscapes, the spiral, the thick lines, the levers,

103

56. The fire of the thorns. Paint on canvas, 1949. 89 × 116 cm. Albert Jacas Collection, Barcelona.

57. Composition. Paint on canvas, 1949. 46 × 38 cm. Santos Torroella Collection. Barcelona.

58. The eyes of the foliage. Paint on canvas, 1949. 97 × 130 cm. Güell Collection, Barcelona.

56 57

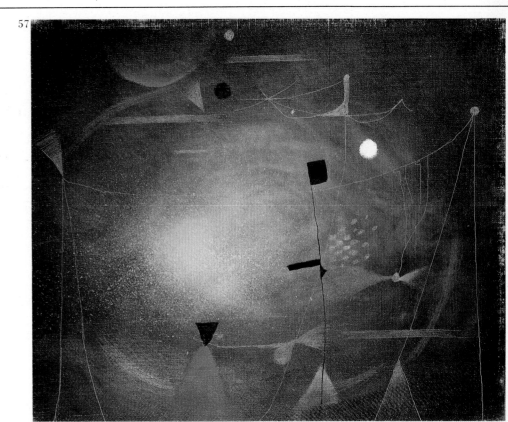

58

59. Dream Garden. Paint on canvas, 1949. 97 × 130 cm. Museum of Cologne Collection.

59

the dotted lines, the splashes and the irradiation. When I asked Tàpies what he was trying to do with these little theatrical compositions of 1948, he told me that they were an attempt *to unite the whole cosmos in one sole image.*

This could only be attempted in a climate of obscurity and mystery, like the act of love, which can only be accomplished when the sex becomes invisible. That is why the atmosphere of the little theatres of the first phase of magic painting is, predominantly, nocturnal.

Some of the pieces have an almost linear texture, upon a world of splashes; they are a sort of ballet, in the style of the *Machine for making the birds sing* of Klee or the *Harlequin's Carnival* of Miró, but the personality of Tàpies makes itself felt in the great stigmata that already appear in them, as also in their nocturnal quality and in the persistence of the themes of the heavy-lidded eyes, the eyebrows,

60. Pastel, 1950. Joan Obiols Collection, Barcelona.
61. Landscape of Urus. Paint on canvas, 1950. 91 × 60 cm. Josep-Lluís Samaranch Collection, Barcelona.

60

61

the teeth and the hairs, all of which come from the self-portrait.

Parenthesis of magic distillation. The year 1949 marked the great moment of expansion of his magic painting. That year Tàpies printed his first etchings, in the workshop of Enric Tormo, and took part in the competition-exhibition organized by the Cercle Maillol of the French Institute. Eugeni d'Ors chose his work for the 7th *Salón de los Once* in Madrid, which gave Tàpies the chance to participate in an historical event of some significance. After ten years of radical Castilianism —or provincialism— Ors was now making up for his omissions. This was the first time that Madrid saw the work of Joan Miró. With it arrived works by Tàpies and the Basque painter Jorge Oteiza, together with an evocation of the work, then incipient, of the architect Oriol Bohigas. Tàpies responded to that necessity that Ors said he felt at the time: *The first thing, my dear sir, is to have one's own cosmos!* Arnald Puig presented his work, saying that in the world of Tàpies there is *the spiritual responsibility for every material particle,* and that the external forms of the objects are replaced in it by internal creative ambiences. These were ideas very close to those of the spirituality of Kandinsky and, above all, the genetics of Klee, of a very typical mysticism.

In the works of 1949 we can still see an abundance of the filiform elements common to Klee and Miró. When I ask him about a balanced ensemble, in charcoal and ink, of lines against a background of splashes, in which Gatt sees *the sense of the painful existential becoming which comes very close to the borders of sorcery*, Tàpies tells me that he did this because he is obsessed by the idea of tightrope-walking, just as he is by that of the razor's edge. Frequently, too, there appears the theme, in common with Miró, of stairs, which for Tàpies are a response to the obsession of climbing.

Generally speaking, the paintings of this period have a very highly-worked background, similar to the most typical backgrounds of Miró, with shadows and nebulosities on which the engraving, the scrubbing and the scratching produce effects of transparency, phosphorescence or pure linear quality in negative.

In the iconography, the themes that respond to the idea of perforation become aggressive, as though the artist wished to combat the dense masses of frightening things —like the trees of the Montnegre by night— and take a violent pleasure in wounding them. This places a nervous accent on a whole series of cracks, eyes, half-open doors, sexes, mouths; gaps between one tooth and another, between cornea and eye, between hair and hair. Thus he became in some sort the contrary of Modigliani, the man of the compressed lips, the opaque eyes, the thin noses and the almond-shaped convexities, tightly closed.

Nocturnal encounters. In these atmospheres, which are often nocturnal, there is a proliferation of landscape elements. The most usual are

62. Nymphs, dryads, harpies. Paint on canvas, 1950. 97×130 cm. Joan B. Cendrós Collection. Barcelona.

63. The legerdemain of Wotan. Paint on canvas, 1950. 89 × 116 cm. Private collection, Barcelona.

the trees by night, rounded recollections of the nocturnal excursions made with Brossa in the woods of Vallvidrera, and those great dark trees with their tops illuminated which evoke the fleeciness of the evergreen oaks he used to see in the Montnegre when he was staying in Sant Celoni. Tàpies has told me that these nocturnal and mysterious masses had much the same impression on him as the buttoned padding of coffins or pincushions.

There is a strange flora, which seems to derive directly from the signs and symbols, or from the graphisms of Miró and Klee, but transformed, multiplied, irradiant, aureoled, so that they come to look like the castles of fireworks. One cannot tell whether they are aerial or submarine plants, but they are bodiless and spectral and seem to admit the rightness of mystical spiritualism. The teeth, the horns, the snakes, the pupils of the eyes, give them an added terror.

This world is inhabited by theriomorphic personages, of an invented symbology, but undoubtedly related to the Mesopotamian ones. There are the flying personages, with written words coming out of their mouths, the phosphorescent cats, sometimes upside down, like that of the *Lunar disconsolation* in Pere Casadevall's collection, the flying fish with the hook-like scales, the submarine animal with horns and so many more. Tàpies says I am right in seeing in them an oriental source, and tells me that he became very well acquainted with them at the school of the Piarist Fathers. He once gave a lecture there on the discoveries of Ur.

When I ask him about the rocks flying over a landscape, he thinks for a while and then tells me that they rather tend to fall, but that in any case he wished to represent the whole in equilibrium.

At times the self-portrait seems to float, as in *Sofar*, under the rope

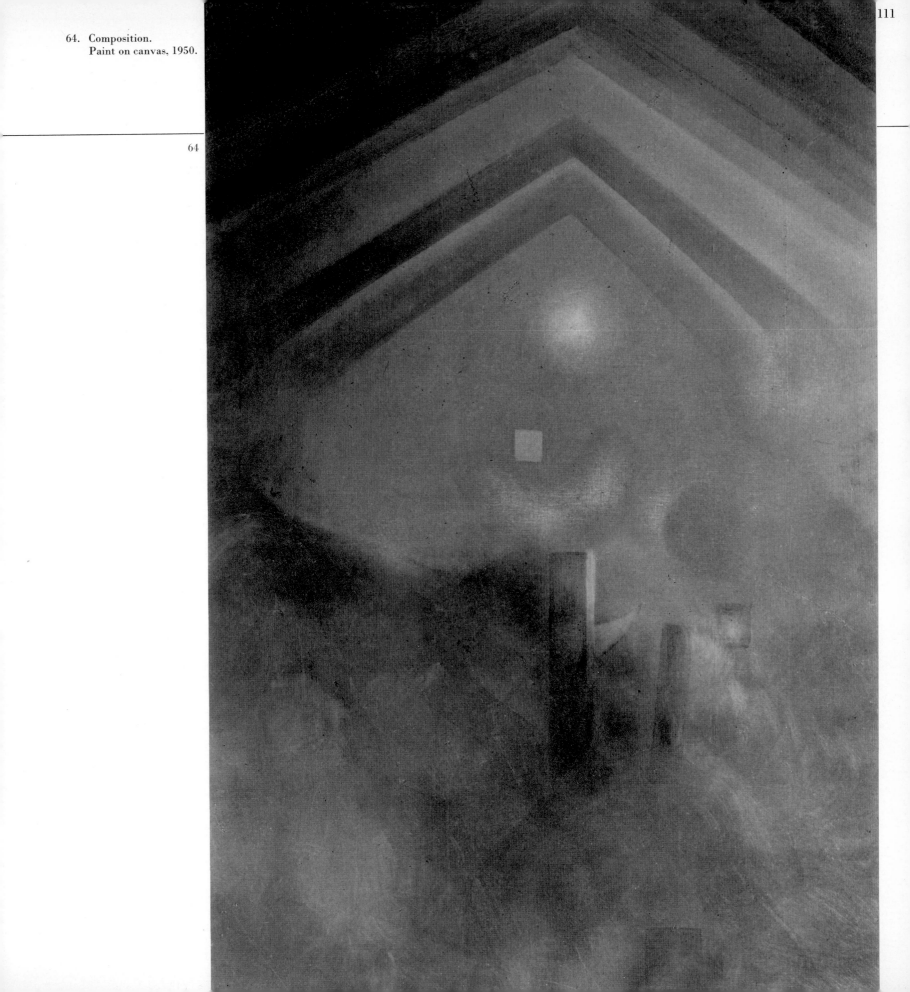

64. Composition.
Paint on canvas, 1950.

64

65. Arromoch, the lion. Paint on canvas, 1949. 81×100 cm. Josep-Lluís
Samaranch Collection, Barcelona.

66. The constructions of Shah Abba. Paint on canvas, 1950. 97×130 cm.
The Albright-Knox Art Gallery Collection, Buffalo, U.S.A.

65

66

67. The probing of the foliage. Paint on canvas, 1950. 81×100 cm. Private collection, Barcelona.
68. Composition. Paint on canvas, 1950.

67

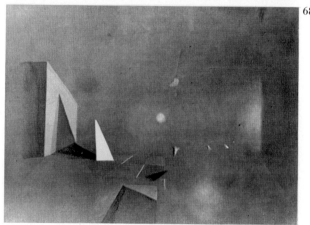

68

of the ropedancer, or to traverse in dreams the field —under diverse moons— of *El blat dels cafres* (The kaffir's wheat), to spy on *Faraga* between the clouds, to melt into the darkness like the chorus of squibs in *El Jardí de Botafocs* (Firebrand's Garden), or to become transformed into a mixture of Hellenistic old man of the river and the Yadwigha of the Douanier Rousseau in *La transformació nocturna d'un lleó en J. Arromoc* (Lion transformed by night into J. Arromoc).

Brossa gave it titles like this, or like *L'escarnidor de diademes* (The scoffer at diadems), the *Miratge d'Oseleta* (Mirage of Oseleta), *El rapte de Batafra* (Abduction of Batafra), *Verdugada*, *Quiriquiguinyol*, *Natura morta de Sirefala* (Still life of Sirefala), *Les constructions de Shah Abba* (The constructions of Shah Abba) or *El dau modern de Versalles* (The modern die of Versailles).

Oracles. These were the sort of works that Tàpies presented on October 28th 1950 in the Galeries Laietanes, for his first one-man show, organized by Josep Gudiol. On the occasion of this exhibition, Brossa published in the *Dau al Set* his really prophetic *Oracle on Antoni Tàpies*.

69. Still life of Sirefala. Paint on canvas, 1950. 81×65 cm. Private collection, Barcelona.

In the year one thousand nine hundred and forty-nine, the ninth month and the thirteenth day of the month, I, Joan Brossa i Sarganta, was resting at home and I heard a voice saying:

Joan Brossa, prophesy of Antoni Tàpies, prophesy, Joan Brossa, and you shall say: Thus says the oracle:

You shall make your estate in a three-year-old calf. The clamour is over... you shall turn your face and all those about you whence they shall not be invoked shall utter cries of joy, for whoever exalts a single hair of your head shall become a lion... And you shall rise to your feet and shall not reach the level... Then the revelry shall give way to anger and a desolate wind shall cross the sun above the sun-dials... [You are... a powerful hook in razed lands, which shall have the shape of a human hand in the end... your stones are the main center of two winds... you shall shut the door at broad noon, with smooth rocks in slippery places...] it will be the end of pride... There shall be a cleft very close to your odorous instruments... rocks will exist mutilated: those which were monumental triumphal carriages...

The Modern Die of Versailles. In this same year of 1950 Joan Josep Tharrats published his little book

70. Composition. Paint on canvas, 1950. 65 × 81 cm. Galería René Métras, Barcelona.

entitled *Antoni Tàpies or the modern Die of Versailles*, which began: *I present Antoni Tàpies to you, a personage who has just made his entrance in the History of Painting and who will be much spoken of,* a phrase which, like the oracle of Brossa, is another sign of the strange fascination that Tàpies immediately aroused among those closest to him. Tharrats explains the relationship between the painting of Tàpies and the poetry of Brossa when he says: *Perhaps, in listening to the readings of his work that Brossa habitually gives you, you identified yourself with that very disconcerting universe which he showed you and you perfumed then with incense, and with a ritual fervour, his most tortuously attained heights.*

Tàpies' first exhibition, from October 28th to November 10th, was presented by a very recently formed group of persons interested in the arts, which crystallized in the *Club 49*; its president at that time was Sixte Yllescas and the prime movers were Joan Prats, Xavier Vidal de Llobatera, Pere Casadevall, Eudald Serra, Ramón Marinel·lo, Josefa Cusí, Jaume Sans, Joan Teixidor and a few others. Shortly afterwards were to follow the first exhibitions of other members of the group.

Closed spaces and double bottoms. During 1950 Tàpies showed a tendency to abandon the great open spaces of the preceding magic period and to develop the theme of closed space.

Beginning in January of 1950, we have the publication in the *Dau al Set* of visions of men seen from behind, placed in cabins, chambers and little back rooms, wardrobes and drawers, intriguing corridors, polyhedra, staircases, traps, hatchways, peepholes, stage-flies, locks and keys. This was the period of the interiors and boxes, influenced by Brossa's great interest in the double-bottomed boxes used by conjurers. It was the period of pictures like the *Dolor de Brunhilda* (Sorrow of Brunhilda), in the Obiols Collection, or the *Escamoteig de Wotan* (Legerdemain of Wotan), in which the optical illusionism of Tanguy and the unsuspected magic of Ernst are blended into a transformism of the spaces themselves, whether as the stage of a popular theatre or a majestic, legendary cavern. In the same way the objects that rest in them are ambiguous, like those of metaphysical painting, half-way between the papier-maché stage-prop and the pure geometrical presence of abstractism.

Despite all this, there are also free spaces, some with the mysterious, nocturnal evergreen oaks of the Montnegre. The objects in the space, within the tradition of Tanguy, appear to humanize themselves, in the ambiguous fashion of Magritte, close to the great female body with swollen veins reclining among sponges, and the ambiguity becomes extremely anguished when, in the sinking vessel in the Museum of Buffalo, we seem to see an immense mummy.

Between the closed spaces and the open there is the theme of the windows, in which Tàpies was to find the graphism of the thick cross, almost equivalent to four corner rectangles, which was to be so often repeated in later periods.

The whole seems to breathe the anguish of things that are concealed but imminent.

THE PHASE
OF CONFLICTS

The first Paris. His friendship with the Brazilian João Cabral de Melo had a great influence on Tàpies' cultural formation during the year 1950. The irrationalistic Wagnerian basis, the forms of a lay mysticism and an empty magic which had bordered on spiritualism and pantheism were now confronted with new intellectual structures. Tàpies began to take an interest in Marxism, read widely about the movement and its doctrines and approached the programme that Cabral made explicit when he said that *one must go beyond formalism to achieve the clash of men.* Cabral was not so ingenuous as to believe that realism is a question of form. *"It is essentially"*, he said, *"a question of substance, of theme."* Cabral wrote in 1950 that *reality is not the idle enjoyment of an object. Reality is rhythmed by a fierce fight, and in it there is no giving up... No dream... Suffering is not an orchard to be dug or a thing to be raised in dignity, but on the contrary a thing that seeks to be overcome. That fight is an essentially virile one, and at bottom, since it is neither subjected nor interrupted, an optimistic one.*

The French government gave Tàpies a scholarship to Paris, as a result of the competition organized by the Cercle Maillol, and this permitted him to remain ten months in the French capital, where he lodged first in the Cité Universitaire and later in a little flat in Saint-Cloud.

71

In Paris he met Cabral again, who accompanied him to buy books. Now he thinks that it was this period that aroused in him a revolutionary enthusiasm very typical of the European intellectuals of the time. Later, though, the knowledge of specific facts such as the phenomena of Stalinism, Ydanovism, the Moscow trials and, above all, the events in Hungary, made him share in a disenchantment, also very generally felt, which, although he still desires the changes necessary for justice to be done, prevents him from accepting them in authoritarian form. On the other hand, though he believes that the artist —considering him as an autonomous thinker— must remain independent of politicians in his work, he still thinks that the great artists have always prepared and collaborated in the most progressive political changes. He does not think, therefore, that there can be such a thing as a great artist with conservative

72. The last hand. Paint on canvas, 1950. 89×116 cm. Guillem Díaz-Plaja Collection, Barcelona.

72

ideas. The works carried out in 1951 begin to reveal the ideological influences that worked upon him, especially during the Paris period, but the fruit of these influences was to be especially noticeable in 1952.

Fait-divers. Tàpies' painting on his return from Paris in 1951 is still a magic vision of places, carried out on backgrounds like those of Miró, scrubbed and scraped, and with the techniques of superimposed drawing or graffito that lend themselves to this way of painting. But the things happening in his work are beginning to abandon the pure themes of the self-portrait, of myths and imminences, and tend to be aimed at the real society of the *fait-divers*, at isolation, cruelty or work.

One of the more characteristic of his *fait-divers* works is *L'atracament* (The holdup), in which architectures and gardens of the sensorial repertoire, with a feudal morphology in the castle and reminis-

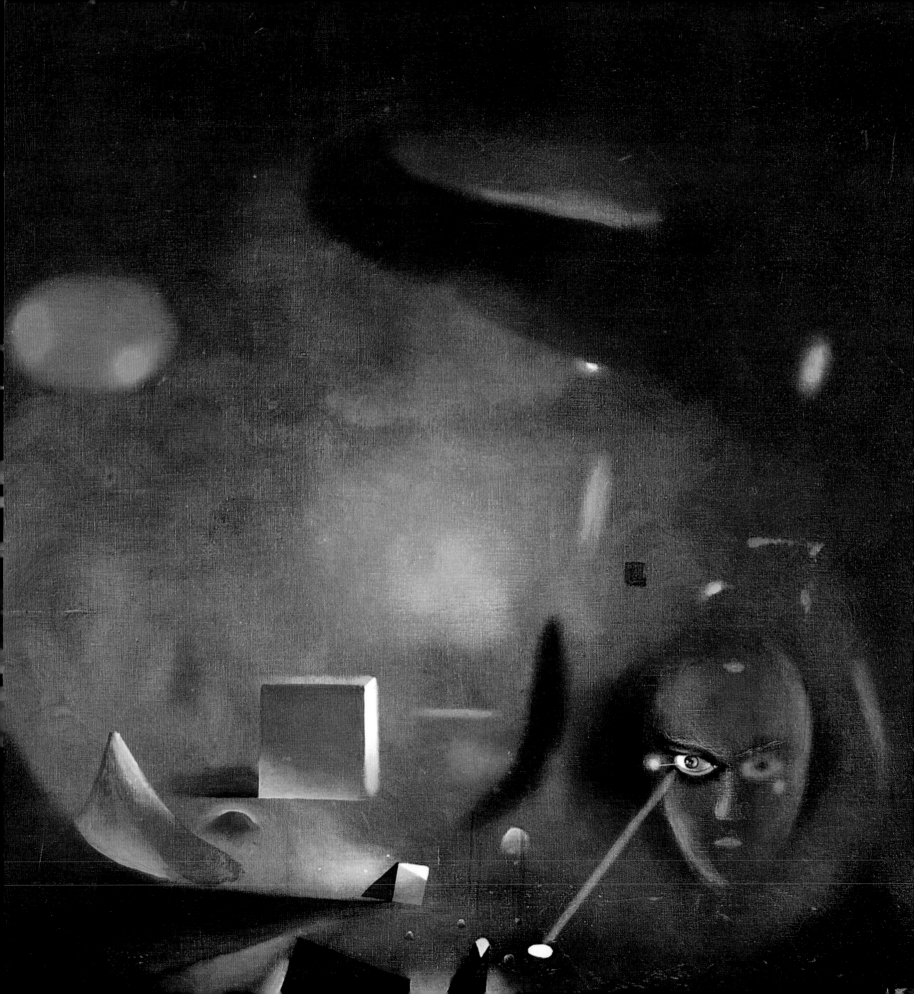

cences of the Benozzo Gozzoli of the Florentine bankers in the trees of the garden under a dense sky, with a mystical vision, serve to situate the episode of the man armed with a rifle who is expelling the naked man and woman from Paradise. There is a clear parallelism between the manifestation of the power of wealth, the force of tradition, and the power and force of the holdup man of our own age. Also between a man and a woman, beautiful and naked, images of men more human but deprived, expelled from the possession of the riches of this world, who have been treated in a way that is reminiscent of the *Adam and Eve* of Masaccio.

All the ambiguities of form and phosphorescences of the magic painting converge in this programme.

Another *fait-divers* work is *L'atropellament* (The collision), in which a sad and enamoured Harlequin, who kisses his Columbine and snatches a black tear from her, is run over by the motor-car in which the indifferent woman follows, with half-closed eyes, a top hat that the man inside does not need to be effective. This is a work treated as a drawing in ink on an abraded Miró-like background.

There are men with knives who want to kill the flying lions, the man half-fainting, in the isolation of the street with closed houses, and the gypsy girl innocently sleeping, surrounded by the threat of the bull's heads.

The work chosen for the international exhibition of the Carnegie Institute of Pittsburgh in 1951 was pervaded with this atmosphere.

Work. Another series, a rather later one, linked the themes of everyday work with an attempt at monumental treatment of social and historical problems, which was to reach its highest point in 1952 and was to set the tone for Tàpies' second exhibition at the Galeries Laietanes.

Still in the year 1951 are the compositions allusive to various trades, such as the great trophy of working implements, linked to a bull, to an eagle, to a big, tall man, which is presented as a great bouquet brandished by a hand across the space.

There are more trophies of work in 1952: the flower man, the man ploughing, the great canvasses which seem to be mural paintings and which evoke, with a style already significant made of light and transparent allusions, the great allegories of the progressives, with personages bearing attributes and with emblems and banners of the 19th century; with work tools, wheels, cogs, shoes and other pieces of clothing.

Plasticity. From his reading, from his contacts and from what he had seen, Tàpies learnt a lesson of simplicity that made him find the works of his magic period complicated and manneristic. A new grandeur, a more unified and more rhythmed plasticity, greater and stronger rhythms, now took the field.

Some of the experiments of 1952 in this direction bring him closer to the purism of Le Corbusier or Ozenfant, opaque and deliberate artists very far from his world of phosphorescence. The centres are dominant; verticals or horizontals appear simple and modulated, architectural, with mechanical forms and thin profiles, like that of the classical vases, the form of the cithara or the silhouette of the gondola.

These works underline the problems of the relationship between the form and the working procedure, and the effects of *grattage*, never so highly purified as now, while the superimpositions of forms tend to destroy the concept of optical space and to block up its perspectives, in a movement towards an art more strictly flat, in

73. The letter. Paint on canvas, 1950. 89×100 cm. Josep-Lluís Samaranch
Collection, Barcelona.

73

skilfully done stratifications which sometimes serve to create, through the graffiti, cameo arrangements.

The re-encounter with matter. The study of the relationships between the tool and the paste, and the suppression of visual spaces, brought an accelerating tendency to return to the material painting practised by the young Tàpies from 1945 to 1947. Undoubtedly he was stimulated in this by a direct acquaintance with the work of Dubuffet and Fautrier; this latter, in 1950, had begun the series of *the boxes and the objects*, in directions not too far removed from those of Tàpies' own old collages. In spite of this affinity, however, there was a substantial difference, which Tàpies emphasizes when he says that he has seen painters working with materials indeed, but with indefinite materials, like chocolate, whereas he chooses materials which say something in themselves.

74

Within the general ensemble of his work in 1953 there is a special significance in the surfaces obtained with light-coloured materials on dark cardboard, in which, like remains of the period of the signs, pieces of straight lines, dotted lines, remains of spirals and round or sometimes oblong holes, crutch- or V-shapes, scratches and furrows create a system of relationships on the flat.

At the same time their character of elements of significant graphism is changed into one of elements of incision, an incision that is temporary, procedural or simply creative of spatial relationships, as if foreseeing what Fontana was later to call spatialism. A painting in Joan Teixidor's collection combines the element of furrowed material with traces that definitively have the effect of superimposed projections of light or of wounds through which an intense brightness filters.

The procedural aspect gives rise to the appearance in the painting of this period of the theme of dilapidation, the *delabré*, which co-exists paradoxically with lights and shades as though the work were a second-degree, objectivist language, built over another, visualist one of the first degree.

There are all kinds of treatments of the material. There are striations, obtained with the imprint of the corrugated cardboard; there are reticulations obtained with the imprint of muslins or else using them as braid, tramplings of woven material, etc.

Transverberation. There was not yet a re-encounter with matter as a wall. The magic space could not withdraw without a fight. It appears to be helped still by the typically procedural texture, produced by the dripping which eliminates a top layer and reveals the one beneath. There are also the modifica-tions on the moulds or braids, as in the case of the torn nets, which create a particular suggestion of a wound through which filters something from beyond, as in the *Foc Interior* (Internal Fire), in the Cominges Collection.

The scribbling theme is now incorporated, no longer with the aestheticism of a Hartung, but rather as a graphism of spontaneous violence, which co-exists with the vertical, horizontal or crossed rulings, almost sadistically, in dialogue or in aggressive conflict with the passive backgrounds. Tàpies asked me for a text on the paintings of this period, for publication in the catalogue of his 1954 exhibition at the Galeries Laietanes; later published by the *Dau al Set* in the form of a little book entitled *Tàpies o la Transverberació*, it was, though small, the first critical monograph to appear on the work of Tàpies. The work of that period was indecisive. In it we can as soon find constructive values as visual, abstract and even geometrical ones, as well as figurative and even anthropomorphic. A striation or a reticulation could co-exist there with effects of light and of darkness, while some plaques like prints by Lardera were at home with a torso like that of a Hermes.

We sought in it for a unity that would show us its significance, or at least a group of connotations capable of giving its sense, and we realized that instead of a logical rectilinear intention there was only the objective fact of the work executed on the material, with a sense of craft and a devotion that were in marked contrast to the usual manner of painters who, thinking of forms and of colours, allow themselves to be distracted from the material and treat it inexpertly. We were then able to affirm: *the technical mastery gives it freedom.*

When we re-examined the elements of this material work, we observed that in those works of 1953 the dominant phenomenon was that of an intercommunication, as a sort of counterpoint to the softer places, a conflict that often came very close to the limit of contradictions.

In visual counterpoint, light and shade, he gave the work effects of transparency, as of two worlds superimposed, rather in the style of a melody and an accompaniment. In conflict, the brightness seemed to attain, by means of a crack, through the shade, to the most violent transverberation.

The same thing happened with the tactile part, the textures. In counterpoint the roughs played with the smooths, while in conflict a crack or a wrinkle was like a boundary between distension and contraction, between pressure and tension. The primings —matter added— often in relief were contrapuntal to the graffiti —matter removed—; and the painting through textures bore witness to the conflict between passage and barrier.

The result, dual and cathartic, was like a translation into new terms of that instinct of the cut, the slit, visible in the magic paintings of 1949, when he separated the lips of the mouths and the sexes and made a space between the teeth, between eyelid and cornea and between one hair and another.

For a moment the painting of 1953 might permit us to have doubts as to the ultimate destiny of its trajectory. Its aim might be to cause the secret to explode, break down the walls and liberate a far-off transcendency that would flood everything, or else, with the bitter lucidity that comes from the knowledge that the glories of the Jesuitical ceilings do not exist, it might let the wounds and cracks close up, leaving us in the outside part, the cold part, of an opaque world. Who knows?

At this point, faced with the alternatives of Byzantinism and realism, between Pala d'Oro and Caravaggio, the latter choice seemed stronger and I wagered all on the future of the Caravaggio line.

SOLITUDE

The closed walls.   Tàpies now takes a clear decision to shut his art up within what Theodor Adorno has called an immersion in himself, by means of a reflexivization of the innerness, in order to reach a higher level of revelation, of brusque approach to reality. This decision presupposes a starting-up of the rupture. In establishing this personal basis, he breaks with all dogmas and all systems. It is a decision laden with subversive significance.

The works of 1954 clearly represent the definitive taking of this decision. If, the year before, we were dealing with the dilemma between the irrationalist trajectory, towards an illusory transcendence, and the lucid, disenchanted trajectory, towards the bitter solitude of an opaque world, now the definite decision was being taken, and in closing up the last fissures of the transverberation, so highly inflamed but by now so hemmed in, we found ourselves, once and for all, facing closed walls.

There is here a total renunciation, which is sometimes presented in the form of a triumph of the existentialist theme of Nothingness, in compositions in which the simple counterpoint between the matt black and the glossy takes up once more the famous *black on black* theme of Rodchenko.

But the great theme is that of the wall, rooted in the constant which, from his childhood, revealed Tàpies' sensitivity to the things that concealed things, like the cushion of the Sacred Heart or the evergreen oaks of the Montnegre. The wall closes, and at the same time it grows and obliges the painter to use the great formats which typify this period, imposing in their grandeur.

On the other hand, the wall needs to accentuate its character of opacity, and this entails the generalization of a change of materials which causes him to replace the transparencies and viscosities of painting in oils with the fleshy muteness, matt and desiccated, of the layers of latex. Side by side with the enlargement of the format and the opacity of the material, the conception of the painting as a wall brings him to a great simplicity through the composition, sometimes almost smooth, sometimes divided by a line into two fields, always very sparingly articulated.

Tactile exacerbation. A sign, as we know, in order to attain a character of significance does not need only the material it contains, in this case the character of a wall, which is its semantic axis. It also needs semantical articulations; there must be a dialectic between opposed manners in order that this axis may exist. If we recall that, before closing the luminous fissures of the period of transverberation, we classified the elements of polarity —counterpoint or conflict— according to whether they were visual or tactile, luminous or textural, it is logical that, once the world of Tàpies has been unified into one sole, uniform proximity, into a kind of wall, there should only remain the counterpoints and conflicts of the texture, of the relief.

It was also logical that, once alone, these conflicts should be exacerbated. This gives a coherent explanation to the development of the theme of matter chastized, trodden down, split, scratched, stigmatized, and also the opposite phenomenon, the excrescence of the cakings, of the rays of corporeal matter like threads, like cylinders, like clots, like incrustations forced from the tube on to the palette, distantly related to the hurled painting of Pollock, to the infinite calligraphy of Tobey, to the signatures of Mathieu. In some of the compositions the light-coloured excrescence is superimposed and counterpoised with the dark masking, in order to introduce new elements of contraposition, as in the *Blanca amb taques vermelles* (White with red stains) in the Samaranch Collection, or the *Composició en blanc i negre* (Composition in black and white) in the Tooth Gallery. In other works, such as the *Ocre i marró* (Ochre and brown) in the Lluís Gili Collection, the counterpoint is carried out according to zones, one zone against another.

Dialectics. Sometimes a dialectic is established between a delimited whole, lying in the centre, and the total ensemble that constitutes its background. There is a compensation of density and extension, a contrast between graphism and smooth tension, between the small scale or small rhythm and the large scale or large rhythm, as when the painter evokes the form of a window, our vision of which seems to be dimmed by some *graffiti* of exceeding fineness.

Sometimes this sort of contrast between a small, dense zone and a larger zone of lower density is created by the presence of a graphic sign, for instance a cross, at one edge of the deserted composition.

When I asked Tàpies whether this composition was in response to an aesthetic quest for balance, for a *point of exactness*, he told me that it was not. He said that once the great, smooth and perfect work was ready, in putting this cross there he had the sensation of cutting something in it. That it was like marking something for destruction, or like rubbing something out or refusing it.

The *de facto* informalism of this kind of composition was not exclusive. Sometimes there was a formal dialectic, and even a bipolarity through symmetry. In some of the works that he sent to his first exhibition at the Stadler Gallery there were twin counterpoised forms, in something that is reminiscent of the double symmetries of Chinese bronzes, such as the two cotyledons of the leaf-lobe of a plant, duplicated upside down.

This theme of the two cotyledons, which was to be developed in paintings of 1955, such as that in the Schmela Gallery of Düsseldorf, or the *Sense títol* (Untitled) in the Albright Art Gallery of Buffalo, initiates an evolution leading into organic morphology that was to a certain extent explicit from the moment when, in the first material works, the *transfert* began between the concept of matter and that of the flesh of man. Here we see once more the lungs in the radiographs of his youth. At other times there are coxal or gluteal structures, of kidneys, of testicles or of lobes of the brain.

Purity. The works of this period take on a specially rich ambiguity, and frequently a great purity of form, as is the case with the great composition in the Dotremont Collection in Uccle (Brussels), somewhat like an enormous torso kneeling, which, ambiguously, can also be seen as a wall which has had its plaster peeled away by the dripping of the rain, and on which some workman from the gas company or some maniac has marked a point, to indicate something unknown. This painting, which was the most monumental of the works he contributed to the Hispano-American Biennale, is related, according to what he told me himself, to the phenomenon of his very accentuated claustrophobia.

As pure as this one, or perhaps even purer, was a great black painting, almost smooth, where one of the lower quarters was marked with an M. I asked him if this was meant to be the initial of Mort (Death), but he told me that he might perhaps have been thinking rather of the M of the palm of the hand, which, in fact, corresponds to the same evocation of the mythology of the unknown destiny. This impressive picture could not be included in the exhibition because the panel of critics voted against it. There was, however, the great pachyderm's hide, in anthracite, marked with a cross, which is now in the Museum of Contemporary Art in Düsseldorf.

In one great reddish painting, in which the combination of the latex with marble-worker's sand produces an effect of great quality, we find the reappearance of a theme which we shall later find frequently, that of the four smooth corners, like the strengtheners of a binding or of a folder. It is one of the most elemental themes of his work. In another picture we find the great ochre tongue in graffito, showing the black of the background through the cracks. In the reddish picture the dialectic was established between the great field of the cross and the little rectangles in the corners. In the ochre, it was between the big, warm, rounded form and the dry presence nearby of a cold, grey rectangle. There is an iconic subject matter which is very characteristic of this phase of ambiguity and claustrophobia: the doorway, often a doorway which has been stripped of its door, and even of its frame, in order to brick it up, and the bucket which conceals the entrance —there is no exit— to a well.

One of these paintings with a white door was exhibited at the *Saló de Maig*.

75. The bird. Paint on canvas, 1951. 41×33 cm. Galería René Métras, Barcelona.

76. Homage to Federico García Lorca. Paint on canvas, 1951. 81×100 cm. Josep-Lluís Samaranch Collection, Barcelona.

77. Asia together. Paint on canvas, 1951. 81×100 cm. Sala Gaspar, Barcelona.

78. The holdup. Paint on canvas, 1951. 81×100 cm. Xavier Vilanova Collection, Barcelona.

79. Still life of a hunt. Paint on canvas, 1951. 90×90 cm. Daniel E. Schneider Collection, New York.

80. The monument. Paint on canvas, 1951. 115×110 cm. Albert Jacas Collection, Barcelona.

81. Chorale of work. Paint on canvas, 1951. 130×162 cm. Galería Biosca, Madrid.

82. Jobs. Paint on canvas, 1951. 89×116 cm. Sala Gaspar, Barcelona.

79

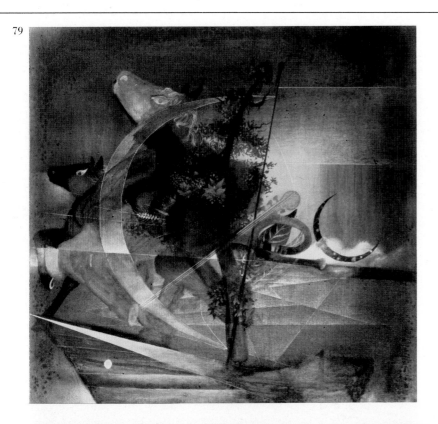

80

81

82

83. The cat. Paint on canvas, 1951. 65×81 cm. Cesáreo Rodríguez-Aguilera
Collection, Barcelona.

84. Figure in yellows, whites and blacks. Paint on canvas, 1951. 38 × 46 cm. Josep-Lluís Samaranch Collection, Barcelona.

85. The collision. Paint on canvas, 1951. Alexandre Cirici-Pellicer Collection, Barcelona.

83

85

84

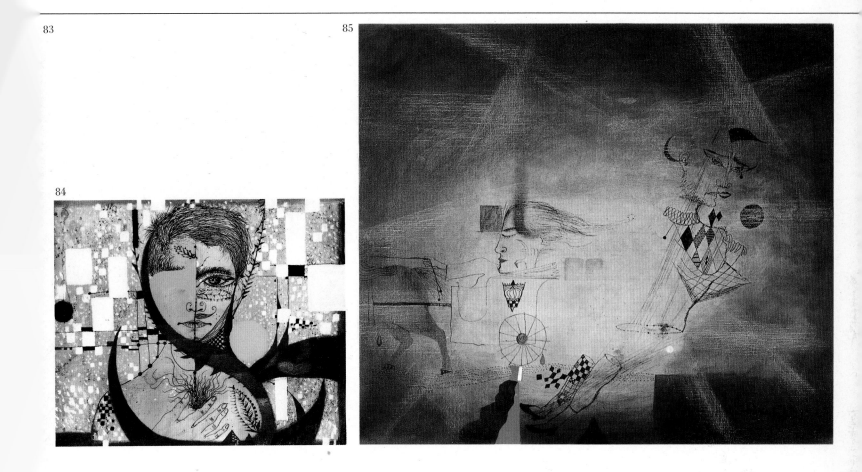

142

86

87

88

Nipple. Half-way between the closed wall and the organic morphology provoked by the *transfert*, in an ambiguity between what painting possesses of the sign of the Alter and of the sign of the Ego, the theme of turgescence was developed. *Remolí de sorra* (The swirl of sand), in the Anthony Denney Collection in London, is a clear example of the origin of this theme, with its ambiguity between technique and representation, between living and looking.

The marble-worker's sand, not dust or ordinary sand, but the hard product of grinding, incorporated in

89

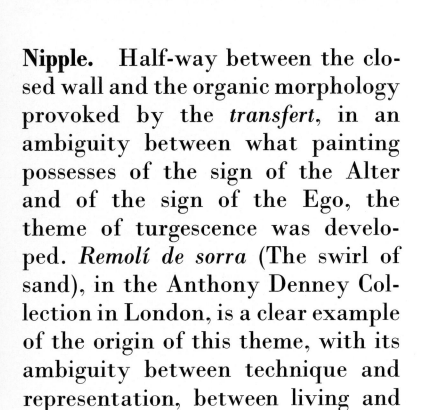

90. Collage of the bank notes. Gouache, inks and sizing on paper, 1951.
26×31.5 cm. Private collection, Barcelona.

91. The bouquet. Paint on canvas, 1951. 100×81 cm. Museum of Modern Art Collection, Venice.

92. Prodigal night. Paint on canvas, 1951-1952. Martín Collection, Barcelona.

93. The furrows. Paint on canvas, 1952. 97×130 cm. Private collection, Barcelona.

91

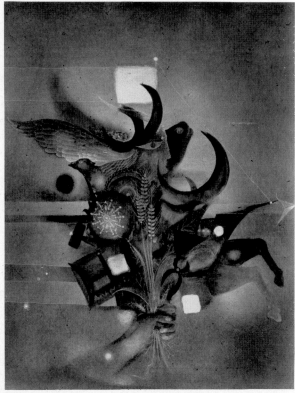

93

92

94. Homage to Miguel Hernández. Paint on canvas, 1951. 116×73 cm. Galerie Beyeler, Basle.

95. Political archaeology. Paint on canvas, 1952. 73×92 cm. Private collection, Barcelona.

94

95

the mass of latex, is used here to produce a swirling turgescence in the middle of a neutral plane, as if it were the inert matter itself that suddenly achieved, in some privileged place, a vitality inspiring it with a desire to project itself beyond its own being. Here we have a problem that resembles certain biological problems, like that of a gland between supporting tissues, which explains the resemblance of the artificial theme created by Tàpies to the natural theme of a nipple on a female breast.

In one way or another, this privileged excrescence, in dialogue with the inert universe, was to be one of Tàpies' themes, at times sharp and erotic, at other times formless, devious, frustrated or malignant, like a cancer.

This isolated theme brings us to that of the purer solitude expressed by the *Tres pinzellades sobre un espai gris* (Three brushstrokes on a grey space), lost near the limit of

96. Composition. Paint on canvas, 1952. Museum of Figueras (Gerona).

97. The plough. Paint on canvas, 1952. 130×162 cm. Pere Portabella Collection, Barcelona.

98. Collage-composition in yellows. Paint on canvas, 1953. 89×146 cm. Private collection, Barcelona.

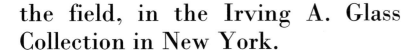

the field, in the Irving A. Glass Collection in New York.

Central structuring. If we observe the evolution of Tàpies' painting between the date of his marriage (1954) and that of the rebuilding of the house at Campins (1960), which covers the period of his great triumph of 1958, we shall be struck by a phenomenon of progressive structuring of the form, accompanied by a certain diminution in the subject matter of sexual origin and an increasingly important personal mythology, based on his memories of childhood. In all of this there is a kind of assimilation between the ideas of evident formal simplicity, stability and deeper probing, on solid bases that communicate with

99. The amphora. Paint on canvas, 1952. 92 × 73 cm. Galería René Métras, Barcelona.

99

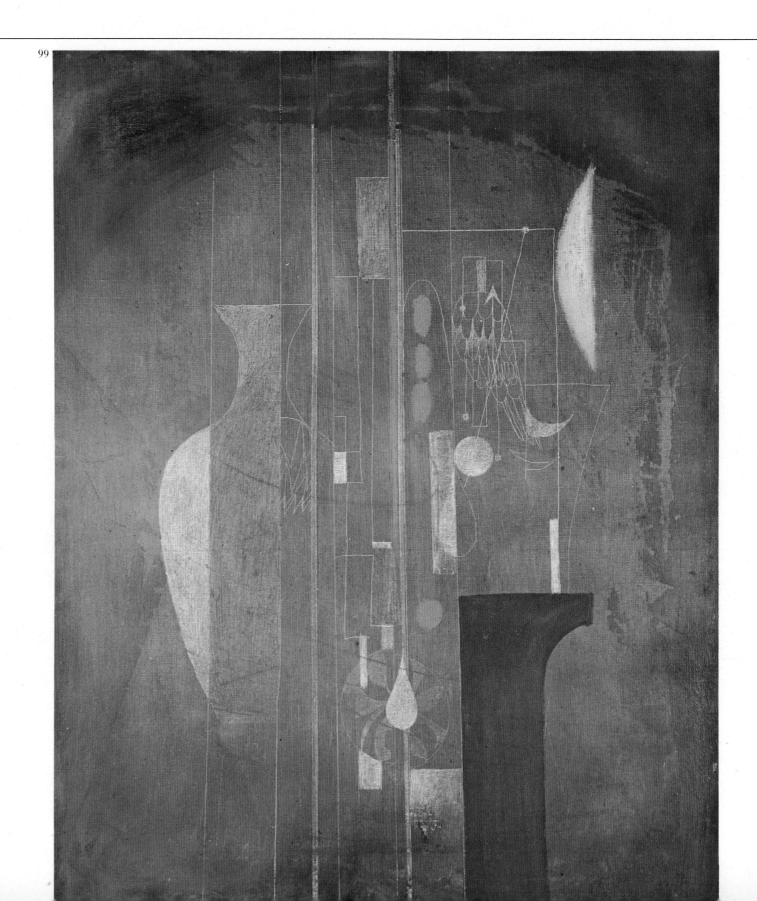

100. Composition of blues and reds. Paint on canvas, 1952. 81 × 100 cm. Sturedgalleri, Stockholm.

the use of strong structures, and a refinding of known morphologies. The past performs the function of roots.

If we have so far been able to speak of informalism, this is quite evidently not the right word for a work full of specific morphologies.

There is the dialectic of the fields, which is stated in many different fashions. Sometimes it is ambiguous, and when we see a rectangle in the picture it is difficult to specify whether the principal element is the surrounding fringe or the central texture. At other times, as in Philip Johnson's picture, it is quite clear that the leading role belongs to the central volume, more or less ovoid and speckled all over, which is animated by a sort of serpent. Even more so when, as in the great *Oval blanc* (White oval) in the Museum of Krefeld, which is fissured all over, the ovoid mass reaches a point at which it is tangential to the frames. At times, however, as

in the *Blanc craquelé* in the Holländer Collection, it becomes evident that, unlike the other examples, the material that speaks loudest defines itself by the distances it takes, around a central void, even though in this case a solitary nipple appears out of the nothingness. There is the flattened white oval, which seems to be a *lavabo*, the vertical oval of mulberry-grey sand and sometimes the specific identification, like the composition with a bow, centered by an oval which is the transference of a washstand looking-glass from Campins.

More determined than determining. Even though it may sometimes contain industrial references, the central structuring usually appears as a natural phenomenon. As the crushing of a ball of mud, as the spilling of a thick drop, as a cowpat in a field. The type of deceptiveness that it admits is limited, as is for instance the form of an omelette or a cake.

When the structuring depends rather on the corners than on the centre, the material naturally does not appear in it freely but subject to conditioning, and its morphology becomes more deceptive. Thus functions, for instance, the theme of the frames (i. e., the vertical supporting elements at the sides), which operate as elements of static construction in connection with a central door, or else as a corset, compressing a thoracic form that often becomes, as though by dint of this lateral pressure, segmented.

It is interesting to note here the counterpoint between the central theme —the nipple, the field, the omelette, the cake— and that other, organic, segmented theme, which leads to the torso or the abdomen. It is a double motif, like that represented in Christian architecture by the central theme of the baptistery or mausoleum —holy places, valid in themselves— on the one hand, and the longitudinal, segmented theme of the basilica —an organ conditioned by the necessity of the ambience— on the other. It is the same double possibility as that created, in Buddhist architecture, by the Indian *estupa* or the Chinese tower of bells, on the one hand, and, on the other, the Indian *chaytia* or the gilded room of the Japanese temples.

A deeper reading would show us that the central theme —the nipple,

152

102. No answer. Paint on canvas, Sturedgalleri, Stockholm.

103. The oxcart. Paint on canvas, 1952. 116 × 89 cm. Manuel Salsas Collection, Paris.

104. Grey ochre. Paint on canvas, 1953. 130 × 162 cm. Private collection, Barcelona.

102

104

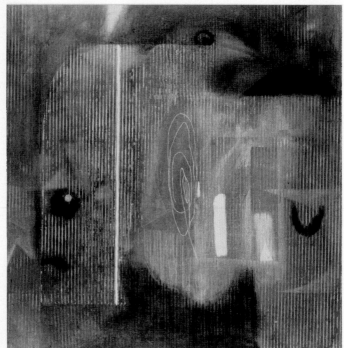

103

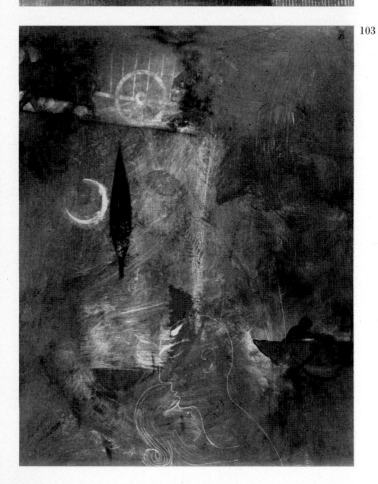

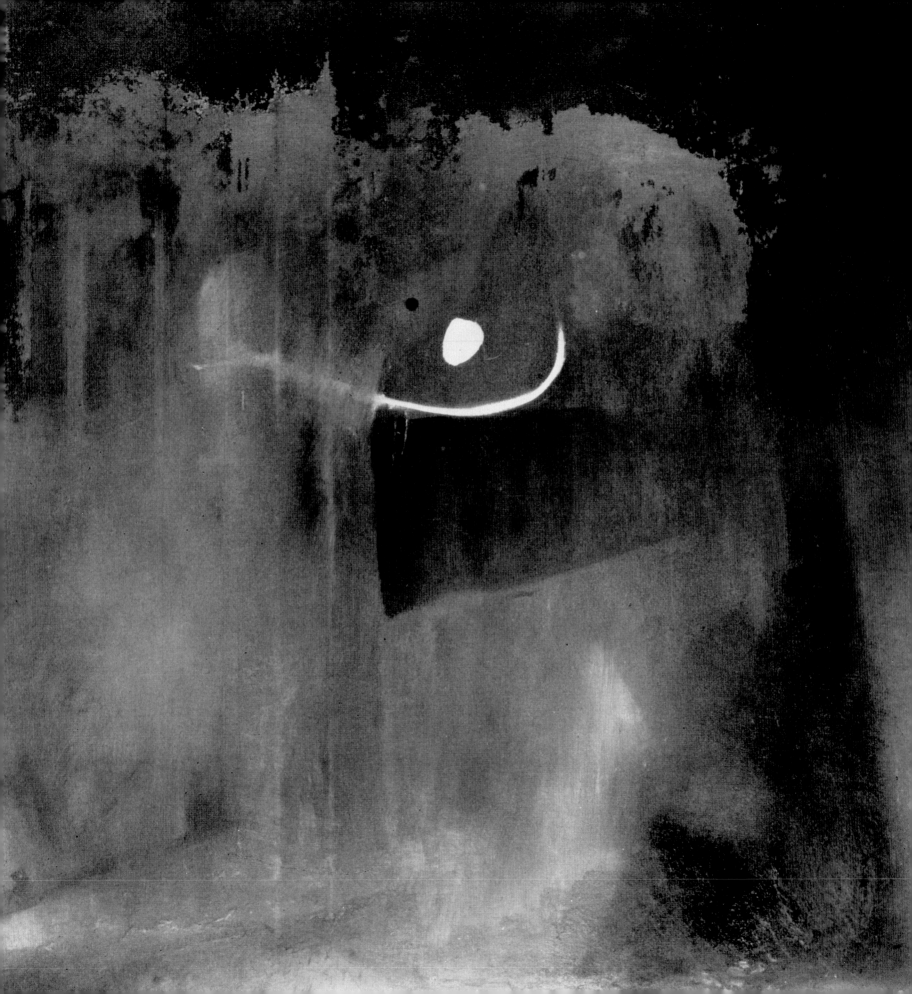

105. Origin. Paint on canvas, 1953. 89×116 cm. Martha Jackson Gallery, New York.

the omelette— is a conditioned theme, just as those of the torso or the abdomen are conditioned themes. The old chiefs of the figurative period, like the solar elements, belonged to the conditioning mythology, which is gradually disappearing, while the conditioned thoracic or abdominal structures will steadily proliferate.

This is a phenomenon which repeats that of the progressive disappearance of the visual luminous factors, which give place to the blind presence, opaque and tactile.

Crosspieces. It is not only the vertical frames that determine the central form, for this is frequently decided by the crosspieces.

Quite often there is a horizontal determination, as when the picture (one in the New York Museum of Modern Art is a case in point) reproduces a typical Sezession dado, with sinusoidal crowning and adorned with typical compressions of cement work, the evocation of one particular dado in the Carrer d'Alfons XII, in the district of Sant Gervasi. At other times the crosspieces are those typical of furniture, like the arcadings in the picture in the Didisheim Collection in Lausanne, which imprison the feeble verticals as if they were those of the headboard of a Viennese bed. In other paintings, like the wedge-shaped relief in blackish ochre which is in the Streep Collection, the crosspieces are like the concave or convex ends of a Mesopotamian stele.

The crosspieces may also appear in negative, as backgrounds or cloud effects, and in this case they also frequently produce segmented forms, this time recumbent.

They may also be like brushstrokes, as a sort of border above and below.

Body and clothing. The ambiguous correspondence between pictorial structurings and certain structurings

106. Violet monotype on paper, 1953. 48×61 cm. Martha Jackson Gallery, New York.

107. Composition with red lines. Paint on canvas, 1953. Sturedgalleri, Stockholm.

108. Scraping on red. Paint on canvas, 1952. 54×63 cm. Galería René Métras, Barcelona.

109. Composition with greens. Paint on canvas, 1952. 80×80 cm. Private collection, Barcelona.

106

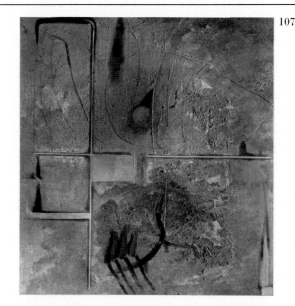

107

108

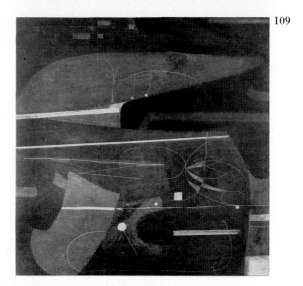

109

of the world of memories often becomes very explicit.

Thus we see the segmented vertical field which, in a green painting in the Piacenza Collection, painted as early as 1955, not only shows the assurance that makes it organic, but presents us with the cotyledonic structure of a pair of buttocks and the visual centre of an anus. The graphism of the red nude already referred to may be recalled here, as may the dense quality —of skin and muscle— of an occasional vertical strip in which the furrows make us think of rolls of flesh at the waist or of ribs and,

110. Screen. Paint on canvas, 1953. Josep-Lluís Samaranch Collection, S'Agaró.

111. Composition. Paint on canvas, 1953. 73×54 cm. Galería René Métras, Barcelona.

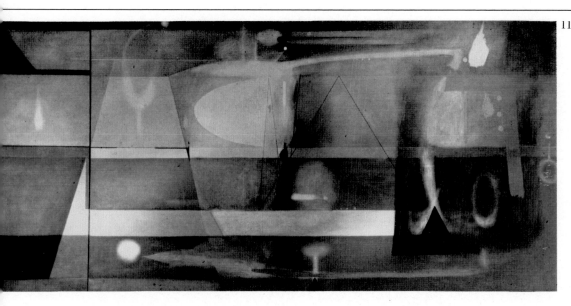

111

when they form an angle, correspond to the groins.

There are also great navels, like the brown and ochre in the Monzino Collection, which should not be confused with the more generic theme of the nipple. Because they are large they make us think of a disembowelling, as a violent reaction against closed things. The disembowelling is sometimes total, and the human body appears really cut down the middle, as in the reddish painting of Panza di Biumo. Sometimes, too, the segmentation of the body leads to multiple tumefaction, as in Jacques Dupin's grey

relief, in which excrescences proliferate; no longer, however, is it the isolated turgidity of the nipple theme, but a deflated and wrinkled multiplicity which, among other things, alludes ambiguously to empty teats or to old hipbones.

Following the obsession of the things that conceal things, the theme of the chest and the abdomen —no heads, no arms, no massive legs, but places that hide spaces— is often replaced by themes of clothing, such as the girdle with hanging folds, the sort of grey shirt with a red sign in the Panza di Biumo Collection, the coattails of grey

112. Epicurean meditation. Paint on canvas, 1953. 92 × 73 cm. Private collection, Barcelona.

113. Collage-painting. Combined process on canvas, 1954. 146 × 114 cm. Nippon Gallery, Tokyo.

112

113

ochre, like a chasuble, in the Tate, the splendid blue dalmatic in Joan Teixidor's collection, an orange-coloured Buddhist tunic, the vest in the Boulois Collection, the curtain-

ing in yellow sand in the Morton Newman Collection, the suspender belt in the Aesthetic Research Center of Turin, or the trodden corseting in the collection of Panza di

114. Yellow and violet. Combined process on canvas, 1953. 97 × 130 cm. Private collection, Barcelona.

115. Painting. Paint on canvas, 1954. 97 × 130 cm. Private collection, London.

116. Painting on cardboard, 1953. Private collection, Paris.

Biumo. The lacerated bodies are not far from the theme of the dirty underpants.

Occasionally the clothing is present in the form of the pattern for making it, as in the dark brown on black in the Guggenheim Museum.

Furniture and house. Beyond the human body, but as its analogical image, the morphology of furniture undergoes considerable development.

There are the vertical elements, like apparitions, of the sides of beds or of chairbacks. There are also the concealing elements, like drawers or cupboards. But where the lyricism is most highly concentrated is around the subject matter that evokes furniture charged with emotion, like the objects on his mother's sewing table, where the little Antoni played and reproduced, sticking pins into the pincushions, the fierce excitement of the red velvet Sacred Heart of the nuns, or like

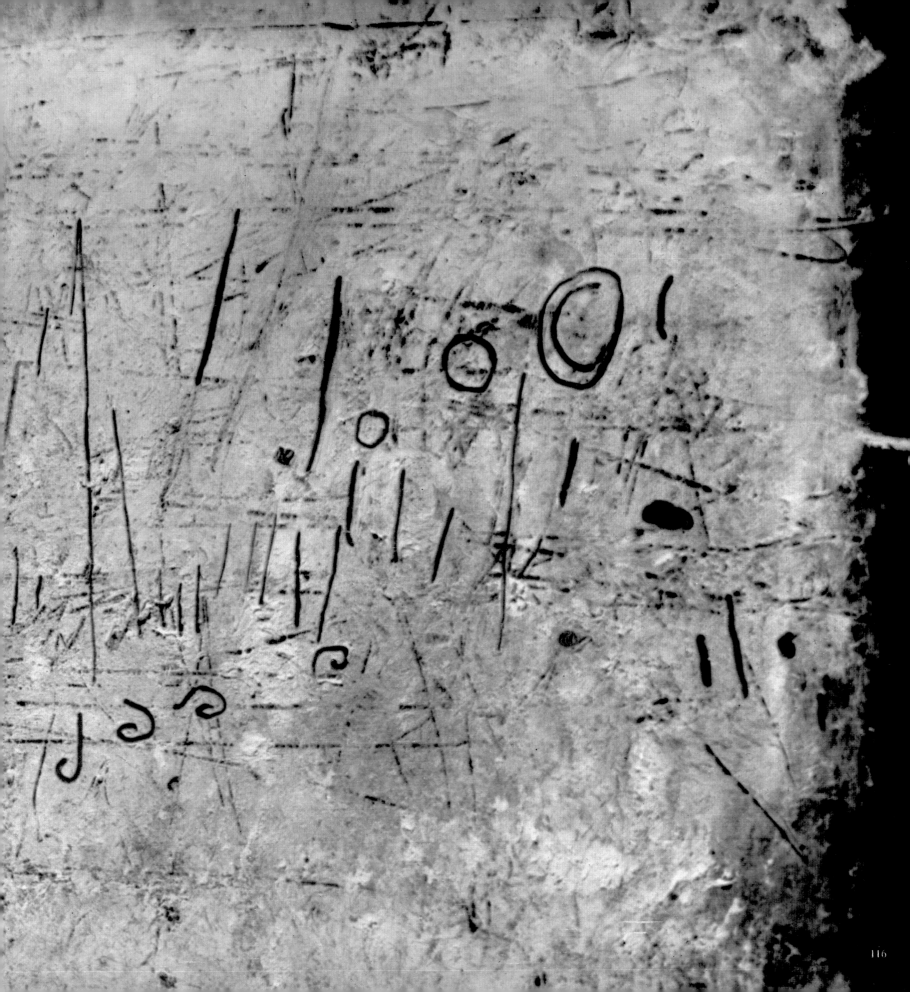

162

117. Black with yellow mark. Paint on canvas, 1953. 100×81 cm. Sturedgalleri, Stockholm.

118. The inner fire. Combined process on canvas, 1953. 60×73 cm. Antonio de Cominges Collection, Barcelona.

119. Relief painting. Paint and varnish on canvas, 1954. 130 × 162 cm. Amos Kahan Collection, New York.

120. White with red marks. Combined process on canvas, 1954. 116 × 97 cm. Josep-Lluís Samaranch Collection, Barcelona.

120

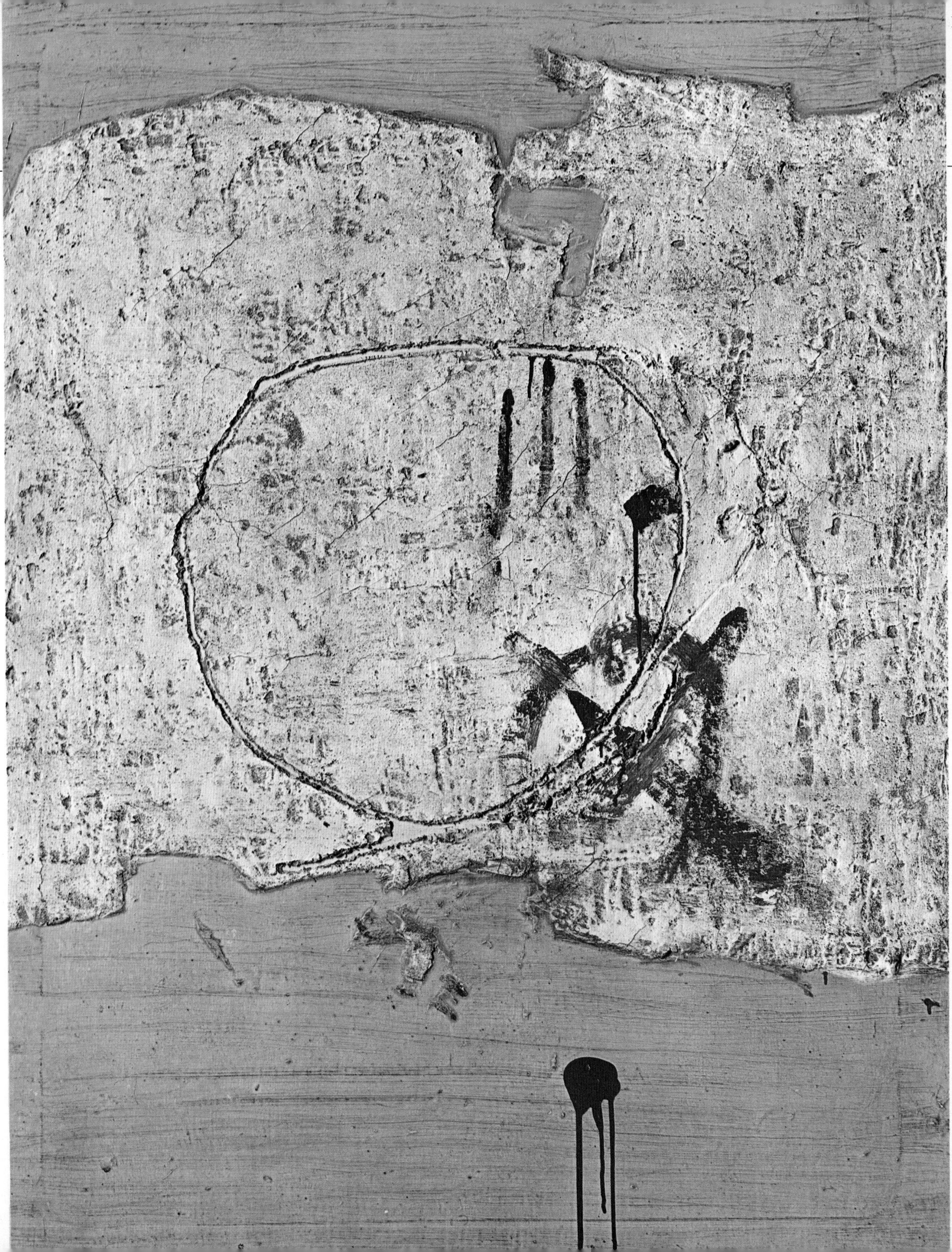

121. Painting. Paint on canvas, 1954. 146×97 cm. Mutschler Collection, Ulm.

122. Grey. Paint on canvas, 1955. 65×81 cm. Pere Portabella Collection, Barcelona.

123. Green painting. Paint on canvas, 1954. 97×146 cm. Marlborough Gallery, London.

121

122

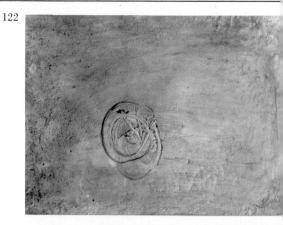

123

124. Grey with black marks. Combined process on canvas, 1955. 162 × 130 cm.
Galerie Stadler, Paris.

124

125. Painting on canvas, 1955. Galerie Stadler, Paris.
126. Painting on canvas, 1955. 97×130 cm. Marlborough Gallery, London.

127. Large grey painting. Combined process on canvas, 1955. 195×170 cm. Düsseldorf Museum.

125

126

the dissecting table seen in a film by Resnais about the Buchenwald concentration camp, or like the family piano.

The little sewing table sometimes appears closed and sometimes open, showing the mirror inside the lid. The famous grey composition in the Carnegie Institute in Pittsburgh presents the sewing table like that, with the lid raised. At other times we see the ensemble formed by the lid of the sewing table, with the four pincushions in the four corners.

There is the form of the beds, sometimes with the disquieting curves of hanging sheets which remake, in matter, a visualistic theme that appeared in the early picture entitled *L'escamoteig de Wotan* (Legerdemain of Wotan). There are the partial organizations of the furniture, like the theme of the buttoned upholstery or the hinges. And there is the ambiguous subject matter of things that might be beds or

128. Painting. Combined process on canvas, 1955. 97 × 130 cm. Sala Gaspar,
Barcelona.

128

129. Painting. Combined process on canvas, 1955. 89×130 cm. Museum of Contemporary Art Collection, Madrid.

129

130. Painting with red cross. Paint on canvas, 1954. 195×130 cm. Galerie Beyeler, Basle.

131. Painting. Paint on canvas, 1955. 81×65 cm. Galerie Stadler, Paris.

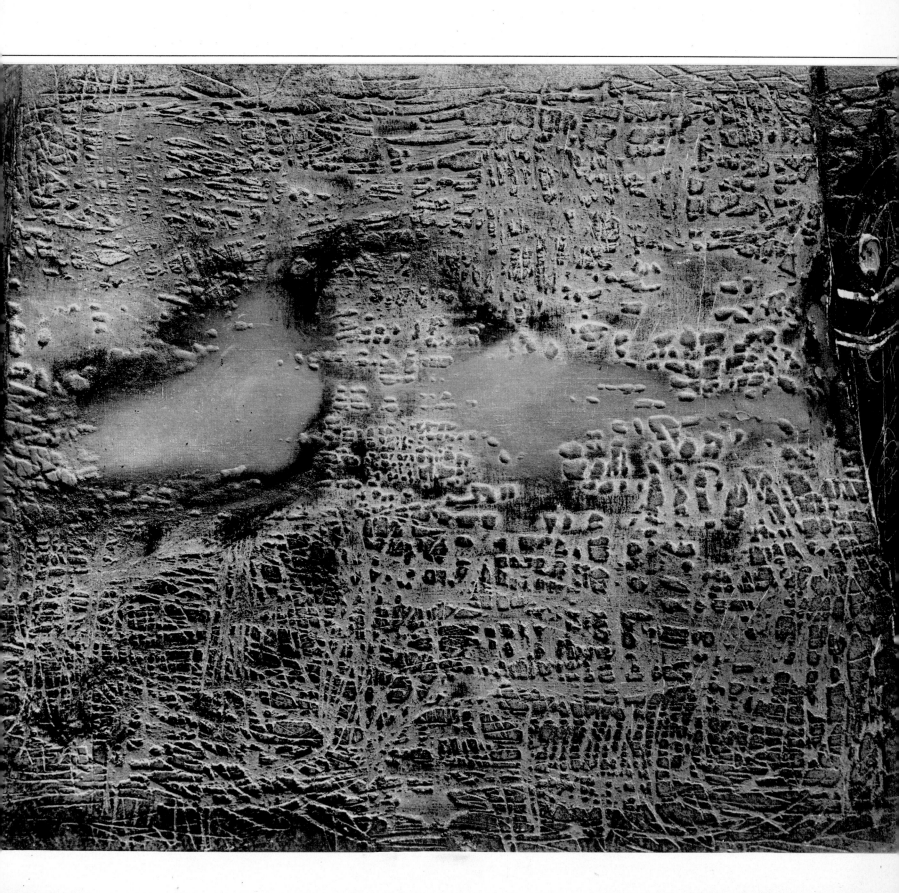

132. Black painting. Paint on canvas, 1955. 146 × 89 cm. Philippe Dotremont Collection, Uccle, Brussels.

133. Painting No. 27. Combined process on canvas, 1955. 162 × 130 cm. Piacenza Collection, Turin.

132

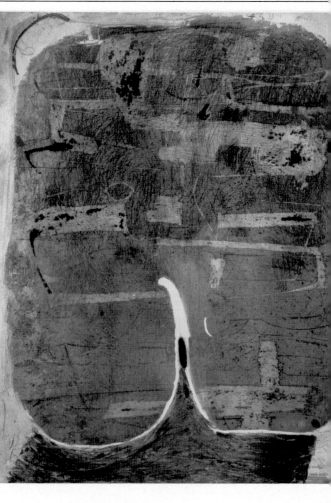

134. Collage-painting. Paint and collage on canvas, 1955. 162 × 130 cm. Kootz Gallery, New York.

134

niches, lintels or biers, fullness or void, the edges of a pyramid or the rigging and shrouds of a boat, a window or a parcel. This last theme, the parcel, becomes an absolute speciality, in which the poverty of the cardboard is matched to the vulgar indifference of the knotted cord, long before the Bulgarian artist Christo made the theme his own.

As a continuation of this morphology there are the forms of the house. We can see the dado, the border, the blind, the iron-link gate that winds up, the window, the staircase, the bricked-up doorway, the beginnings of the projections of a building, the arcade, the archings, the leather-padded doors in the doctor's house and the lunettes in which the intense red and blue suggest the old stained glass in houses of the Romantic period.

Above all there is the wall, the partition, the fence, with stuccoed appurtenances at the sides, often peeling and forming vermiculations,

and sometimes with graffiti, or even with the quadrant of a sun-dial.

Vermiculations. The vermiculations are complex. Some of them are engravings or incisions of a calligraphic character. There are some that are like wall-peelings directed by verticals and horizontals, after the fashion of the barks of pines or of plane trees. And there are some that are broken lines, crossed furrows, rulings, points or strokes, or made up of continuous or vibrant scratches. There are positive ones too, in caked form, as though formed by the crushed elements of a bombardment, like showers of splashes, solidified but in the minority, for the active character of these elements does not accord with the general entropy of Tàpies' work, in which the conditioned forms predominate over the conditioning ones. Sometimes the vermiculations are genuine *graffiti*, evoking organic forms, like the nude in the *Figura*

135. Painting. Paint on canvas, 1955. 146×97 cm. Martha Jackson Gallery, New York.

136. Painting No. 2. Combined process on canvas, 1955. 146×97 cm. Panza di Biumo Collection, Milan.

137. Grey with graphic signs. Combined process on canvas, 1955-1956. 195×114 cm. Gates Lloyd Collection, Haveford, Penn., U.S.A.

138. Relief-painting. Combined process on canvas, 1956. 162×130 cm. Landeau Collection, Paris.

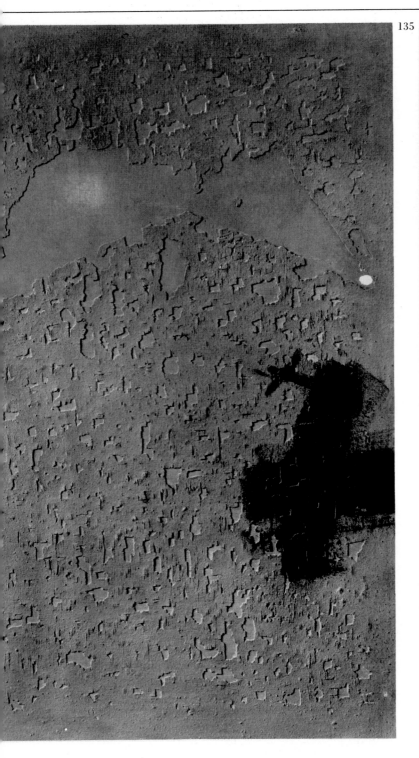

135

136

138

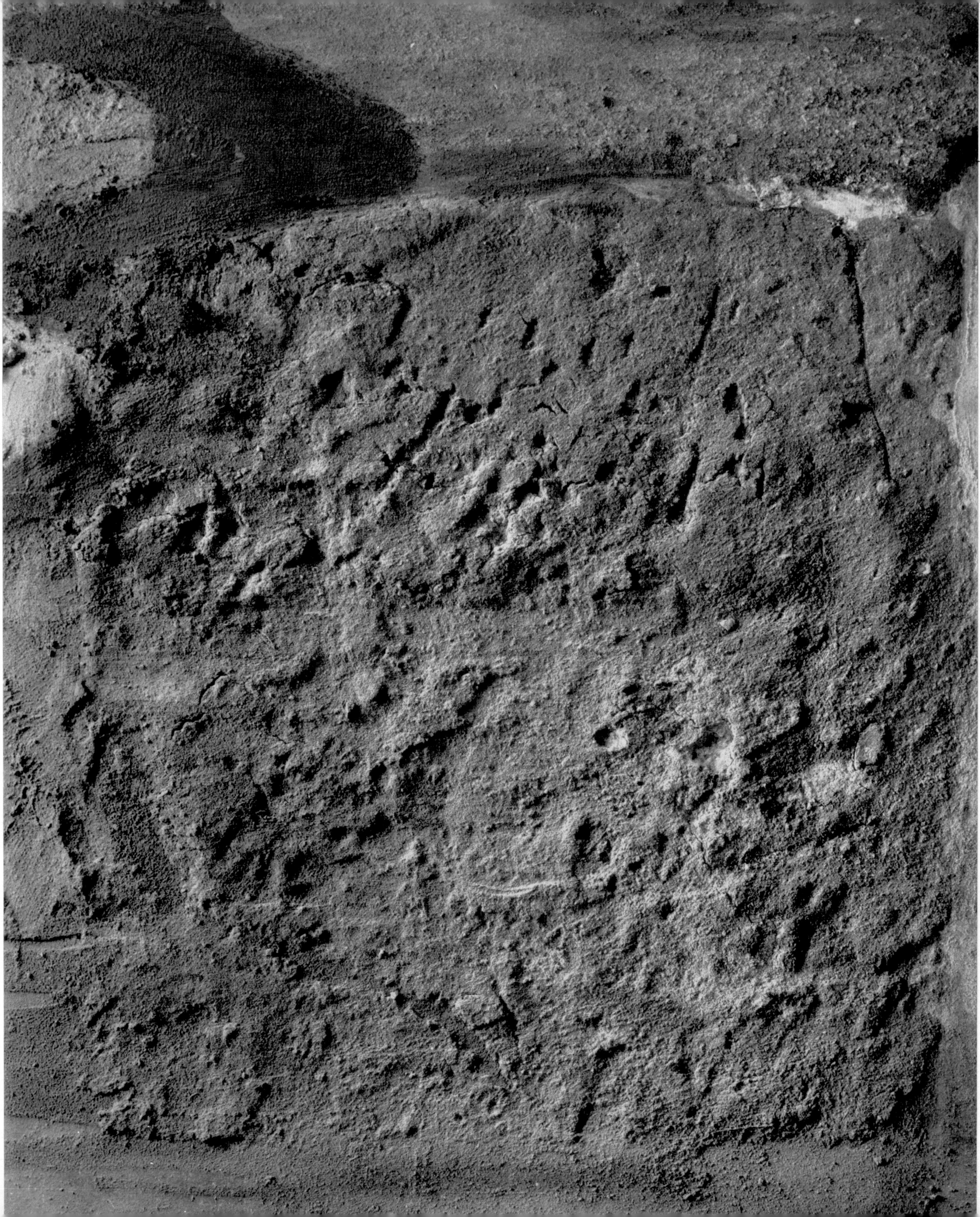

paisatge en vermell (Landscape figure in red) in the Lee Ault Collection (1956).

If we were asked to sum up the general lines of Tàpies' painting during the period of the stabilization of his life, from 1954 to 1960, we should emphasize not only the growing and frequently dominant structuring, which presents very clearly the characteristic of the living forms determined by causes that are alien to them, but also the backward gazing into a world of obsessive memories, though also, sometimes, of an epic character, as seen in the visions of the dissecting table and the cremating furnaces of Buchenwald, revealed by Resnais.

Letters of death and of love. This world of nostalgias might have placed Tàpies' painting in danger of a relapse into the figurative, which would have been the absolute negation of his continual ascent towards reality, from distant representation to peering nearness, from the visual to the tactile, from representation to presentation and from presentation to the matter presented. The touchstone of the sureness of this trajectory is the specific character of the significance, which is unwilling to give up those of its features that are independent of the significance. Possibly to strengthen himself, Tàpies makes this very evident around the year 1960. Between 1960 and 1963, indeed, he gives great momentum to the reincorporation of graphism. In yellow-varnished ochre paste on a dark brown ground, filling the whole of the pictorial field, we find a great M, the theme of the palm of the hand, the signal cut on trees marked for felling, the initial letter of *Mort* (Death). On a smooth grey ground appears the great X which denotes things that are to be suppressed, executed in glued-on hair. We can see the same sign in a kind of suitcase with a collage of cloth dyed the colour of blood.

On the big dark brown picture, two lone brushstrokes of material in ochre. Sometimes they are elements of the graphic language of decoration, like the themes in blue that rhythm the romantic curtaining in ochre, or the subject matter, also rhythmical, of the little dark red chest.

There are also the letters A and T, the initials of his own name, and also those of Antoni and Teresa, in white on a dark brown ground. Sometimes the A and the T are superimposed, becoming ambiguous and taking on a form like that of a draughtsman's table seen in profile.

Then there are the series of orthographical signs, like the X, or the hyphens which fix the forms after the fashion of overcasts, stitches or seams.

There is the net sign of the set of strings, like the crossings of strings on a background of black wood, and there is, on more than one occasion, the parenthesis, which often only encloses the ambiguous notation of a series of hyphens. There are also the commas, often transformed into lowered eyebrows or whiskers presenting a special evocation of the patient attitude. There are some very personal themes; the triangle, the tress, the angle or the four oblique corners.

The signs are not always confined to being superimposed on the background. They are often incorporated into the morphology of memories. Thus we can see the sign in X side by side with the theme of the hinge, the M pointing to a cotyledonic structure, which looks like two lungs, just as if death were being read by the doctor in a radiograph of the thorax; on other occasions, more indirectly, the same great M of the thorax is placed over the front of a tunic or beneath the neck of a vest, sometimes superimposed three times. It is also written in the form of *graffiti* on a decrepit wall, or it figures, upside down, at the foot of a cemetery niche. The X, likewise, is incorporated at the head of the great bed in Joan Prats' collection, with its matt chocolate-coloured headboard and blue counterpane of ribbons, violently indicating the big dismembered cardboard box.

The wound of time. As if the presence of the signs had given him greater tranquillity, Tàpies let himself be carried away by a romantic aura in the early nineteen-sixties. He declared that he took any theme at all, often from memory, in order to develop it as musicians do, but at the same time he was seeking to let something show through, something analogous to what happens when we see an orchestra in a concert-hall, but we hear behind the walls the voices of a choir singing Bach.

One of the aspects of this romanticism is his preoccupation with destruction and ageing, complementary to his investigation into the letters of death. And thus, using a technique that involved placing quick-drying plastic material on a mass of still soft paint, he obtained the gnarled fists of an aged body or a flaccid curtaining.

Another aspect is the identification between the new conception of procedural painting, made of his own vicissitudes, and a visual concept, when with a scratch on the brown-stained wood he obtains a transparency of the tone of the wood which makes it seem as though two hidden eyes were watching us through the paint.

There is also an accentuation of the nostalgic content. The theme of the tray, which is revealed in its ambiguity as a sign of the female sex; the theme of the skin stretched at the four corners, as if it were rehearsing its quartering, in a violent red obtained by means of some excellent German pigments; the theme of the botchy pencil-stroke on the delicate and fragile pale rose, the torn cardboards, the folders, the copybooks, the ruled pages and blotting paper of his school-days, also torn or stained; the plaits of the little girls, the parallel mouths, the theatre with the curtain down and the niche with the tombstone in place; the dining room with chairs, table, bulb, lampshade of braided cord; the pink corset on the brown skin of a negress; the orthopedic apparatuses, the girdles and the trusses, the play of the heap of white sand on the white cloth, the buttocks that blend into an apple and take on its pale green tone; the fans, the spectacles, the dunce's caps, the great sheets and blankets, the tarpaulins of lorries, khaki-green, and forms from his old repertoire, now isolated and magnified, like those of the sewing-table pincushion in collage.

Just as we translate these forms of the pictures into terms of objects from the real world, if we were to translate the background music that comes to us from behind the walls we should need to tape-record a whole polyphony of children's voices, voices of parents and brothers and sisters, cries of terror heard in the night and many anguished silences.

Gelsomina's stone. When we attempt to seek an interpretation at a very deep level of the work done in the years of solitude, from 1954 to 1963, we must revise the lesson of the closed walls, the renunciation, the tactile exacerbation, the dialectic of ensembles, purity, the isolated theme of the nipple, the themes of central structuring and the themes determined rather than determining. After this we shall observe the nostalgic subject matter, themes of the body, of clothing, of furniture, of the house and of all

139. Three marks on grey space. Paint on canvas, 1955. 146×89 cm. Irving A. Glass Collection, New York.

140. Undulating grey painting. Combined process on canvas, 1956. 195× 140 cm. Raoul Levy Collection, Paris.

139

141. Black and ochre painting. Combined process on canvas, 1955. 100 ×
81 cm. Claude Vulliet Collection, Paris.

140

141

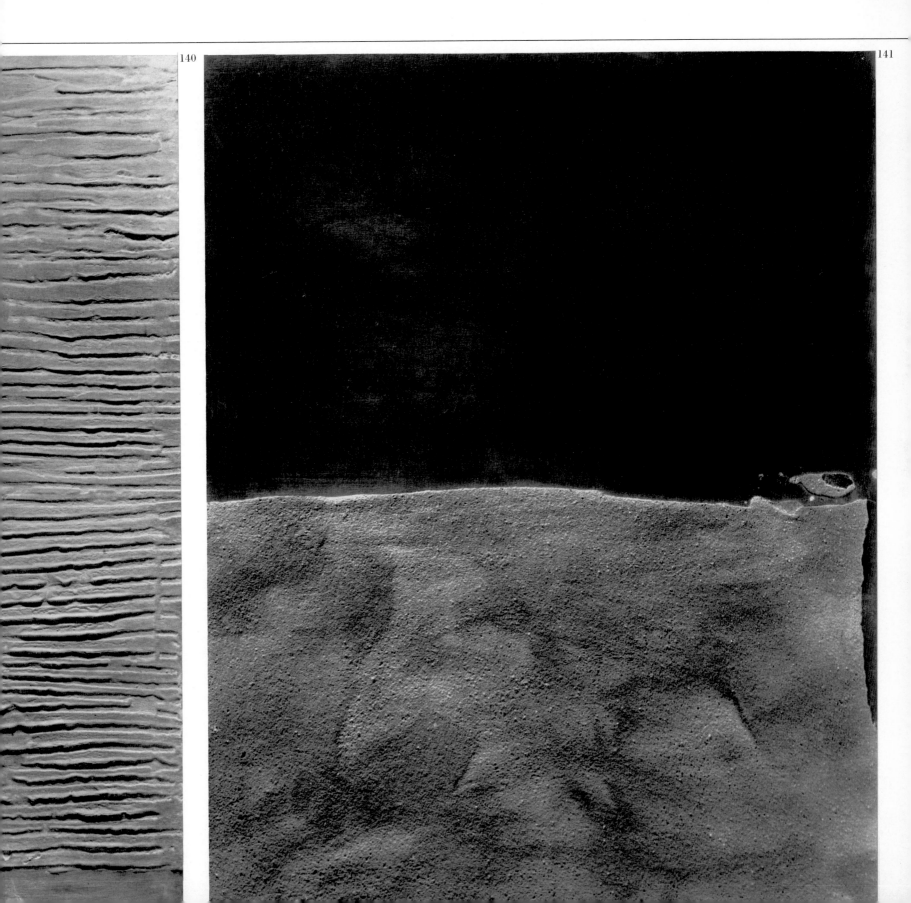

142. Brown. Paint on canvas, 1956. 97 × 162 cm. Museum of Hamburg Collection.

143. Painting on canvas, 1955. Galerie Stadler, Paris.

144. Winding relief. Paint on canvas, 1956. 65 × 100 cm. Rosier Collection, Lyons.

145. Crackled white. Paint on canvas, 1956. 81 × 100 cm. Holländer Collection, U.S.A.

146. Grey and black. Paint on canvas, 1956. 81 × 81 cm. Eva de Buren Collection, Stockholm.

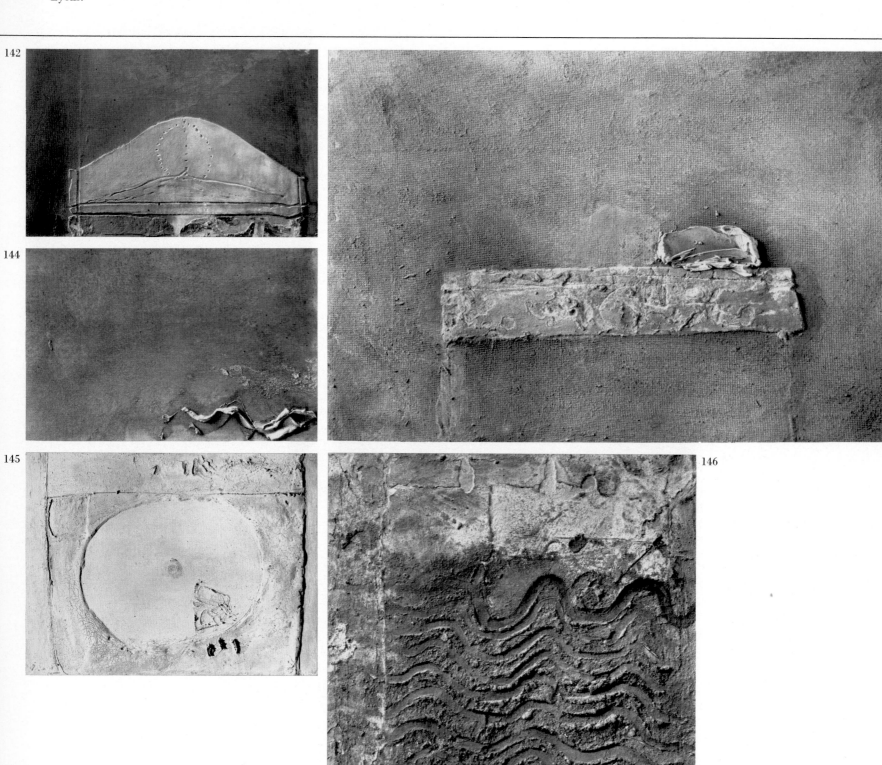

147. Landscape-figure in grey. Paint on canvas, 1956. 146×114 cm. Martha Jackson Gallery, New York.

148. Untitled. Paint on canvas, 1956. 130×97 cm. Staatsgalerie, Stuttgart.

147

148

149. Grey with black cross. Combined process on canvas, 1955. 146×114 cm.
Panza di Biumo Collection, Milan.

149

150. Large oval. Combined process on canvas, 1956. 195×170 cm. Paul Larvière Collection, Montreal.

150

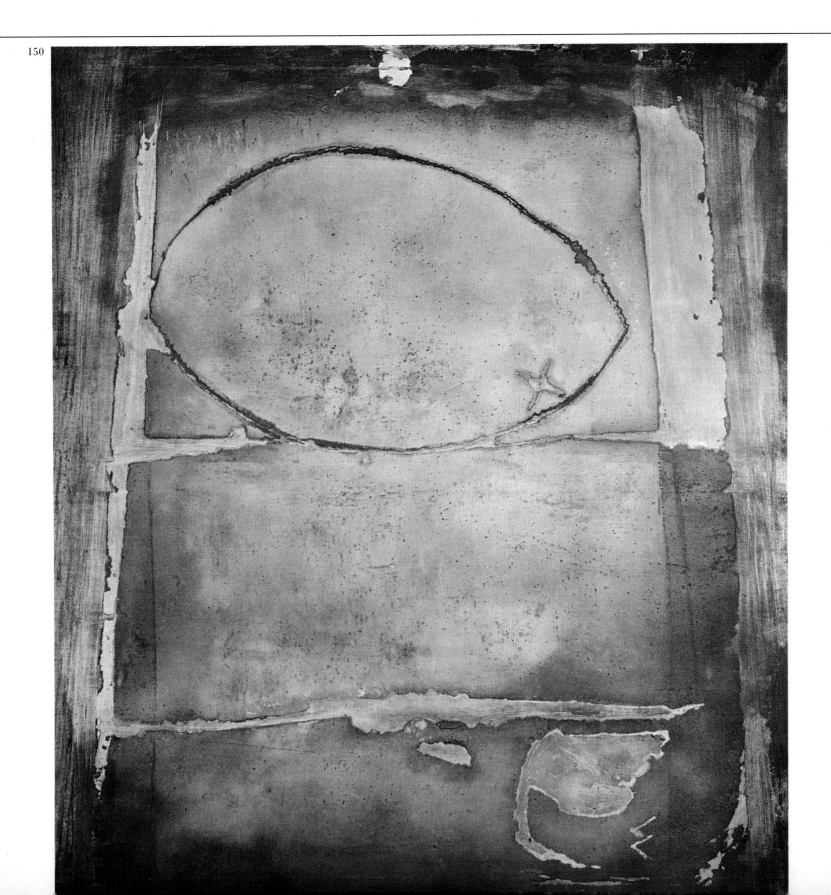

those procedural factors that lead us to feel the wound of time.

If we peel away the top layers of semantics to feel a common layer beneath, we shall find it in a simple system of values which in Tàpies' work assumes an identification with the values of the old realism of the seventeenth century, possibly through a sensibility influenced by existentialism, which prevents it from falling into the nullification towards which it would have tended if left to itself, the ancient orientalism of negation. This sensibility to nothingness, in fact, still favours his realism.

Like Caravaggio, like Ribera, he gives a value to things by contrasting them with nothingness. The Byzantine mosaic-workers and the painters of the Catalan Gothic altarpieces had also made human existence stand out in contrast against a neutral background. But with them it was the solar gold of Plotinus, of spiritualism, of the belief or hope in a happy perfection, eternal and incorruptible. The realists of the seventeenth century were more ambitious or more desperate, for they made things stand out, not by comparing them with a pattern of fullness, of essence, but with a pattern of emptiness, of darkness.

The feat was an ambitious one. While the Byzantine and Gothic artists were obliged to improve men, to make their eyes larger and to endow them with perennial youth and health, the seventeenth-century realists knew how to take the sick, the old, the wretched, the mad, and dignify them through the mere value of their presence in front of nothingness. Thus the idiots of Velázquez not only do not repel us, but do not even inspire us with pity, but rather with respect, full as they are of a humanity that impresses us, a humanity that comes from the fact that their personality appears before us in isolation, as something unique and irreplaceable.

Tàpies performs the same feat. He isolates inner worlds in a rarefied universe, close to the black emptiness under the prison of the limits, the supports, the crosspieces, the cords. And he presents this isolated material to us, as do the realists, in its poorest, most desolate, most abandoned and mortified aspect. Like the realists he gives it nobility, even though it be simply sand, clods or torn cardboard, by means of the artifice of displaying it in its solitude. Thus it comes to be like that stone in Fellini's *La Strada* which the trumpeter showed to Gelsomina to cheer her up, saying that it was like her, for even though it was just an ordinary stone from the roadside, it was unique and irreplaceable and the Universe would be incomplete without it.

Interrogatory about the world. At the end of the period of solitude, some long conversations on all sorts of subjects enabled me to hear some opinions expressed by Tàpies which may help us to understand his work at that time.

I began by asking him about all that is most remote. The stars, the galaxies, the constellations. He is interested in cosmology, but not so much in astronomy, and hardly at all in the idea of space travel.

Space:

He is interested in space to the extent to which Relativity has proved the identity between space and time, or rather, the space-time complex.

From physics the conversation turned to mathematics and logic. He has always envied people who are versed in mathematics, which he believes to be something of the greatest importance. He has the same opinion of logic. He thinks that speculative thought engaged in with logical deductions has had extremely important results, and he believes that in this method Nagarjuna coin-

151. Swirl of sand. Combined process on canvas, 1955. 81 × 100 cm. Anthony Denney Collection, London.

152. White with graphic signs. Paint on canvas, 1956. 200 × 175 cm. Washington University, St. Louis, Missouri.

151

cides with Einstein or Heisenberg.

Landscape:

He loves the landscape, especially mountains, woods, Nordic scenery.

Plants:

Big trees and the atmosphere of the woods.

Animals:

He likes all animals. The only ones that annoy him are mosquitoes and flies, but he respects them, remembering that they are the food of the birds.

Music:

Wagner, Schumann and Brahms, above all others. Also Schoenberg, Webern, Alban Berg, Varèse and Cage, and the music of the Far East.

He listens to music every night and believes that it has a very powerful influence on his work. He considers, above all, that music communicates sentiments and makes it evident that there are forms which do not belong to visual reality, but are not thereby inexpressive.

Poetry:

He is most particularly interested in all the poetry of the Far East. The Song poetry of China, the Japanese Hai Kai.

He is also interested in Edgar Allan Poe, Mallarmé, Rimbaud, Breton, Eluard... and, among the Catalans, Salvat-Papasseit, Foix and, of course, Brossa, who has had such a great influence on him.

Cinema:

He tends to discard American cinema in general, with the exception of Griffith, Von Stroheim, so-

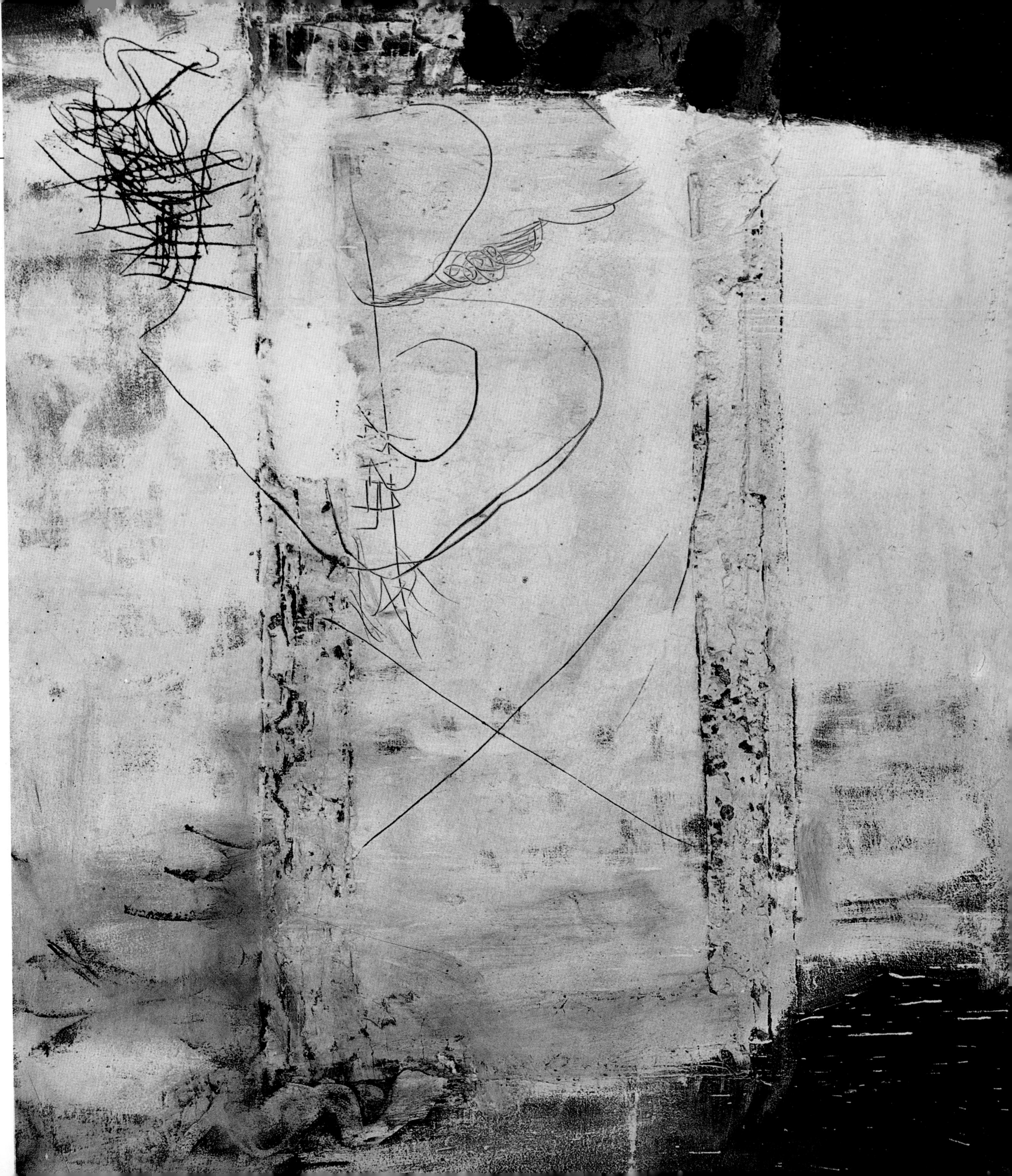

153. Grey cloud effects. Paint on canvas, 1956. 50×61 cm. Cardazzo Collection, Milan.

154. Blackish ochre with perforations. Combined process on canvas, 1957. 146×114 cm. Martha Jackson Gallery, New York.

155. Graphic signs on blackish-ochre relief. Combined process on canvas, 1957. 65×81 cm. Streep Collection, New York.

156. Composition No. LXII. Combined process on canvas, 1957. 114×146 cm. Galerie Beyeler, Basle.

153

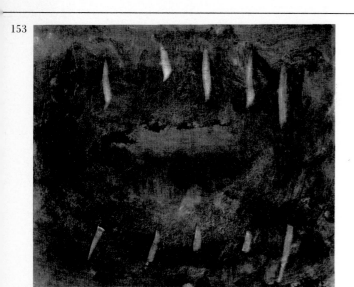

155

156

154

157. Grey painting. Paint on canvas, 1957. 81 × 100 cm. New London Gallery, London.

158. Black relief. Combined process on canvas, 1957. 81 × 65 cm. Willy and Fänn Schniewind Collection, Neviges-Rhld.

159. White, shadows and relief. Combined process on canvas, 1957. 162 × 130 cm. V. Langen Collection, Düsseldorf-Meerbusch.

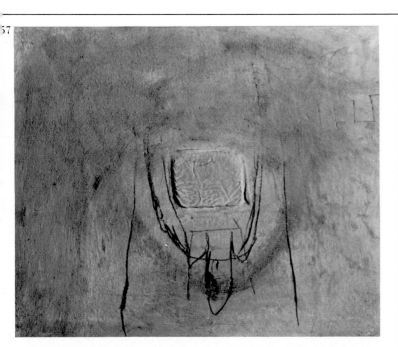

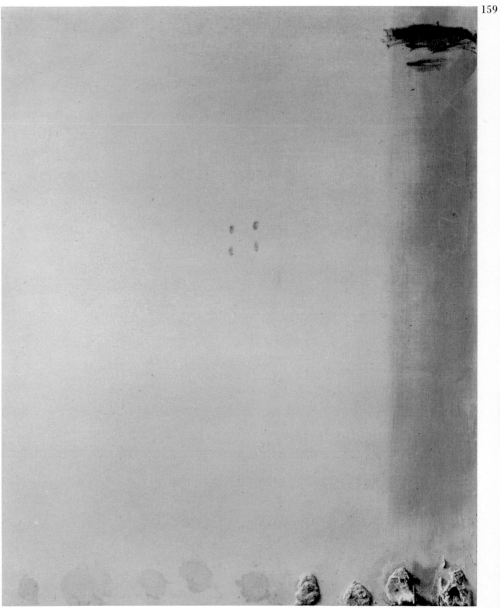

160. No. VII. Combined process on canvas, 1956. 162×130 cm. Private collection, Milan.

161. Brown and grey. Combined process on canvas, 1957. 97×130 cm. Torsten Anderson Collection, Stockholm.

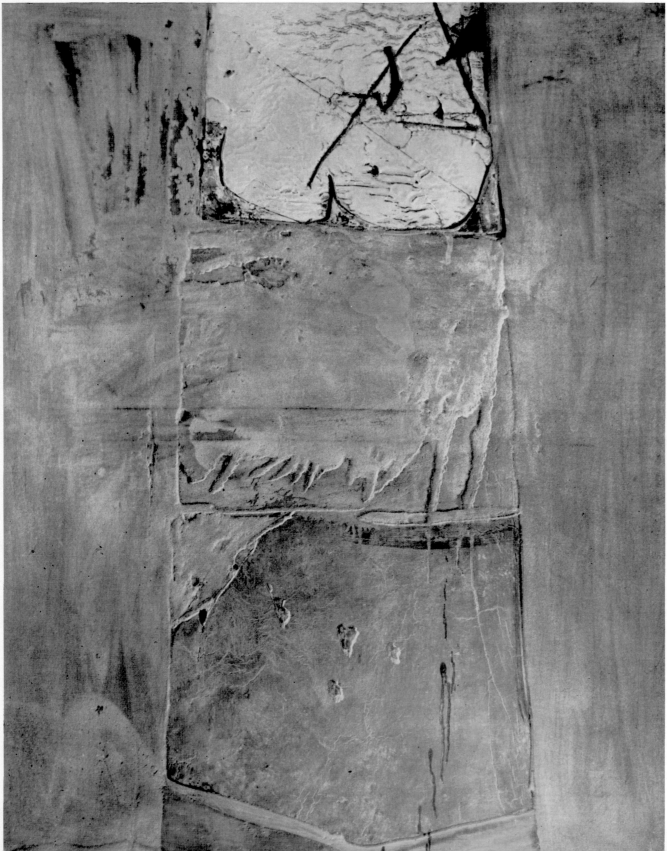

160

162. No. LXVI. Combined process on canvas, 1957. 162×130 cm. Franz Meyer Collection, Basle.

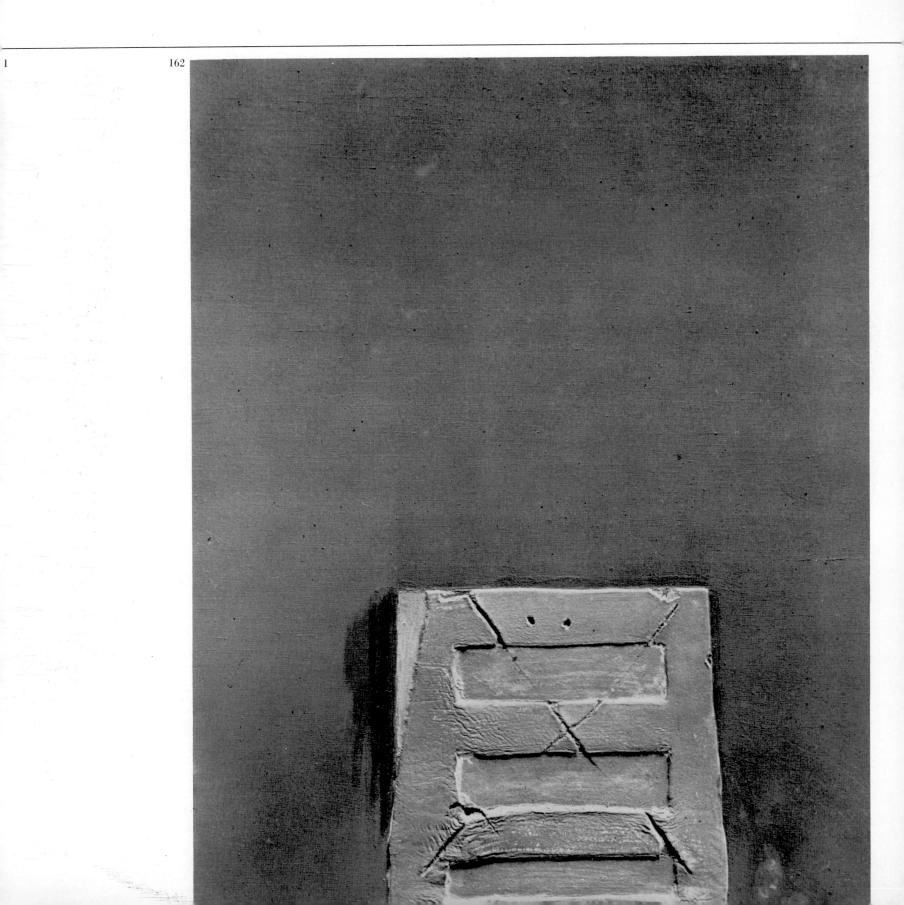

163. Graphic ochre. Combined process on canvas, 1960. 162 × 130 cm. Niedersächsische Landesgalerie Collection, Hanover.

163

164. White oval. Combined process on canvas, 1957. 100×81 cm. Municipal Museum of Krefeld, Germany.

164

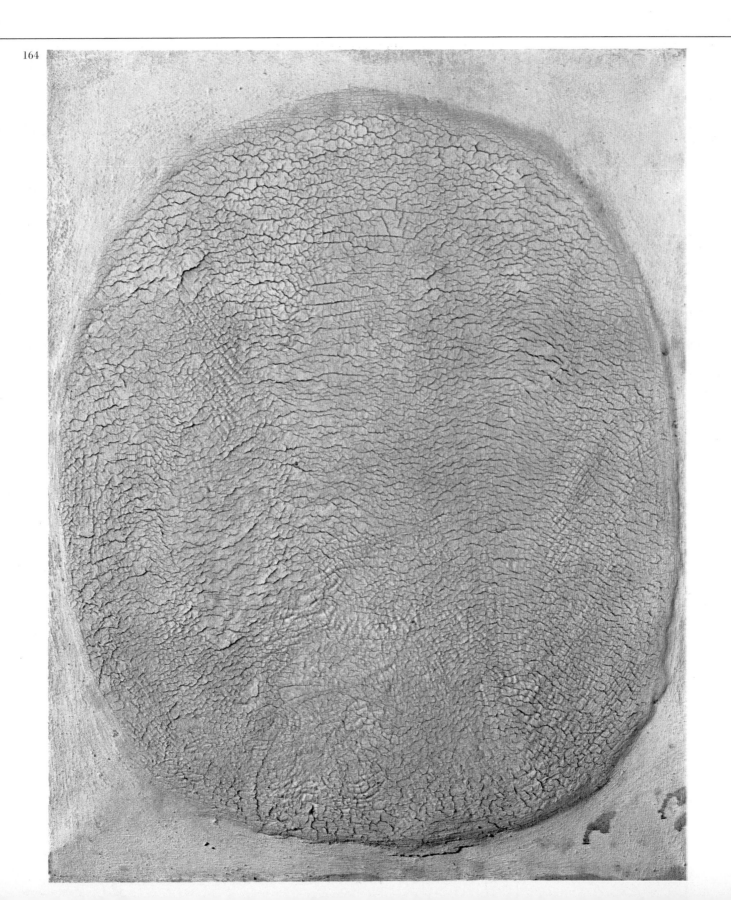

200

165. Painting. Combined process on canvas, 1957. 146×97 cm. Museum of Modern Art, New York.

166. Relief with five perforations. Combined process on canvas, 1957. Galerie Stadler, Paris.

165

166

167. Black oval. Combined process on canvas, 1957. 89×116 cm. Anthony Denney collection, London.

168. Grey over white. Combined process on canvas, 1957. 130×162 cm. Panza di Biumo Collection, Milan.

169. Ochre sand. Combined process on canvas, 1957. 195×130 cm. Panza di Biumo Collection, Milan.

169

170. Calligraphy. Combined process on canvas, 1958. 195×130 cm. Morris Pinto Collection, New York.

171. Ochre relief on white. Combined process on canvas, 1957. Fernando Rivière Collection, Barcelona.

172. Grey relief No. VIII. Combined process on canvas, 1957. 130×162 cm. Jacques Dupin Collection, Paris.
173. No. XXXVII. Combined process on canvas, 1957. 130×162 cm. Marlborough Gallery, London.

172

173

174. Composition with white sand. Combined process on canvas, 1958. 162 × 97 cm. Sala Gaspar, Barcelona.

175. Brown relief. Combined process on canvas, 1958. 114 × 146 cm. Martha Jackson Gallery, New York.

174

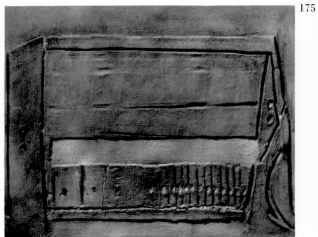

175

176. Blackish-ochre reliefs. Combined process on canvas, 1958. 195×130 cm. Galleria dell'Ariete, Milan.

177. Graphic signs. Combined process on canvas, 1958-1960. 95×130 cm. Van der Loo Gallery, Munich.

176

177

178. Grey furrows. Combined process on canvas, 1956. 89×116 cm. Toni Slick, San Antonio, Texas.

179. No. XLV. Combined process on canvas, 1957. 146×97 cm. Claude Vulliet Collection, Buchillon, Switzerland.

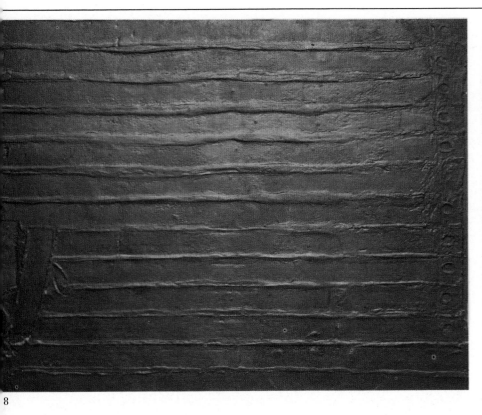

180. The broken plate. Homage to Gaudí. Combined process with china plate stuck on canvas, 1956. 130 × 162 cm. Galerie Beyeler, Basle.

181. Large painting. Combined process on canvas, 1958. 200 × 260 cm. Guggenheim Museum, New York.

180

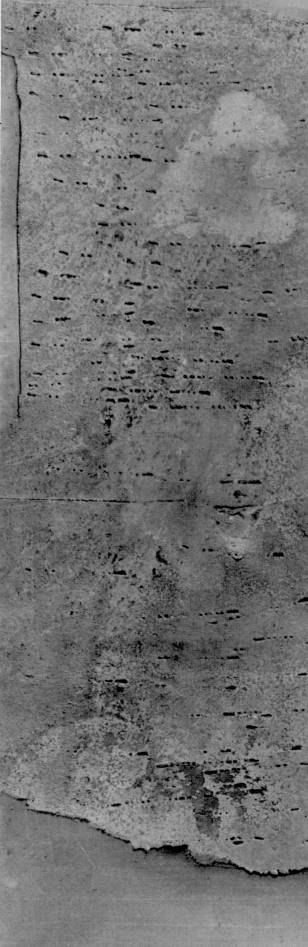

181

me of the comic actors and very little else. He finds it cold and industrial, though well made. He has a real weakness for German expressionist movies and for the cinema of Sweden, Russia and Japan.

Entertainment:

He is interested in ballet. He is also interested in the circus and the music hall, though by this he means the popular music hall, what you see in the *Molino* in Barcelona, not the mechanized show business of *Radio City.*

He is not particularly interested in pop music, which he usually finds superficial, considering it more interesting as a sociological phenomenon than as music. Even Piaf he does not find any less superficial than the others. What is she, after all, beside Stockhausen or our own Carlos Santos?

Design:

He finds it quite wrong that any little lamp-designer should be considered in the same category as an artist. Design, in general, is aimed at comfort; the reverse is the case with art. But one cannot generalize.

Objects:

He is affected by certain objects, and also by certain furniture.

Art:

Here his taste for the Far East is still dominant. Chinese and Japanese painting. Tantric art. He is not particularly interested in the things to be found in the art museums of the west, what was until recently identified with capital-letter *Art.* He likes visiting the Egyptian rooms, the ceramics, the Sumerian things from Ur. He prefers the Musée de l'Homme or the Guimet to the rooms of paintings in the Louvre.

Travel:

Air travel terrifies him. He wishes he never had to take an aeroplane.

Interrogatory about men. *Men:*

He feels himself to be a humanist. He has a great love for Buddha, Lao

182. Reddish painting. Combined process on canvas, 1958. 114×146 cm.
Panza di Biumo Collection, Milan.

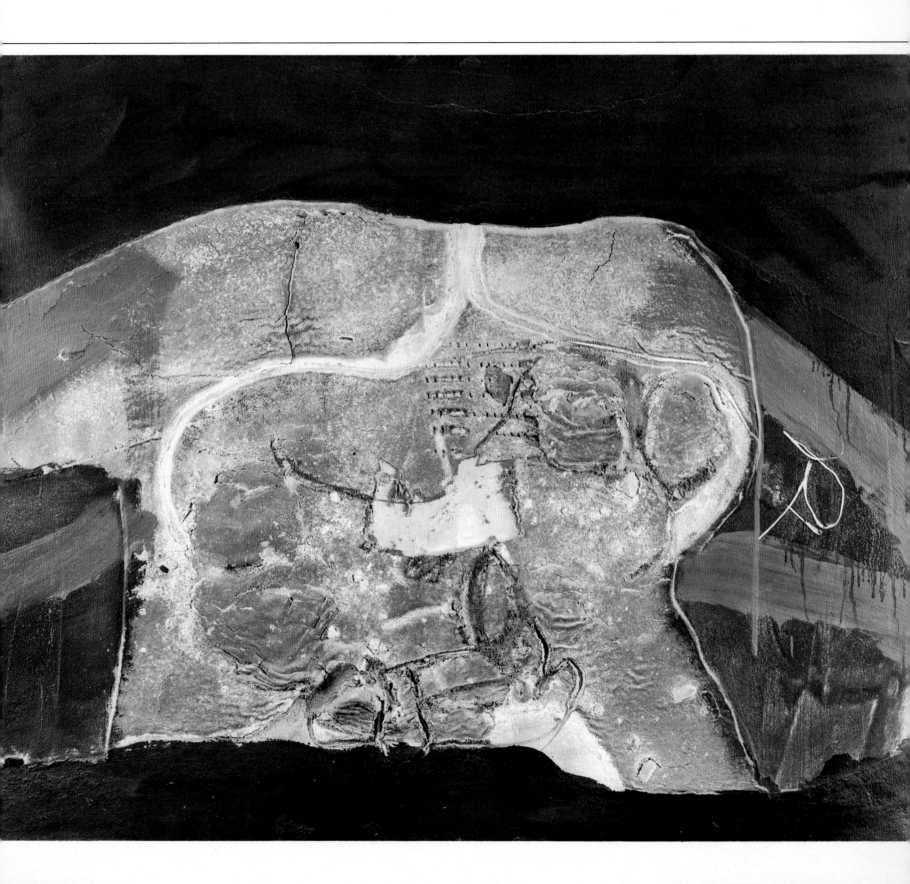

183

Tsze and their confluence in many Hindu and Zen masters. He is conscious of the importance of Marx and Freud, but his direct acquaintance with them is slight. He likes Gandhi, Thoreau, Bertrand Russell, Huxley, Allan Watts (whom he has known for ten years); he particularly likes C. G. Jung (with whose work he is well acquainted), Dreier, Chaplin, Einstein...

He is enormously interested in Vivekananda (an Indian pilgrim in America), Aurobindus (the pantheist of *divine life*), D. T. Suzuky and many other orientalists.

Religion:

He has a certain religious feeling which is mingled with his sense of wonderment in the face of mystery, but he does not see any necessity for giving the name of God to this mystery.

He does not know whether things happen in obedience to any purpose and considers, as an agnostic, that the real sense of the universe is unknown to us. He feels a great dissatisfaction at not knowing the meaning of things, but perhaps things have no meaning.

Revolution:

He wishes to live for mankind in general, but he does not think that the Revolution is coming any time in the near future. He feels anguish at the heedless spilling of blood and at those social and economic plans that treat human material coldly (the Draconian measures taken by Stalin to transplant whole peoples, etc.).

Economy:

He despises abundance and esteems simple things.

Friendship:

He believes in friendship as he does in progress, despite the fact that the experience of life is so persistent in disenchanting us.

Love:

This, for him, is of the greatest importance. Without love there can be no true knowledge. But he feels aversion to the representatives of certain ideas and to immoral behaviour.

His wife:

She has saved him. He might have gone on drifting, but she has meant clarity for him.

His children:

He suffers for them, thinking of what lies in store for them.

Instinct:

He is a great believer in instinct. He admires women because they have more instinct than men. Men often lose themselves, but women have a clearer idea of where they are going.

Morals:

He believes that if there were a return to natural, instinctive morals everything would be better. But he accepts the existence of moral principles as a way of making life work better.

Pleasure:

He certainly likes eating and drinking, but they are not important things for him. Sexual pleasure attracts him more strongly and he thinks that it should be given its proper place in the scheme of things. He likes to be at peace and to eat sparingly. When he drank as a young man, it was not so much for pleasure as to stimulate his imagination. In this sense he would like to take wine, and he regrets that it should be harmful in the long run. There are better natural stimulants. Perhaps certain drugs. Generally speaking, he is more concerned with health than with pleasure.

Interrogatory on his work. *Taste:*

Through his wife, Teresa, he has learnt not to esteem sophisticated things. Now he loves simple things. He is not interested in elegance. He likes people who are natural and unburdened with prejudices, a quality independent of whether they are rich or poor. His wife has extremely clear ideas. She feels an aversion to jewels, preferring total simplicity. This Tàpies accepts, but he also feels a total, authentic and primitive affection for poor things. The value of things dwells in their origin.

In one's life, as in one's work, one must try to strip away everything superfluous until one is left with the final truth.

Action:

Since he was a child, Tàpies has had the feeling that he holds certain basic ideas more clearly than other men, and that he has the capacity and the obligation to inculcate these, for the sake of mankind. But when it comes to sitting down to do this, he is filled with doubts and sees before him a perspective of total failure. He feels that his career is questing after a chimera.

Like Maragall with poetry, he once thought that he would change the history of painting. That the first thing was to view the world with intelligence, the second to paint well. He began by following Van Gogh and Picasso, but then he felt the desire to express himself in a way that was his and his alone, however bad it might be. He scraped, tore and glued, did things that were rudimentary, but did them right from the start with his whole soul. Sometimes he is disappointed that people do not listen to him, and he often thinks that they have not seen all the qualities that he has put into his work, so he sometimes feels undervalued or misinterpreted.

His pictures:

He makes projects and works them out in his imagination, sometimes with great precision, but he rectifies the project if he is dissatisfied with the result.

Colour:

He is deeply concerned about the existence of colours, for he tends to see metric structures rather than colours. The colours he likes in nature, such as green, he cannot stand in a picture. He hates the colours in a tube of paint. There are so many industrial colours now, and such good and varied ones, that their very abundance takes away the excitement. They are too easily consumed. It is not that he despises them, it is simply a matter of attrition. Besides, there is an over-abundance of conventional colours, like those of the cinema, and these finally disgust him.

Why he paints:

His purpose in painting is to seize the mystery of the world that surrounds him. The outer world, not the experience of the world. In his own words there is a kind of self-definition: *I should like to be a thinker who meditates on existence in order to get to the bottom of it, and with my works to help others to «achieve illumination».*

184. Cards crossing on wood, 1960. 56 × 76 cm. Sala Gaspar, Barcelona.

184

185. Crossed canvas. Combined process and sizing on canvas, 1962. 170 × 195 cm. Martha Jackson Gallery, New York.

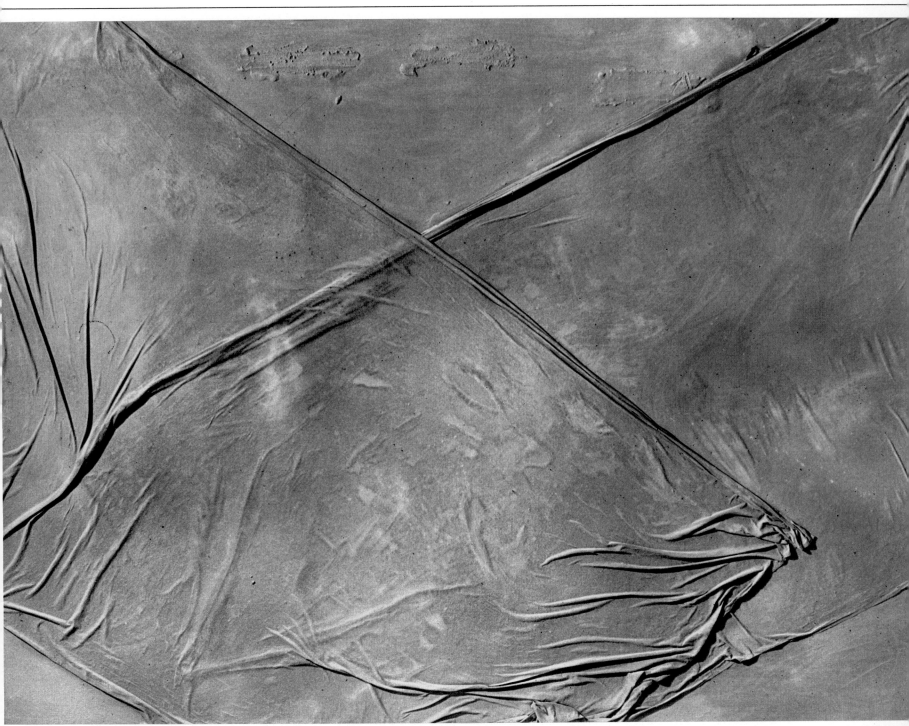

185

186. Grey canvas. Sizing on canvas, 1963. 70 × 100 cm. H. Richter Collection, Düsseldorf.

186

THE HUMAN TRACE

The days of Pop art.   At the cross-roads of the early sixties, when the Pop group in the United States were hurling themselves with the fury of optimism, as though in a cruel and entertaining game, into the discovery of the shrill and gaudy morphology of the world of industry and the consumer society, Tàpies had already made several experiments on the incorporation of the object, experiments that went beyond abstraction, though charged with many different connotations.

The objects among which Tàpies, like the Pop artists, sought the human trace were not those of the consumer society brought up to date, but the hereditary objects of the past. Frequently the Pop artists, like him, gave their mor-

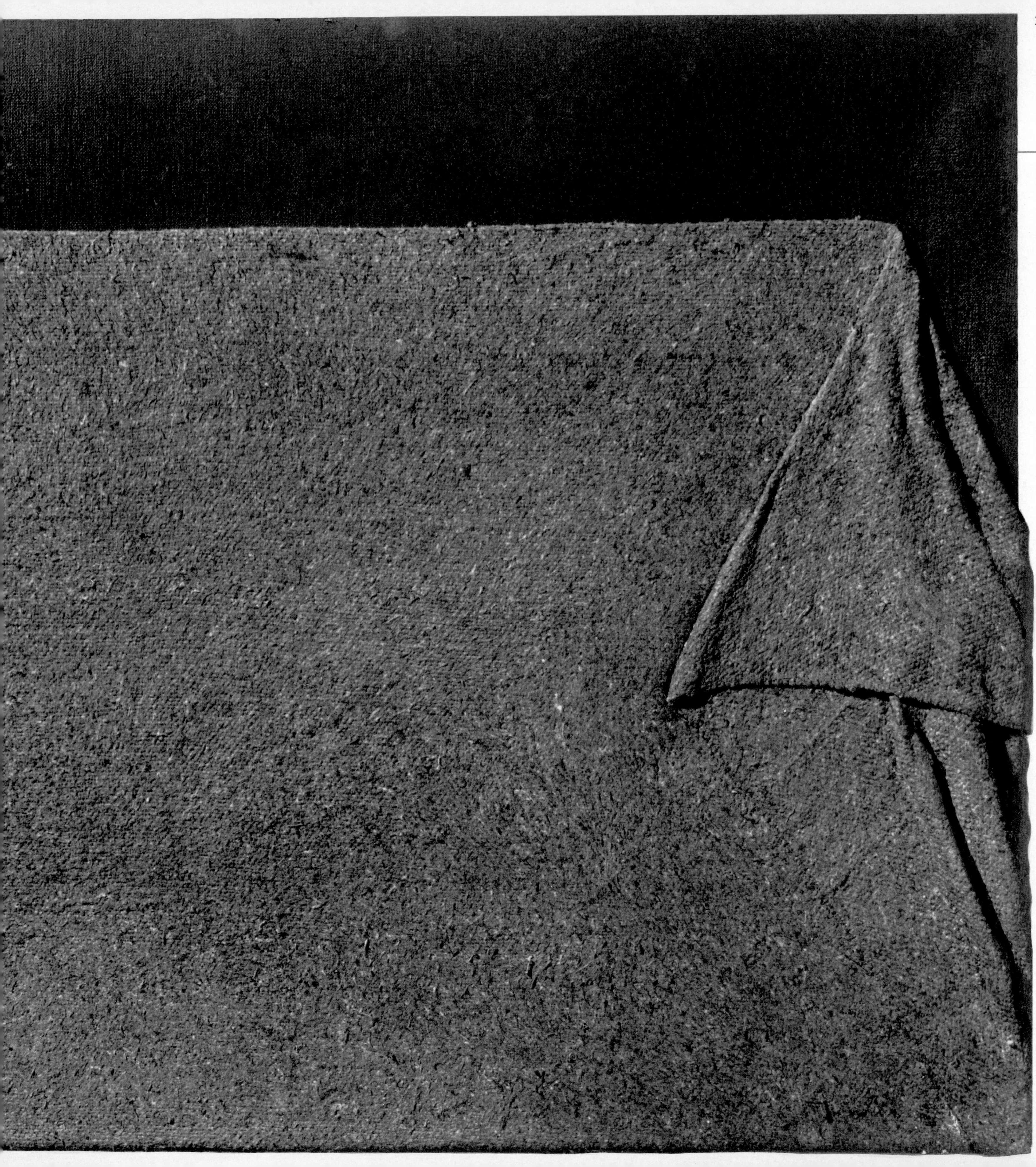

187. Cardboard and string, 1959. 16×48 cm. Private collection, Barcelona.
188. Pot-bellied canvas. Sizing on canvas, 1964. 65×81 cm. Joan Teixidor
    Collection, Barcelona.

187

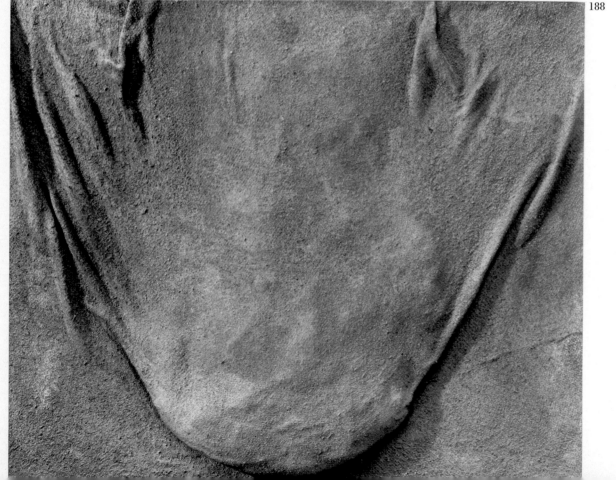

188

189. Collage of comb on cardboard, 1961. Private collection, Barcelona.

189

190

phology a nostalgic character, full of tender feelings for their own childhood, but there is evidently an enormous difference between a childhood spent surrounded by Coca-Cola bottles and one spent among the velvet pincushions of the sewing table, prolonged into an adolescence in a country at war.

However much the Pop artists may condemn, with laughing irony, the inhuman aspects of the industrial society, it does not stop them from accepting the screeching publicity, the erotic beauty, the visual impact and the perfection of form of industrialized techniques. Tàpies, on the other hand, ignored the screeching, abjured conventional beauty and eroticism, sought to arouse a lingering contemplation rather than a sudden visual impact and systematically destroyed any idea of industrial perfection by making soft, organic and vacillating all those forms that in real life are rigid, such as, for instance, the struc-

191

tures of carpentry. His repertory, moreover, is totally craftsmanlike and ancestral.

If we were to generalize the concept of Pop art as regards what is plastically interesting, i.e., in the transition from abstraction to the incorporation of the object as such (not the object as a suggestion of something else, in the style of Dalí and the other Surrealists), then evidently Tàpies would have to be considered as a forerunner of Pop. But if we restrict it and define it in relation to its socio-cultural interest, as a typical manifestation of response to the consumer society, then Tàpies must evidently be classified as totally opposed to this tendency.

But however this may be, if we examine the facts objectively we shall see that a generalized tendency of cultural dynamics leads to a necessity to approach the object, as a trace of man. In Tàpies' case, as in that of the Pop artists, this approach is clearly made, but Tàpies seems to go beyond its limits and reach an identification of man with his trace by a kind of *einfühlung*. Moreover, whereas Pop art made a sort of class-conscious selection of objects and eliminated certain things, Tàpies defended the rights of the most despised objects.

New themes for old. If we make a graph or chart of the morphological themes of Tàpies' painting between 1960 and 1970, we shall observe some very appreciably descending curves during the years previous to 1963, replaced as from this year by ascending curves. The change was slow at first, but quickly gathered acceleration. The years 1964, 1965 and 1966 are distinguished by their low semantic level, gradually reaching a maximum of nakedness, after which his work takes on a new skin.

If, in 1963, we have finished with the panorama of solitude and we think it useful to choose this year as the starting-point for a new group of works, it is because it is the last year in which the previous subject matter, with its maximum of structuring, is of any importance, while at the same time a very significant new theme begins its ascendant: that of fabric —folded, stuffed, inflated or tied. While the evocations of furniture and the house, the trestle table, the folder for drawings, the tray, the doorway, the glass door and the arcade all still appear, with something of a monumental character, as though they were funeral commemorations, this new textile theme appears in the form of slip covers, antimacassars, patches (first cousins to those of Burri), folds, drapings, wrinkles and bindings, with tailor's marks on them, as though prepared for cutting up; and in the inflated, almost biological forms of a bed made up or of a well-stuffed sofa. This theme, often linked to the weave of a blanket of cheap wool, like those of soldiers or of the poor, continues in 1964 in dramatic forms, like a pregnant belly or the wrinkled face of an old woman. As a counterpoint, there is the thin fabric stuck on, like cloth that is wet from the rain that falls on the shelterless, like the tarpaulin over a shapeless load, or like the lining of crudely-fashioned flies on a stage, or the pathetic canvas of an old marquee or circus tent. Grey or dirty, indefinite colours characterize its poverty.

The soft form of these works makes the imprint of the structuring give way in such a fashion that, to a certain extent, the road followed from the pastose material to the rigid now continues from the rigid to the flexible. Generally speaking, this evolution is linked to a style that is very laconic, elliptical, quiet and light.

The Luther King period. In the historical context there were also some changes.

The Tàpies before this new Tàpies had undoubtedly been one of the results of the closing of the frontiers, a reaction against the dead weight of the postwar profiteering and a concentration round the embers of Surrealism, the last remains of prewar fires.

At the beginning of the fifties we observed the impact of his physical contact with the outer world, and at the same time his contact with wider ideological horizons, which offered him new perspectives. The agreement between Spain and the United States had opened a crack through which a certain light could enter. Two years later, the thaw in Russia after the death of Stalin coincided with the disappearance of the mystic aspect of conflict for the mentality that Tàpies' painting revealed, and with a tranquil rationalization in the face of the closed walls, where the conflicts were transformed into a dialectic between tangible structures. The fact that his triumph in the United States took place at the same time as that of Fidel Castro in Cuba helps to explain the casting-off of some of his ideological moorings and the formal strengthening of his firm, stable structures, a phenomenon that appears not only in his painting but also in his private life, with his marriage and the rebuilding or building of the houses in Campins and in Sant Gervasi.

The milestone of 1963 and its change correspond to a perspective that goes beyond that of the cold war. It is one that embraces the Kruschev thaw, the opening to the west of Evtuchenko and the Ecumenic Council. There are the *Pacem in Terris* Encyclical and the assassination of Kennedy, which idealized its image. Martin Luther King is about to receive the Nobel Peace Prize.

Then come some years of strife and of hope which no longer respond to the old moulds. In 1965

192. Painting. Combined process on canvas, 1959. 55×46 cm. Galería René Métras, Barcelona.

193. Blackish brown. Combined process on canvas, 1959. Private collection, Barcelona.

194. Grey form. Paint on canvas, 1959. George Guggenheim Collection, Zurich.

195. Cardboard tied with string, 1959. 53×68 cm. Tooth Gallery, London.

193

196. All red. Combined process on canvas, 1959. 65×81 cm. Martha Jackson Gallery, New York.

197. Pleated cardboard, 1959. 54×71 cm. Tooth Gallery, London.

198. Blue Waves. Combined process on canvas, 1959. 60×92 cm. Galleria dell'Ariete, Milan.

199. Composition. Combined process on canvas, 1959. Fritz and Nanana Herlt, Weiden, Germany.

200. Composition. Combined process on canvas, 1959. Victoria de los Ángeles and Enric Magriñà Collection, Barcelona.

201. Blue with double oval. Combined process on canvas, 1959. 81×65 cm. Guy Dixon Collection, London.

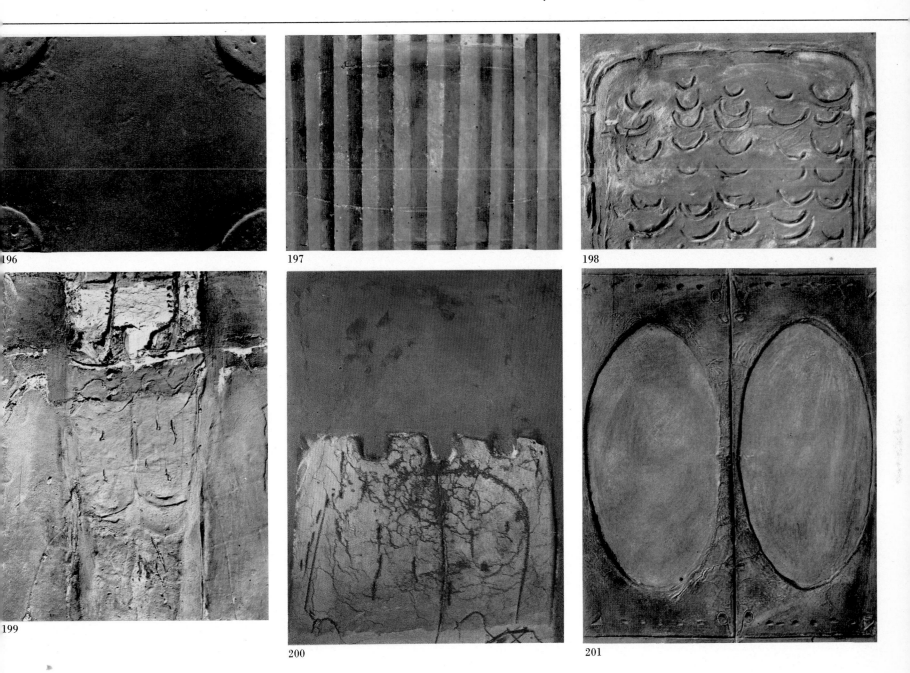

196

197

198

199

200

201

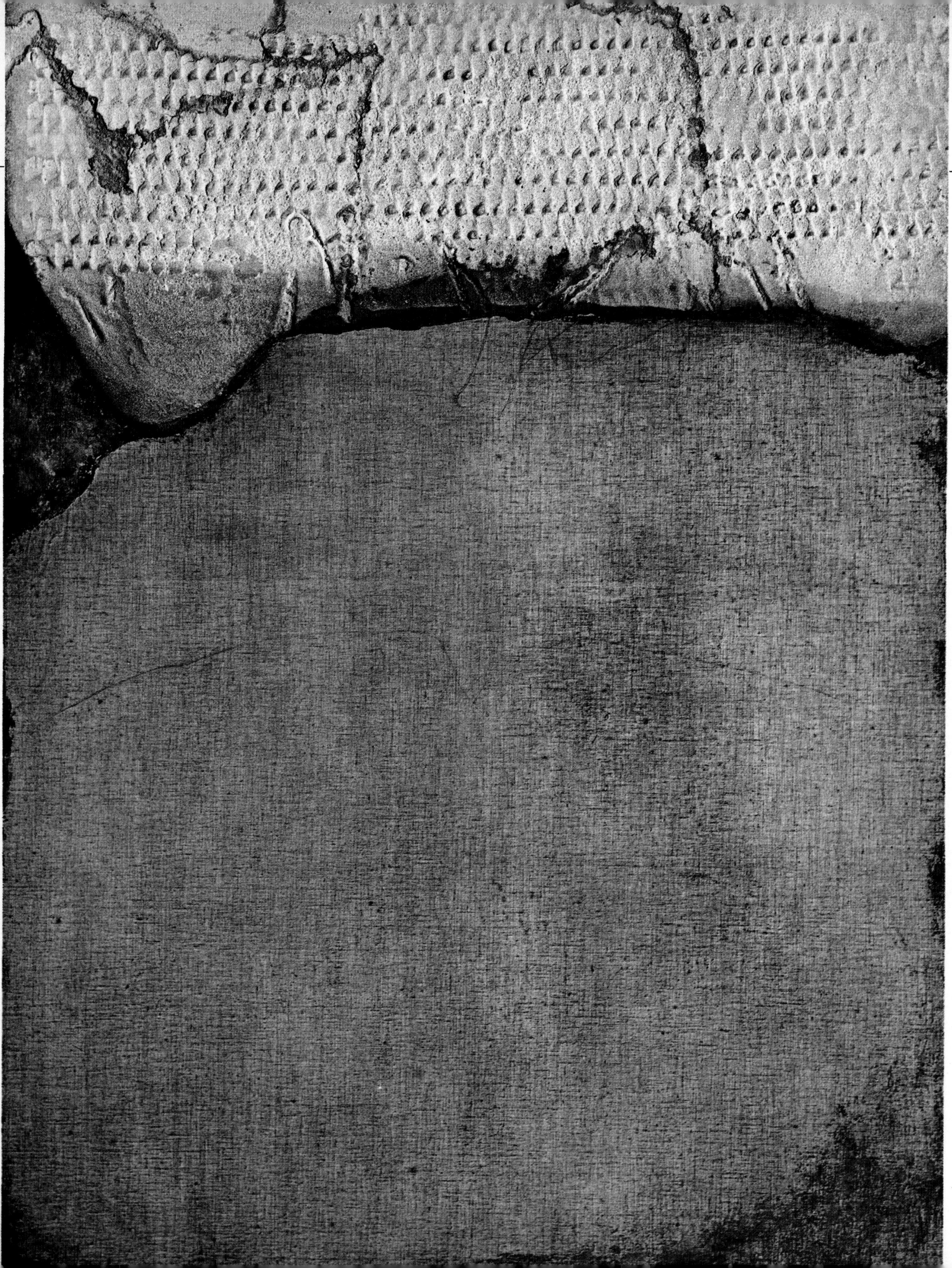

202

202. Grey fragment over canvas. Combined process on canvas, 1958. 130×97 cm. Van der Loo Collection, Munich.

203. Painting. Combined process on canvas, 1958. 195 × 130 cm. Museum of Modern Art, Rome.

203

230

204. Brown door. Combined process on canvas, 1959. 195 × 130 cm. Washington University, St. Louis, Missouri.

205. Grey with two black marks. Combined process on canvas, 1959. 75 × 109 cm. Martha Jackson Gallery, New York.

206. Grey with two bags. Combined process on canvas, 1959. 130 × 130 cm. Eva de Buren Collection, Stockholm.

207. Paper cut-out in violet, 1959. 58 × 72 cm. J. Ferreró Collection, Barcelona.

204

205
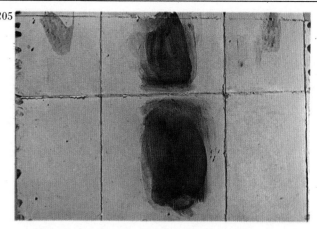

206
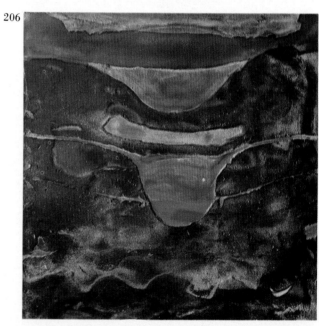

207

208. Crackled white over brown. Paint on canvas, 1959. 170×195 cm. Lebworth Collection, New York.

209. Grey with oblique lines. Combined process on canvas, 1959. Museum of Modern Art, New York.

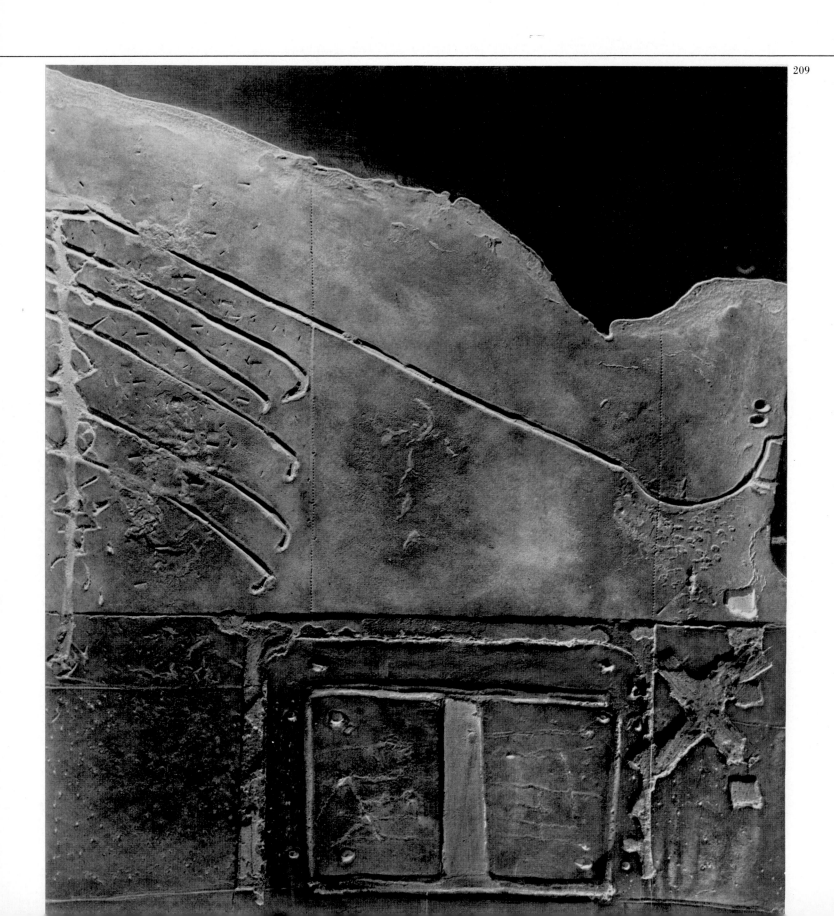

210. Grey space. Paint on canvas, 1962. 130×81 cm. Gómez Collection, Oakridge, Tennessee.

211. Marble-worker's sand with six footprints. Combined process on canvas, 1959. 265×190 cm. Panza di Biumo Collection, Milan.

212. Ochre painting. Combined process on canvas, 1959. Town Hall of Barcelona.

213. Grey corners on brown. Combined process on canvas, 1959. 195×130 cm. Town Hall of Barcelona.

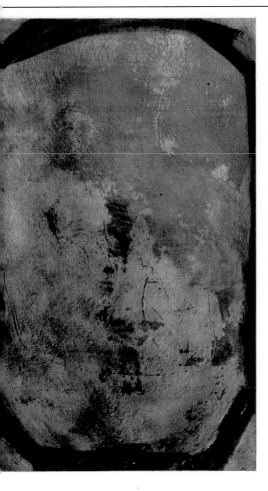

210

211

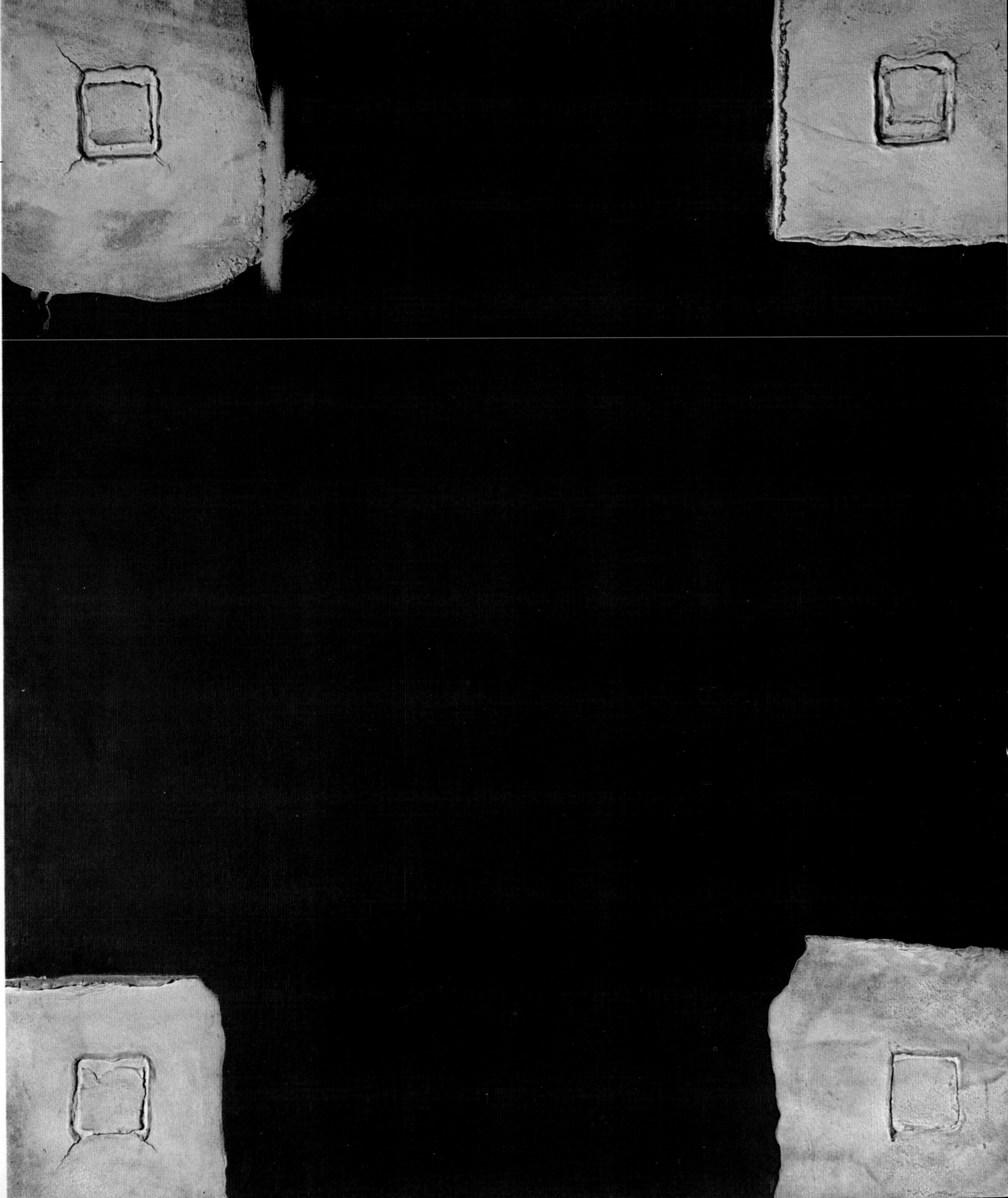

214. Grey with black fringes. Paint on canvas, 1959. 162×130 cm. International Center of Aesthetic Research, Turin.

215. Black with transversal band. Combined process on canvas, 1959. 162× 130 cm. Galerie Stadler, Paris.

214

216. Cardboard, 1959-1960. 58×107 cm. Tooth Gallery, London.

217. Torn papers on canvas, 1959. 130×97 cm. Dr. Bloom Collection, Zurich.

218. Four forms. Combined process on canvas, 1959. 60×73 cm. Galleria dell' Ariete, Milan.

219. Beige with black circle. Combined process on canvas, 1959. 81×81 cm. Galerie Berggruen, Paris.

216
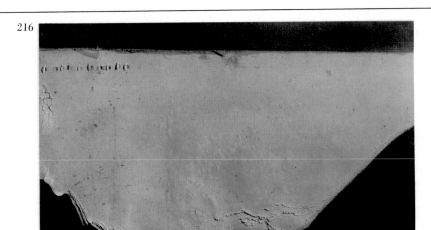

217
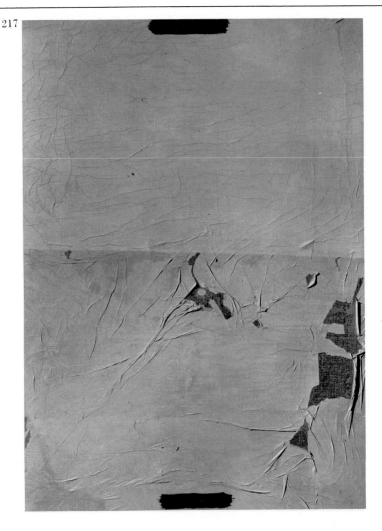

218
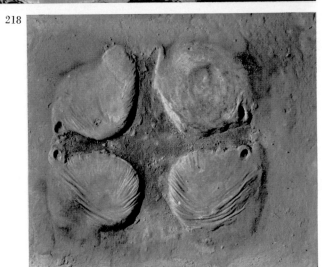

219
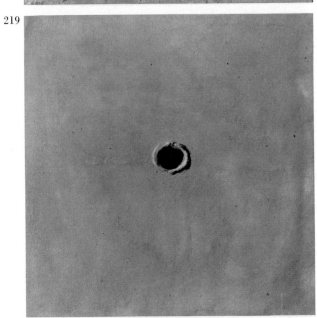

220. Grey with a vertical cross. Combined process on canvas, 1960. 54 × 85 cm. H. Neuerburg, Cologne.

221. Triangle. Combined process on canvas, 1960. 89 × 116 cm. Martha Jackson Gallery, New York.

222. Wood on canvas, 1960. 45 × 99 cm. Victoria de los Ángeles and Enric Magriñà Collection, Barcelona.

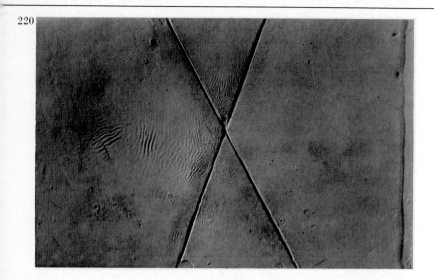

220

221

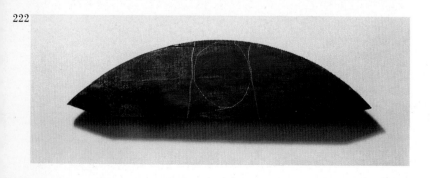

222

there was the Montgomery march, in 1966 the revolt of the students at Berkeley, in 1967 we heard the name of Che Guevara, in 1968 those of Dutschke and Dubcek.

In Catalonia 1965 will be remembered as the year of the *Comissions Obreres* (Workers' Commissions), the great crisis of the students and the demonstration of the priests; 1966 was the year of the university assembly in the Capuchin Monastery in Sarrià, at which Tàpies was present and because of which he was sent to prison; 1967 was the year that saw the apparition of artists' protest groups; 1968 the year of intellectual agitation.

The retrogression after the attempted assassination of Dutschke, the failure of the Paris May Revolution, the assassination of Luther King or the fall of Dubcek, all indicated with a new style the time of poor art, from 1968 on. We must make use of the whole of this perspective in movement if we are to

223. Pink and black collage-painting. Paint and paper on canvas, 1960. 89 × 116 cm. Winterthur Museum.

224. Piece of paper. Victoria de los Ángeles and Enric Magriñà Collection, Barcelona.

225. Painting on wood, 1960. 51 × 91 cm. Private collection, Barcelona.

223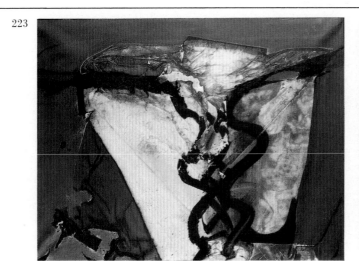

224

225

226. Brown space. Paint on canvas, 1960. 65 × 81 cm. Martha Jackson Gallery, New York.

227. Purple. Paint and sizing on canvas, 1960. 130 × 162 cm. William Janss Collection, Thermal, California.

226

227

228. Black matter over sack. Combined process on canvas. Victoria de los
Ángeles and Enric Magriñà Collection, Barcelona.

229. Grey with black marks. Combined process on canvas, 1960. 195 × 170 cm.
Claude Hersaint Collection, Paris.

229

get into proper focus the context of the anthropoidal accentuation of the trace of man in Tàpies' paintings during the Luther King years, between *Pacem in Terris* and the May Revolution.

The patient man. The nostalgic subject matter of closed objects still continues, though now in retrogression. In 1965 there are cupboards, niches, doors, baskets, cushions, folders, and there are the stretchers turned upside down, no less laden with a sense of concealment. In 1966, the hat, the sofa and the bed, stuffed and fleshy, the spectacles, the cup. More doors, cupboards and boxes in 1967.

On the other hand, within the lightening of the rigid structures we shall see the reappearance of the signs of orthography or musical notation, more laconic than ever, the cardinal points, the corners, the lines of points and the hyphens, which cross the whole surface of the canvas, in the same direction or crossing one another, as though they were the trajectories of invisible personages passing behind.

This hypothesis is borne out by a work done in 1969 which alludes to Frègoli, where the sign = on the right of the picture is joined to the sign = on the extreme left by a line of hyphens which represents the trajectory of the famous mime, passing behind the picture, incorporated in the décor of the stage.

When there is an ear at the end of one of these trajectories, it confirms the invisibility of the theme and reminds us of Tàpies' idea of following the example of the classical composers, who provided for the performance of the choir or orchestra behind a wall.

This ear of 1965 indicates the apparition of the anthropomorphic theme, which appears very suddenly and assumes grandeur and prominence, being clearly identified in the end with the hitherto generic

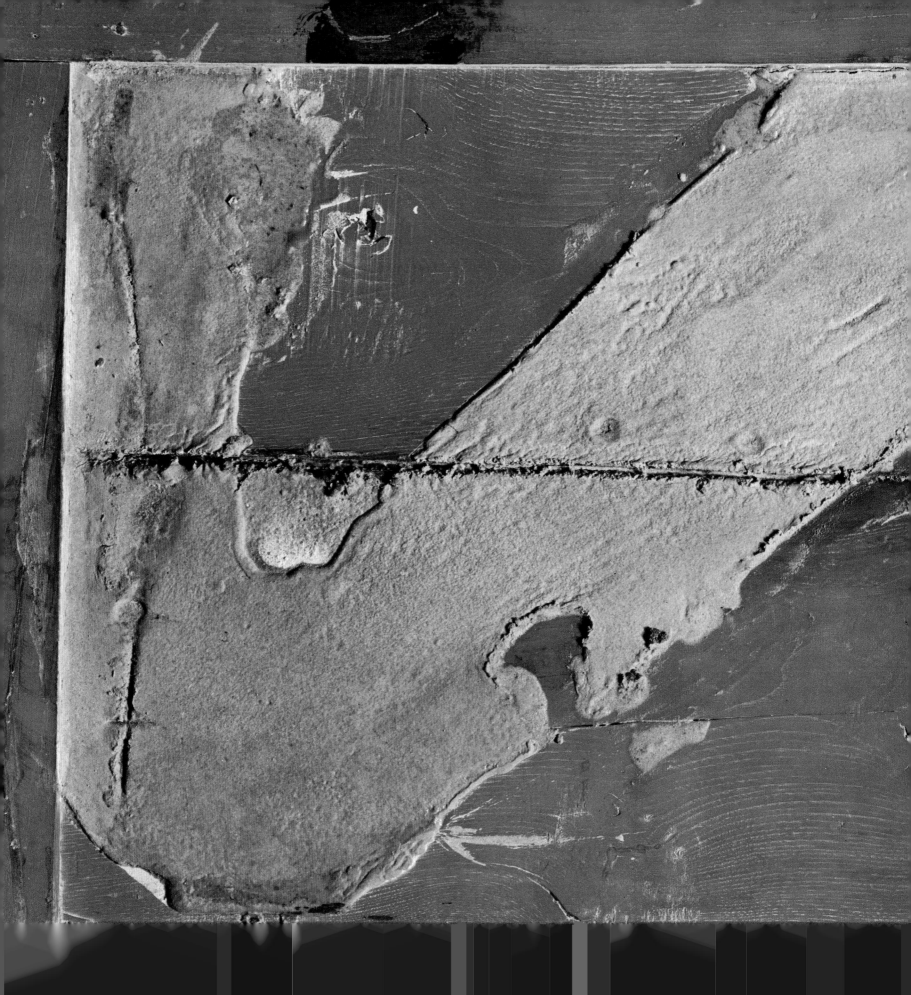

230. Painting on wood, 1960. 51×91 cm. Private collection, Barcelona.

material. It is the real material itself that becomes anthropomorphic. It is not, therefore, a neo-figurative phenomenon, but a presentation.

It is interesting to note that the most monumental theme of 1965 is a foot, an enormous foot, that foot which is to be the most poignant icon in the *Novel la* done with Brossa. A working man's foot, swollen, weary, defeated. Not the head, not the breast, not the hand. Not the seat of thought, nor the heart, nor yet any mainspring of activity, but the passive part, the one that bears weight and weariness, that treads upon the earth.

When a personage appears almost full-length, like the woman kneeling with drooping breasts, the feet are more prominent and the head disappears under a heavy load. The following year, 1966, sees the appearance of another monumental image, the great woman scrubbing, on hands and knees, composed of soft material, with her head hidden, which an alphabetical notation characterizes as something suitable for a census, a payroll, an identity card or a death certificate.

Man profaned. On the other hand, these anthropomorphic themes often appear at this time as the results of scribbling, of an instinctive, cursive trembling of the hand, which cannot prevent itself from remembering things. In a mixture of fragments, as if in a mosaic or in a *cobra* painting, there are some forms that come to the surface. There are the things, the buttocks, the hairy legs of the men, the mouths with big cigars, the swollen breasts of the women, the hair and the smoke blended into a poor, disordered image.

One year later, in 1967, this vision of man stripped of his dignity is accentuated. There are the images of the anus dropping excrement, of the open legs showing the sex, of

231. Architectural. Combined process on canvas, 1960. 265×190 cm. Instituto di Tella, Buenos Aires.

231

232. Two reliefs in space. Combined process on canvas, 1960. 195 × 170 cm.
Martha Jackson Gallery, New York.

232

233. Sized canvas, 1961. 195×170 cm. Private collection, Barcelona.

233

250

234. Three marks on white. Combined process on canvas, 1962. Martha Jackson Gallery, New York.

235. Four cardboards, 1959. Claude Vulliet Collection, Paris.

236. Sign on cardboard, 1961. Leopold Pomés Collection, Barcelona.

237. Cardboards sewn together with strings, 1960. 46.5×69.5 cm. Sala Gaspar, Barcelona.

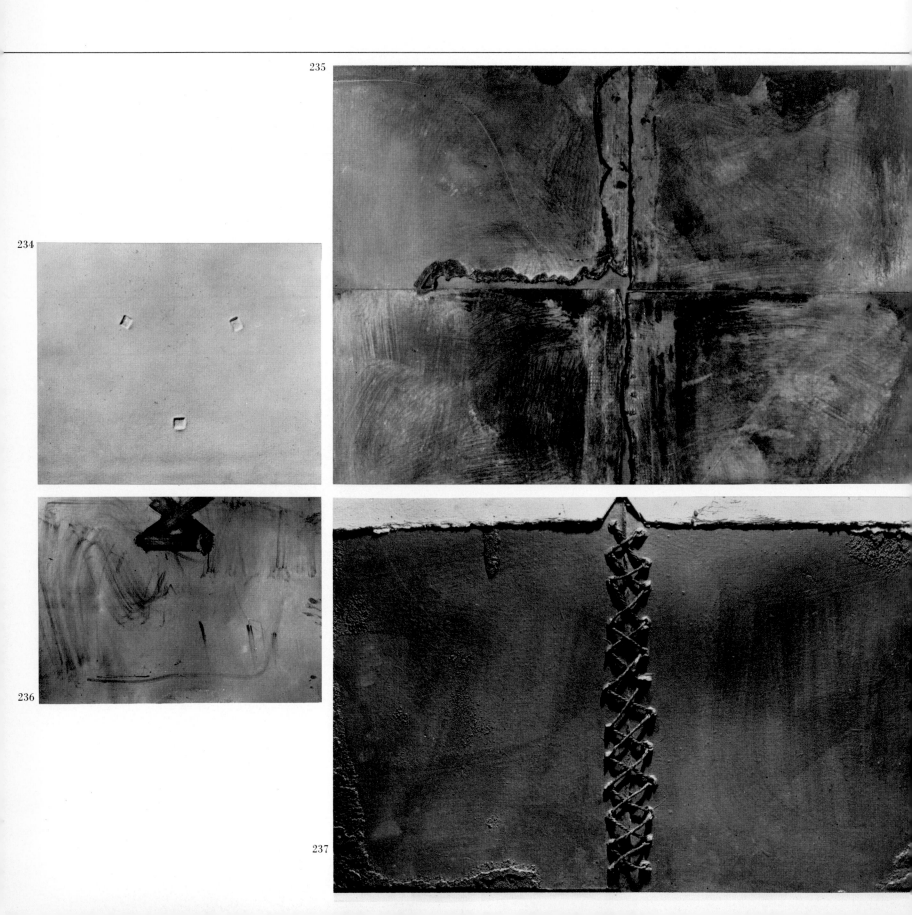

235

234

236

237

238. Triangular form on grey. Combined process on canvas, 1961. 195 × 130 cm. Galerie Stadler, Paris.

239. Grey with wavy red lines. Combined process on canvas, 1962. 162 × 97 cm. Luciano Pistoi Collection, Turin.

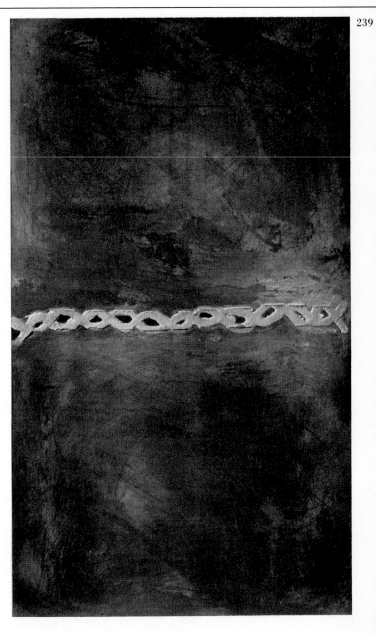

239

238

240. Dark space. Combined process on canvas, 1960. 265×380 cm. Martha Jackson Gallery, New York.

241. Cardboard box unfolded, 1960. 128×85 cm. Joan Prats Collection, Barcelona.

242. Paper on painted canvas, 1960. 100×100 cm. Tooth Gallery, London.

241

242
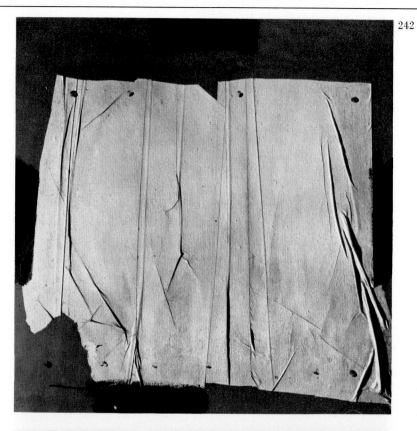

243

244
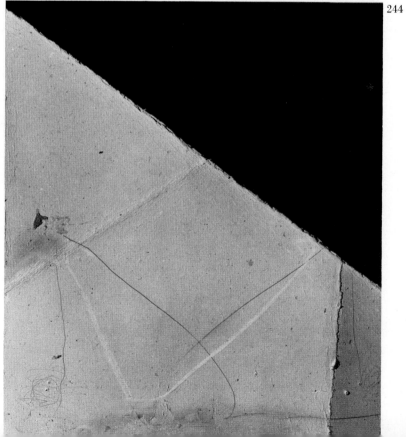

243. Vertical on white. Combined process on canvas, 1959. Herlt Collection, Weiden, Germany.

244. Cardboard cut diagonally, 1960. 60×44 cm. Private collection, Barcelona.

245. Large brown with graphic sign in black. Combined process on canvas, 1961. 195×260 cm. Galerie Maeght, Paris.

256

246. Grey with graphic signs in black. Combined process on canvas, 1962. 195×310 cm. Museum of Basle.

247. Brown bed. Combined process on canvas, 1960. 195×130 cm. Private collection, Barcelona.

248. Grey with black band. Combined process on canvas, 1962. 195 × 130 cm. Private collection, Turin.

249. Collage with a dish, 1962. 76 × 55 cm. Sala Gaspar, Barcelona.

248

249

the mixture between these two themes and between them and the theme of the foot, and of the ambiguity that confuses the two legs spread wide open and the M of the palm of the hand, of destiny and of death. The imprint of the

hand sunk deep in mud or that of the foot, the barred belly, the knees marked with crosses, like the brands made on animals, the presence of the theme of the basin, so closely linked to the most disagreeable aspects of physiology, all

250. Painting on pieces of cardboard, 1960. 104 × 75 cm. Sala Gaspar, Barcelona.

250. Painting on pieces of cardboard, 1960. 104 × 75 cm. Sala Gaspar, Barcelona.

the sex of an old woman; a box, torn, wide open and soot-stained, is like an image of rape. So are the fabrics, crushed, glued together, creased or tied. In one picture a big, ugly scapular, stuffed and swollen, majestically symmetrical and ridiculously rounded, is like the image of a self-satisfied bourgeois, in contrast to the poignant images of man profaned.

The function of the orgasm. Ever since Wilhem Reich published *The function of the orgasm*, the conjunction of Freud and sociology, which had been established in the Weimar period by men like Theodor Adorno or Erich Fromm, and which Marcuse or Ernest Bloch were to reveal to the younger generation in the sixties, has been an active fact. The politico-sexual revolt of the S.D.S. in Berlin, in Hamburg or in Munich, the May Revolution with slogans like *The more I make love the better I help the revolution*, these are mani-

complete the protesting vision of man transformed from outside himself into something ignoble. This operation, at times, is done with objects.

A shrivelled, rotten nut evokes at the same time the buttocks and

251. Blue and brown. Combined process on canvas. Eudald Serra Collection, Barcelona.

252. Flesh colour. Paint on canvas. Victoria de los Ángeles and Enric Magriñà Collection, Barcelona.

253. Graphic signs in green. Drawing on paper, 1961. Private collection, Barcelona.

251

252

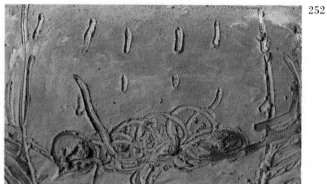

253

254. For the victims of the Vallès floods. Combined process on canvas, 1962.
Antoni de Moragas Collection, Barcelona.

254

festations of a phenomenon that ranges from the violent consciousness of the *enragés* to the more pacific approach of the hippies and from rationalized militancy to the erotic frivolity of those who cultivate *La dolce vita.*

Integrated within this vast phenomenon, Tàpies' painting since 1968 has not only thrown over even the themes of constructive structuring, which were so strong up to 1963, but has alternated the laconic, poor, feeble subject matter which was already developing in recent years with the new sexual theme. This is not an apparition. It is a re-encounter with a theme which had interested him greatly in his first period and which he never altogether abandoned. In 1968 this theme reappeared, with a monumental character, in works such as a red canvas entirely occupied by a superimposition of male and female sexual organs of great size. There has been an abundance since then of characters with their legs spread open, the outline of the legs intertwined with the fateful M. Frequently the zone of their sex is mutilated, trodden upon, soiled, severed, stigmatized, as though by somebody's immense rage.

At times the sexual theme is evoked indirectly, as in the painting of a soft, fleshy matter, with an armpit encrusted with real hairs. Horsehair and straw are associated with the theme of sex and that of poverty at the same time. There are straw calves, bellies with straw stuck to them, improvised cushions made of cotton waste and filled to bursting-point with straw. By 1969 it is no longer the mere presence of the sexual theme but the coupling itself that becomes the theme.

An insubstantial wooden lath forms the frontier between two tufts of horsehair touching each other, one on top of the other. Couplings in multiple postures are superimposed, without any concession to beauty and sometimes coexisting with images of defecation. The sexes are superimposed, penetrate one another, blend together in a mingling in which there are neither eyes nor breasts nor hands, something blind and poor, without thought or feeling or desire.

When there are mouths accompanying these blind bodies, they are either instruments of the orgy or else, like enormous sacks full of rice, images of gluttony.

Poor art. The phenomenon of poor art was possibly the most interesting manifestation of the plastic arts in the later sixties. This is an art that was born with the protest movement, one that seeks to destroy altogether the social statute of objects of art that have become mere merchandise and of the artist as a man who works for a market and who is measured by the stock-exchange quotations of success.

Against these realities, poor art is voluntarily ephemeral and mortal, tending to destroy all possible assimilation to whatever has an exchange value, and it is a moral attitude rather than a work.

The phenomenon has become fairly widespread and there is a group in Catalonia who practise its tenets, especially the young artist Antoni Llena, a friend of Tàpies, who shared a room with him during the siege of the Capuchin Monastery of Sarrià by the police.

Tàpies himself finds the phenomenon interesting, despite the fact that he does not altogether agree with the bases of its programme. He believes that one must work with the spirit of an amateur, but that a professional artist may possess greater concentration in his work. He still considers the present system of the circulation of works of art within the cycle of sales and gallery quotations of the capitalist world as a fatal lesser evil, even though he has no special interest in things not being managed otherwise. To a certain extent he stays aloof from the commercialization of his work, because he finds that speculation belongs to a secondary level and that it does not affect the significance of the work.

In spite of these radical differences, he has discovered that the subject matter, the desires and the poetry of poor art are his own, are what he has sought for years, ever since his first material works and since the first works he sold. That is why he is sympathetic to this tendency, which is now coming close to where he used to be.

In 1969 I published a text entitled *L'art mortal*, in which I expounded my idea that the loss of a centre in the vision of the physical world after Einstein —like the destruction of the unitarian vision of society after Marx, or that of a person's own personal identity after Freud— had ended in the off-centre world in which we live. Brought up still to believe in certain stable values, we see that the castles of our childhood were only painted cardboard and everything comes to pieces in our hands. We had felt the security of our homes, of our parents, of our models, and now we find ourselves completely orphaned, without any points of reference, mounted on tigers racing through the night which we cannot abandon for fear they will devour us.

But at the end I urged the reader not to mourn his lost security, but rather to find the beauty of the night and the danger, of change, of the unknown, of fear itself, and I quoted a verse by Tagore which says that when people weep because the sun is setting, their tears prevent them from seeing the stars.

This text of mine, which elicited warm words from the young philosopher Eugeni Trias, also brought me a letter from Tàpies which read:

I found your article ART MORTAL very interesting. I am enclosing the book (about me) by Teixidor, which you may not already have, for there are reproductions in it of some things I did with similar intentions... I thought you would be interested in knowing this, remembering that you are preparing a book on my work.

Expansive testimonies. The works exhibited at the end of 1969, in effect, were not only expansive testimonies of orgastic energy, but also a conscious blend of this problem with a position of clear social significance. The non-acceptance by Tàpies of the bases of the programme of poor art does not mean that he does not accept or that he has not felt, and long before at that, the bases of their problems. The pictures of the horsehair and the board, that one in which a number of meat hooks half-support a piece of bloodstained cord, the mouth drawn full of real rice stuck on or, above all, the stained canvas covered with a shabby plastic bag, half transparent, half milky, all these bear witness to the exacerbation of this awareness.

The simultaneous sharpening of this poverty and of the sexual factor makes us think of what Wilhem Reich asserts when he says that in 1930 sexuality was a subject for rather doubtful reform groups, but that since 1940 it has become the cornerstone of social problems. Reich emphasizes that fetichisms were a response to an immense desire to live, but on account of the old psychical slavery this desire could only be manifested in perverse forms. Only the post-fetichist world will be capable of manifesting that enormous desire to live in a healthy spirit.

Repairing the entropy. This commentary helps us to place Tàpies' role in its proper place in history. Attracted as a boy by the great force of libido with which the music of Wagner is impregnated, later disenchanted or filled with disgust at stupidity and cruelty (which may possibly have helped to foster the escapist aspect of his magic world), he now finds once more his bio-electrical charges; no longer, however, in the glow of Valhalla, but in the sad darkness of the world of the poverty-ridden slums. It is important to point out that Tàpies does not select from this world those aspects that come from the scourings of industry, as is the case with Pop art or the films of Antonioni, but rather seeks primitive aspects in it that correspond to his method, which is also primitive and which we may describe, with Cassirer, as the application of a general feeling of synthetic life, which rejects the scientific system based on classifications and systematizations.

This decision forms part of an effort to achieve significance that

255

256. Ochre and black paper folded and sized, 1963. 123×91 cm. Van der Loo Gallery, Munich.

256

he considers indispensable. In a world in which, as Lévi-Strauss has shown quite clearly, the elementary structures of opposition with vigorous transformations, when they circulate in the symbolic world through all the sociological code, are gradually giving way to structures of reduplication and of successive episodes, to a point at which the reduplication ends by playing the part of a structure and the transformations and positions seem to be totally extenuated: in such a world it is a matter of urgency to readjust the current of this entropy.

The process of purification is nothing but a radical suppression of tautologies, of rhetoric, of everything that stains and —which is worse— tends to replace, within the ordinary forms of artistic communication, the true trunk of the original dialectic, from which so much rubbish comes.

Tàpies refuses to accept anything institutional or mechanical

257. Stretcher-painting, 1962. 162×130 cm. Private collection, Barcelona.
258. Composition with cords. Combined process and sizing on canvas, 1963.
195×130 cm. Luciano Pistoi Collection, Turin.

257

258

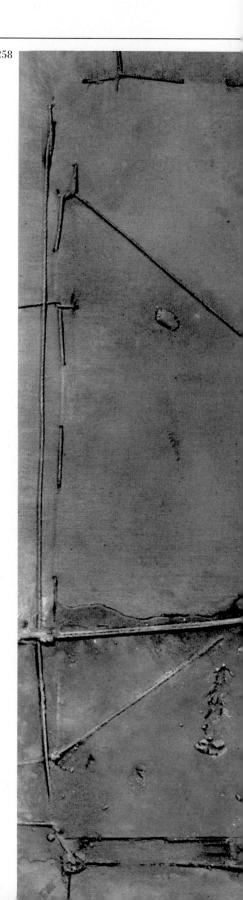

that there may be in a plastic language, and he identifies his work especially with what Barthes calls the word, which means the personal act of selection and bringing up to date with which the artist modifies the codes of the forms

259. Painting on stretcher, 1962. 130 × 81 cm. International Center of Aesthetic Research, Turin.

259

260. Brown, ochre and black. Combined process on plywood. 162×130 cm. Gustau Gili Torra Collection, Barcelona.

261. Cardboard with strings, 1962. 85×75 cm. Galerie Stadler, Paris.

obtaining around him in order to express through this break his personal thought.

PRAXIS, beyond the sign. Despite the importance of the communicative aspect of his art, we think that the conquest of the Tàpies of 1970 is the apparition of something beyond the signs. Signs, typical of our civilization of interchanges, were of great importance in his work. Perhaps because, as Chklovski said, every work of art begins in rela-

262. Large grey paper with white sign. Acrylic paint over sized paper on canvas, 1965. 193×137 cm. Van der Loo Gallery, Munich.

262

tion to other works of art, and the world of art has been that of the signs, the symbols and the icons. But it would appear that his work now becomes aware that there is an ideology implicit in the sign —like all symbolism— and that this ideology is a very negative one, for it presupposes the act of hiding the work behind the value, the production behind the image.

At the same moment in history that neocapitalism sets up an altar to information and goes so far as to place the transmission of information at the very highest level of a way of life, Tàpies makes us feel that he understands that his work can be *praxis*, but not communication. His redistribution of forms, his deliberate wreckings or crushings of recognizable structures, are like thoughts transformed into acts. into pure production, which dispenses with communication and calls attention to the scandal of those who convert all art into pure information (as they would any merchandise into money). Now he brings us nearer to the radical eroticism of art demanded by Susan Sontag instead of hermeneutics, and to the *praxis* beyond the symbol demanded by Julia Kristeva. In

272

263. Relief in grey with three small holes. Combined process, 1964. 24 × 41 cm. Buren Gallery, Stockholm.

264. Sized canvas, 1964. Martha Jackson Gallery, New York.

265. Grey relief in four parts. Combined process on canvas, 1963. 150 × 217 cm. Museum of Cologne.

266. Grey with white angle. Paint on canvas, 1963. 97 × 130 cm. Zwirner Gallery, Cologne.

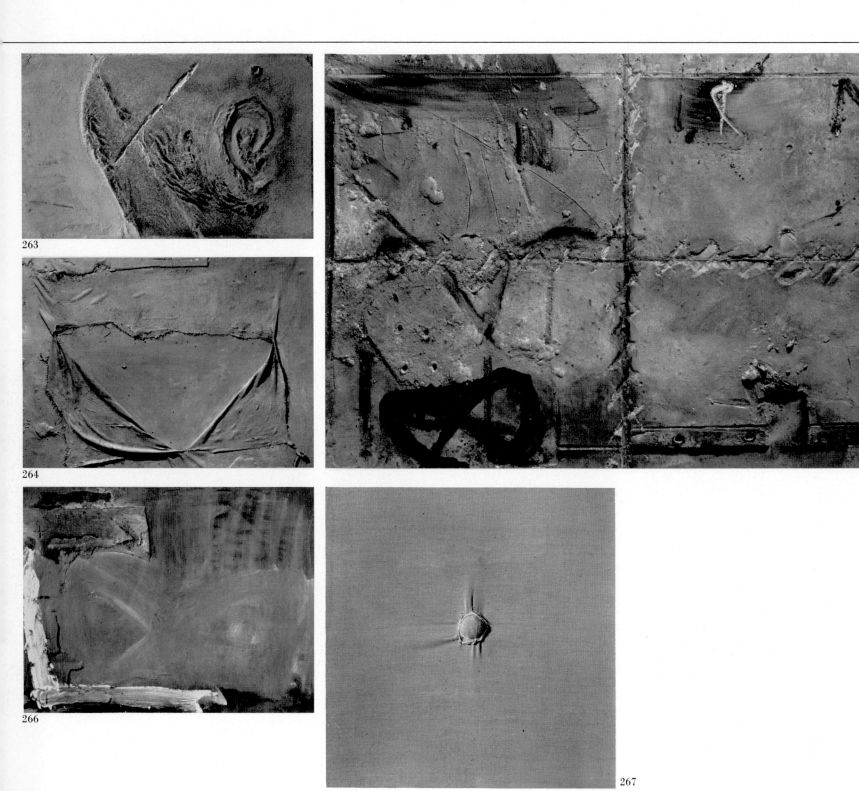

263

264

266

267

267. Canvas and string, 1964. 80×80 cm. Martha Jackson Gallery, New York.

268. Ochre with five incisions. Combined process on canvas, 1964. 162× 130 cm. Galerie Stadler, Paris.

269. Paint on isorel and white collage, 1964. 130×97 cm. Private collection, Barcelona.

268

269

270. Reddish contour. Combined process on canvas, 1963. 92 × 60 cm. Martha Jackson Gallery, New York.

271. Grey with three pink stripes. Combined process on canvas, 1964. 97 × 146 cm. Dr. Dalen Collection, Stockholm.

272. Folder covers, 1964. 41 × 64 cm. Dr. Krüppel Collection, Neuss.

273. Relief with cords. Sizing and paint on canvas, 1963. 162 × 130 cm. Private collection, Barcelona.

270

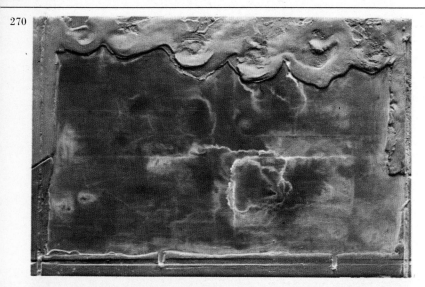

271

272

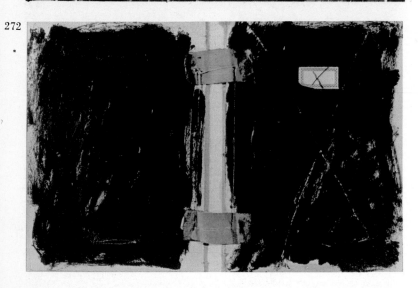

this way Tàpies helps us to realize the enormous mental block to which the signs have subjected us, and to enrich ourselves with what Chklovski already called singularization, the capacity —in which Kafka excelled— of seeing the world as if we were seeing it for the first time.

He does not show us signs, nor even things, but places in evidence functions or dialectics in which all that comes from the language of communication is deformed until it becomes unique. It is an investigation of differences (values of use) which ridicules —as Foucault does so well— the traditional sciences of resemblances (values of interchange).

There is a radical incompatibility between this world of different things, the only one that becomes known, because it is production, and the immanentist world of commercial design, which is gradually submerging us and becoming a gigantic tautology.

273

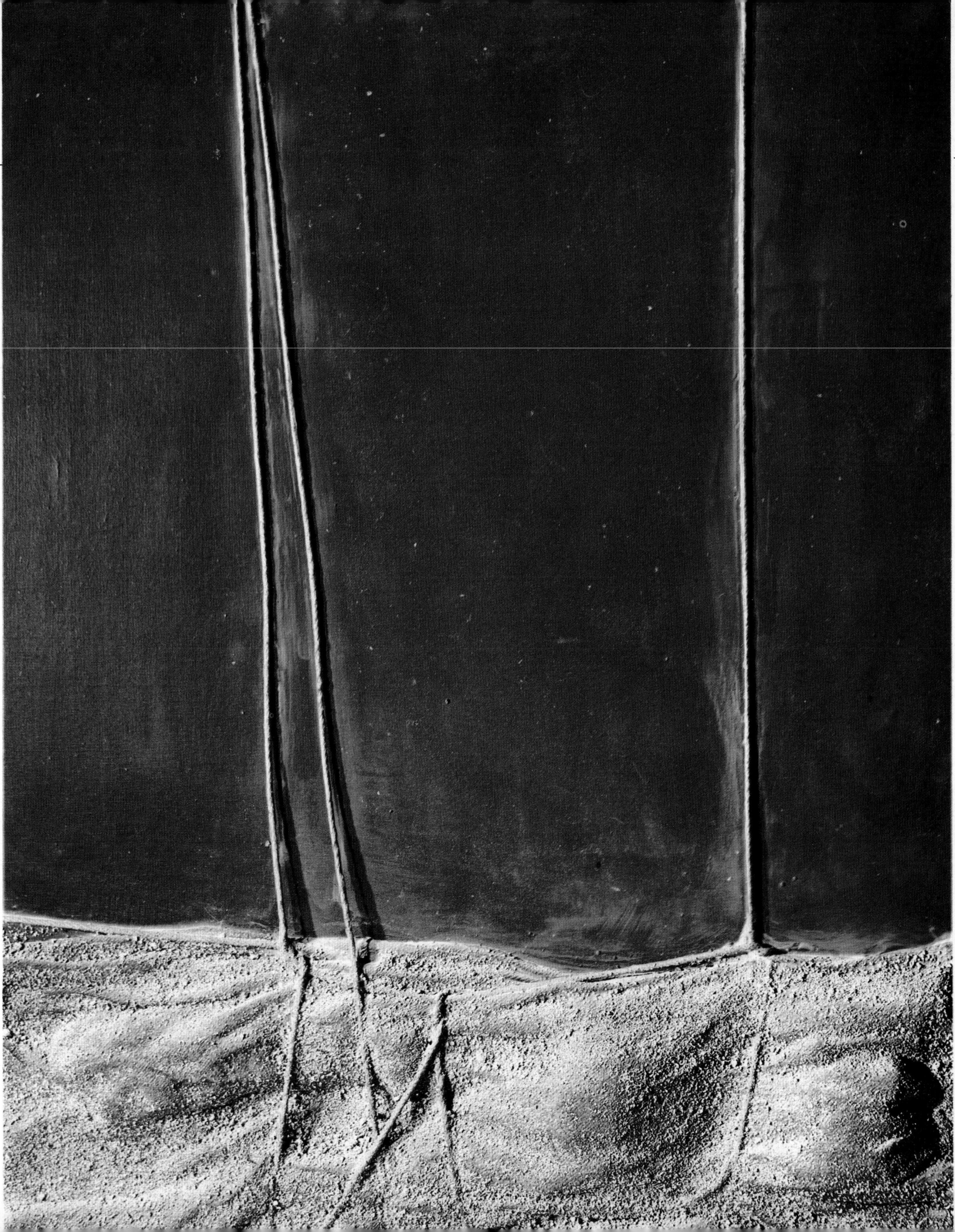

PARTICIPATION

From the suburbs to the city. It is interesting to observe the existence of a very significant curve in the degree of participation of Tàpies' work within the society that surrounds him.

At the age of twenty he attempted to create an environment of his own in the world of the young would-be artists who, following the dictates of the traditional cliché and with no more possibilities than those of a poor and confined world, had chosen the bohemianism of a tavern as their meeting-place and were satisfied to exhibit their work in a suburban centre. This was the period of disorder, in which there was a contempt for the outside world projected from within a nucleus standing voluntarily on the sidelines and trampling on established principles. This was a stage of encystment.

His connection, through Foix, Prats, Miró and Gomis, with the prewar Avant-garde of Spain opened up for Tàpies the first perspective of a positive action directed outwards. At least within the limits of a narrow angle, there would be a sector of society which could connect with the creative nucleus and be at once its culture and its sounding board.

This was the way in which the young artists wanted to move out of their open, disordered bohemianism and into that group protectionism so typical of the avant-garde, that is to say the entry into the competitive system of production with an eye to the market of a limited, but international, sector. The review *Dau al Set*, that tenacious and obstinate organization of Tharrats, made great efforts to reach this goal.

The first polemical area of this sector was undoubtedly the Club 49 of Barcelona. Afterwards came the scholarship to Paris, Tàpies' discovery by Washburn, the Carnegie Institute and the Venice Biennale. The later intervention of Martha Jackson, followed by Michel Tapié and Stadler, created a privileged international position for Tàpies, cutting him off definitively from his early suburban bohemianism, and also cutting him right away from the limited, local struggling of the *Dau al Set*.

Star system and cosmopolitanism. Thus, in the early sixties, Tàpies' participation in society seemed to be marked by a decreasing solidarity. From the unlimited and undemanding bohemianism of *La Campana* to the group protectionism of the *Dau al Set*, and from that underground temple to the total solitude of a headlong advance, protected by efficient switchmen. If the first period had been marked by a certain dispersion, in the second Tàpies had participated very fully, illustrating texts by Brossa, plays like *El Crim* or poems like *L'estoig del Sha de Pèrsia o l'estrella del Nord*, *Das verfinsterne Blumenbukett o Les esquerdes s'omplen*, *The Oracle*, etc. He had, in short, really participated in the underground

274. Relief in ochre and pink. Combined process on plywood, 1965. 162 ×
114 cm. Morris Pinto Collection, Paris.
275. Paper and strings, 1964. 85 × 54 cm. Van der Loo Gallery, Munich.

274

275

276. Blackboard, 1965. 130×162 cm. Stedelijk Museum, Amsterdam.

277. Collage with envelope, 1966. 32.5 × 25 cm. Buren Gallery, Stockholm.

278. Collage with paper and string, 1965-1966. 77 × 57 cm. Buren Gallery, Stockholm.

279. Lacerated relief. Combined process on canvas, 1966. 116 × 89 cm. Martha Jackson Gallery, New York.

280. Calendar. Sizing on paper, 1966. Private collection, Barcelona.

281. Small material and collage, 1967. 32 × 42 cm. Martha Jackson Gallery, New York.

277

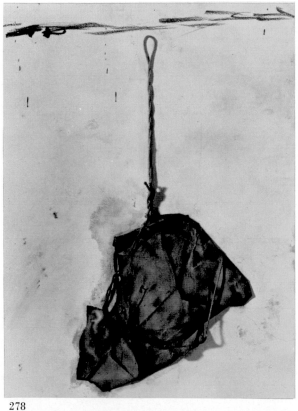

278

279

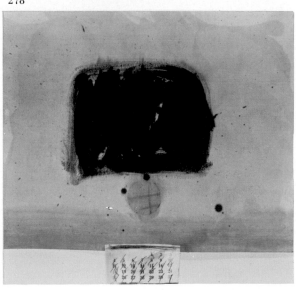

280

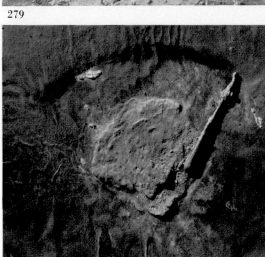

281

282. In the shape of a slate. Combined process on plywood, 1967. 81 × 100 cm. Private collection, Paris.

283. Newspaper with black stain, 1964. 11 × 13 cm. K. H. Müller Collection, Düsseldorf.

284. Landscape. Combined process on canvas, 1965. 89 × 116 cm. Private collection, Barcelona.

285. Line of dots. Marble-worker's sand on canvas, 1964. Sala Gaspar, Barcelona.

282
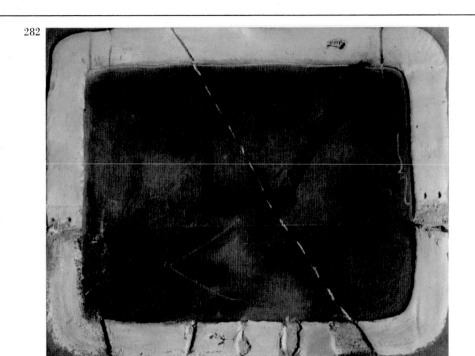

283
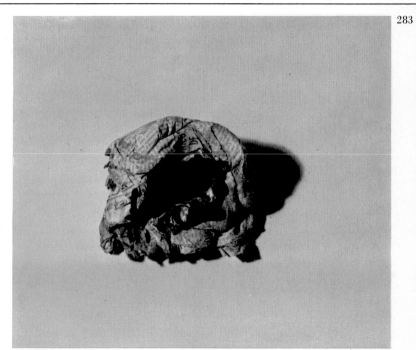

284

285
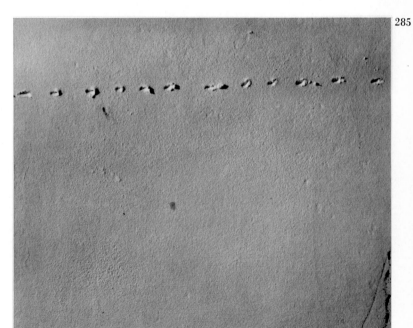

286. White stripes on material. Combined process on cardboard. Manuel de Muga Collection, Barcelona.

287. White on white. Marble-worker's sand on canvas, 1965. Sala Gaspar, Barcelona.

288. White arch on wood, 1967. 170×195 cm. Private collection, Barcelona.

286

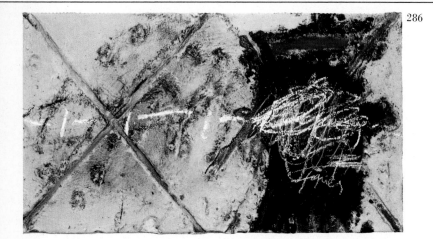

288

287

289. Small black and red. Combined process on canvas, 1969. 33×55 cm. Eva de Buren Collection, Stockholm.

290. Painting with graphic signs. Combined process on canvas, 1969. 89× 115 cm. Jacques Neubauer Collection, Paris.

291. Yellow band. Combined process on canvas, 1966. 74×117 cm. Galerie Maeght, Paris.

289

290

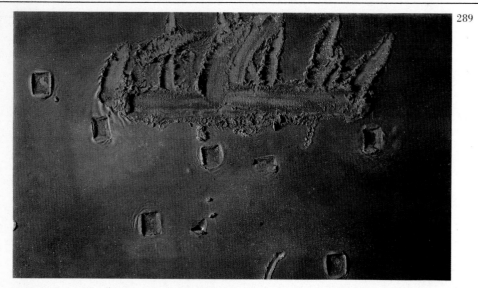

291

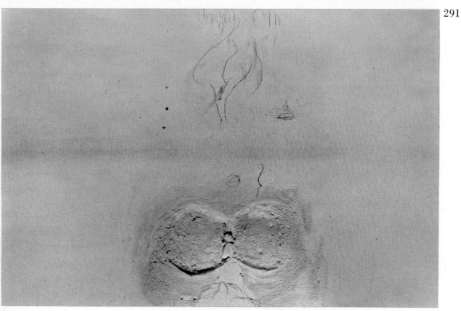

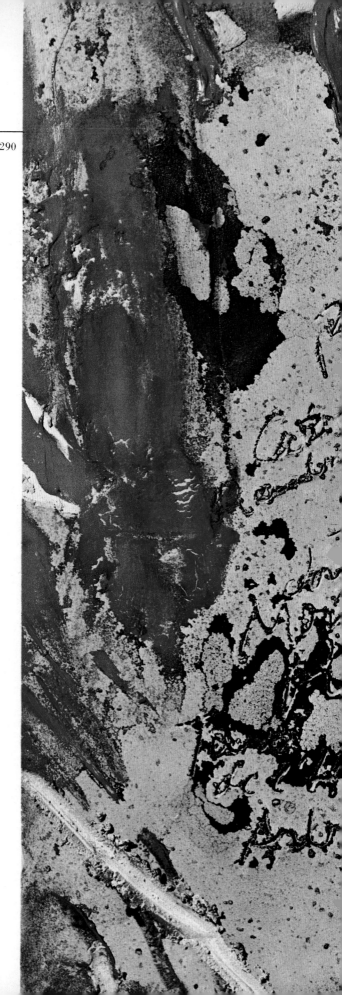

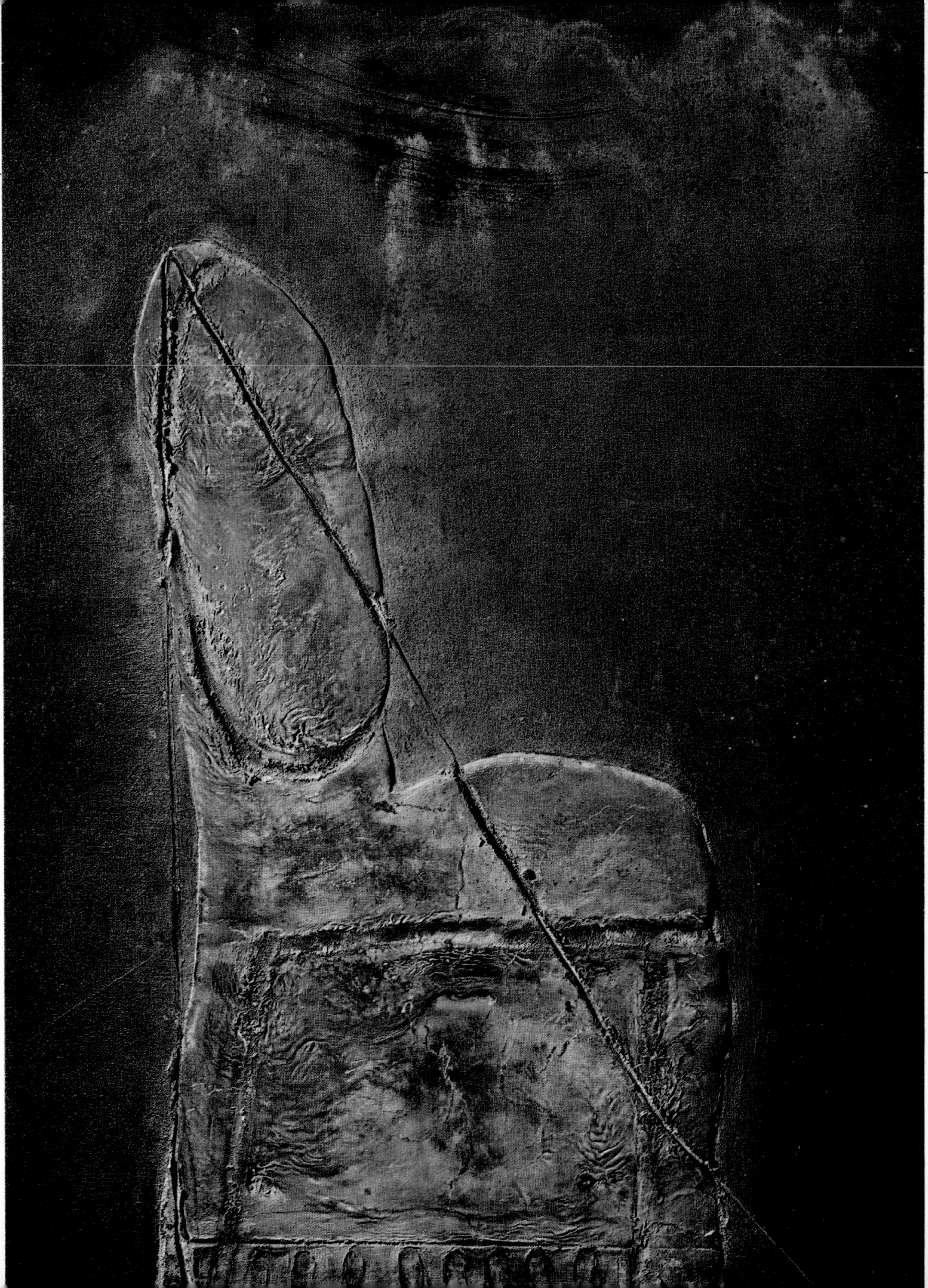

292. Cardboard on dark canvas, 1969. 162 × 130 cm. Martha Jackson Gallery, New York.

293. In the shape of a chair. Combined process on canvas, 1966. 130 × 97 cm. Private collection, Barcelona.

world. When the Club 49 opened up to him an incipient area of projection, he extended his participation to it at once. Not only did he exhibit at the *Salons del Jazz*, but he illustrated, together with Tharrats, Planasdurà, Surós, Guinovart, Poveda (Sànchez Poveda), Sucre, Brotat, Guansé, Roca, Ciria, Saura, Aleu, Ponç, Matilde Tarrés, Rogent, Subirachs and Aulèstia, the literary opuscule published about jazz by the Club 49 and the Hot Club in 1952.

This opuscule marked Tàpies' highest point of adaptation to the protectionism of the group and to the local area of the moment. Afterwards, in 1953, his accelerated advance was to convert him into an increasingly lonely figure on the star system. On parallel lines he had begun, with Cabral de Melo, a new development which would not have gone the way of the galleries and art-dealers but would have taken an ideological path, but he felt the need to keep ideology at a distance, since he believes that independence is vital for art. In spite of everything, a trace of this ideology remained in his paintings by way of manifesto, allusions to social and national realities of combat; and this not only in the evidently ideological and programme-inspired works of 1953, but even in some of the later ones, in which he repeated the symbology of the tool-arms, the Phrygian cap, the four bars (of the Catalan flag), etc. There was a picture called *Arqueología política*, with a red background on which a girl dressed in black and an engraved dove of peace accompanied a bell-shaped vase and the incandescent bar; there was *Himne*, in green, agitated by a spirally ascending construction, halfway between the *Carceri* of Piranesi and the monument to the 3rd International of Tatlin; there was *L'Esforç* (Effort), a great yellow picture with a pistol-hoe, a peasant's cap-fire, a nosegay-tongue and a furrow-4 bars; there was the *Veu de la nit* (Voice of the night), where in the desolate lake of quiet and darkness we see inscribed in a filigree of graffiti the clarity of a possible rose, a yellow, a luminous green; and there was the *Voluntat humiliada* (Humiliated will), evoking something like the atmosphere of a mine, with blue light, thick with black trees seen against the image of a necessarily underground world.

The promotion he received within the star system, a promotion for which the artist naturally cannot be blamed, represented a certain eclipse of his participation. A certain stage of cosmopolitanism.

Theatre and poetry. But the fact of Tàpies' taking deeper roots in Catalonia, with the purchase of his Gothic manor in 1960, initiated a stage of nationalization, which was a logical way of closing the dialec-

tic that had led him from borough bohemianism and the local avant-garde to cosmopolitanism. He had saved himself from the culture of splashes and had gone in search of new seeds. Now he was ready to sow them in his own garden once more and to give up cosmopolitanism in favour of a firmly-rooted universalism.

There are some milestones to be noted with regard to this participation in his context. In 1953 he painted the portrait of the Catalan poet Carles Riba. In 1954 he illustrated a book by J. V. Foix, exhibited his work as part of a show organized by *grup R*, a group of forward-looking young architects, and did the drawings to accompany a text by the present writer in the *Dau al Set*. In 1955 he exhibited in the underground room of the Sala Gaspar, made various statements on the occasion of the Hispano-American Biennale and gave a lecture at the Summer University in Santander. In 1956 he exhibited, for the *Club 49*, at the Sala Gaspar. In 1958 he did his first Barcelona lithographs and in 1959 the paintings for the Barcelona Town Hall. In 1960 he did the drawings for the special number of *Papels de Son Armadans* and the poster announcing the birth of the short-lived Barcelona Museum of Contemporary Art. Shortly after that, in 1961, he created the décor for Joan Brossa's *Or i Sal*, which was presented by the *Agrupació Dramática de Catalunya*, directed by Frederic Roda, at the Palau de la Música Catalana, in an evening sponsored by the *Club 49*.

The explanation Joan Brossa gave of his concept of theatre at that period also explains his new confluence with Tàpies:

With *Or i Sal*, he said: "I have set myself the task of writing the play "as it is". I do not believe in dehumanization, and if the spectator finds a startling, impromptu side to this play, I may say that this has been deliberately done in order to create through the voices of the characters a sort of "theatrical reality" of phases; for I am convinced that any work of art must show the signs of its own laws. If art is not a convention, then it is hardly anything at all. My purpose here, apart from any question of plot, is to destroy and create at the same time, deeply and taking matters to their furthermost consequences.

I do not believe in the confetti of the escapist theatre, but I also think that a reduction to "photography" is a limitation and a contradiction —poetry is fundamental—, and in the midst of lying and deceit it becomes the sun, the wind, life itself."

Tàpies confined his efforts to certain arrangements of the curtains, the creation of a paper wall provided with a sort of doorhole and the external manifestation of the wooden wings of the scenery, in full view of the audience. It was rather like the world of the *Escamoteig de Wotan* (Legerdemain of Wotan) under the new walls and new incrustations of poor materials.

In 1962 Tàpies contributed a printed folder to Brossa's *Acció Espectacle*, directed by Carlos Lucena, a sort of *happening* intended to represent a communication between real life and art. In 1963 we witnessed the apparition of the first of Tàpies' great books, *El pa a la barca*, published by the Sala Gaspar, with 22 lithographs and collages accompanying a text by Joan Brossa. This work was, in the most transparent sense, a cry for freedom, a freedom of which the mere scandalous presence of the walls and bars made it the indirect apologia.

One of Brossa's poems gives a good idea of the general sense, contrasting the images of collective freedom with those of individual slavery.

THE BIRDS

*A bird crosses the river. The birds
are flying ever farther
one after another, from bush
to bush. A bird
feeds in the late afternoon.
The birds disperse. Other
birds take flight.
But look at this poem:*

THE BIRD

*I watch a bird hopping
a chattering bird,
a bird shut up in a cage.
I listen to the bird's song
a white bird.
a little, long-tailed bird.
The bird sings from its world
in the shape of a cage.*

For man. Two years later, in 1965, Tàpies published his *Novel·la*, another book produced in collabora-

294. White with two angles. Combined process on canvas, 1964. 81×100 cm. Buren Gallery, Stockholm.

295. Grey and black sand with chain. Combined process on plywood, 1968. 130×162 cm. Martha Jackson Gallery, New York.

296. Angle on blue. Combined process on canvas, 1968. 114×116 cm. Juan March Delgado Collection, Madrid.

294

295

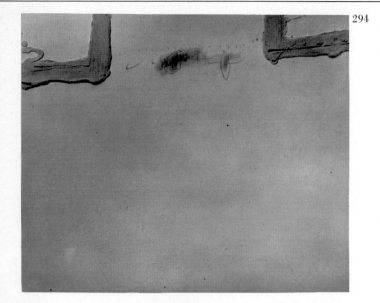

296

297. Canvas with cords, 1967. 116×89 cm. Galerie Maeght, Paris.

297

rators and discovered, later, as a prodigious coincidence of vision.

This book is a vision of man within the Coercive Society. It begins with a quotation from paragraph 2, article 5 of the regulations of the Spanish Pigeon-shooting Federation, which reads:

Any pigeon that finishes within the enclosure shall be considered a fair hit when it falls into the hands of the club servant employed to take it up, or when the dog catches it in its mouth, even if it subsequently escapes.

The 31 lithographs by Tàpies alternate with other testimony contributed by Brossa: birth certificate, ordinary medical certificate, papers from a schoolboy's handwriting copybook, school sports records, conduct reports, finger-prints, military service papers, a diary, a travelling salesman's credentials, a tape-measure, identity card, marriage lines, receipts, accounts, an old-age pensioner's card, an underta-

tion with Brossa. This time it was not a matter of illustrations to literary themes, but of a work thought out separately by the two collabo-

298

ker's invoice and inventories of the dead man's personal effects.

It is a tragic vision, and one that is accentuated by the lithographs, with their numbers, the erasures, the scratches, the holes, the torn material, the allusions to physical necessities, to excrement, to a sexuality without beauty, to swollen feet, to the macabre funeral mound.

There is a final theme, in the epilogue, which Tàpies was later to develop. There are some lines by Brossa, after he has made the wretched inventory of what the dead man has left, which read:

—*Els encenalls i les fustes son aprofitats? —algú pregunta*
Responden: —No; els cremarem aquest mateix capvespre.
("Has any use been made of the chips and shavings?" someone asks. And they answer: "No. We'll burn them this very evening".)

Speaking to Gasch. Tàpies has often given voice to his thoughts. In an interview with Sebastià Gasch, published in *Destino* in 1954 (an interview not quoted in the bibliographies), Tàpies said that *the*

299. Material in the shape of a nut. Combined process on canvas, 1967. 195 ×
175 cm. H. Neuerburg Collection, Cologne.

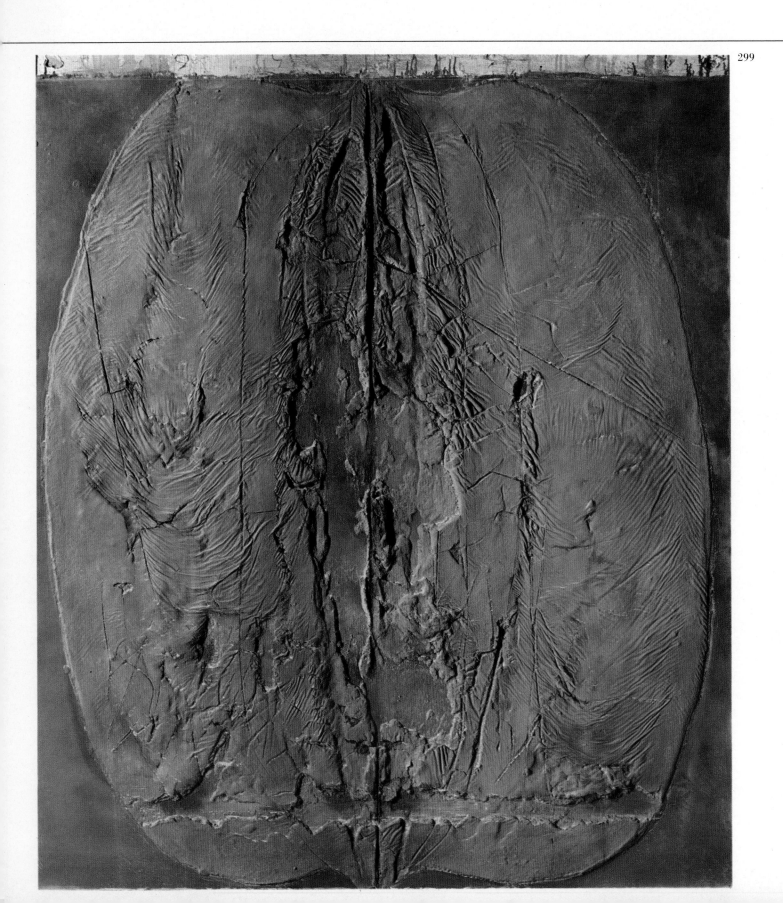

300. Two marks on white canvas, 1967. 162 × 130 cm. Galerie Maeght, Paris.

300

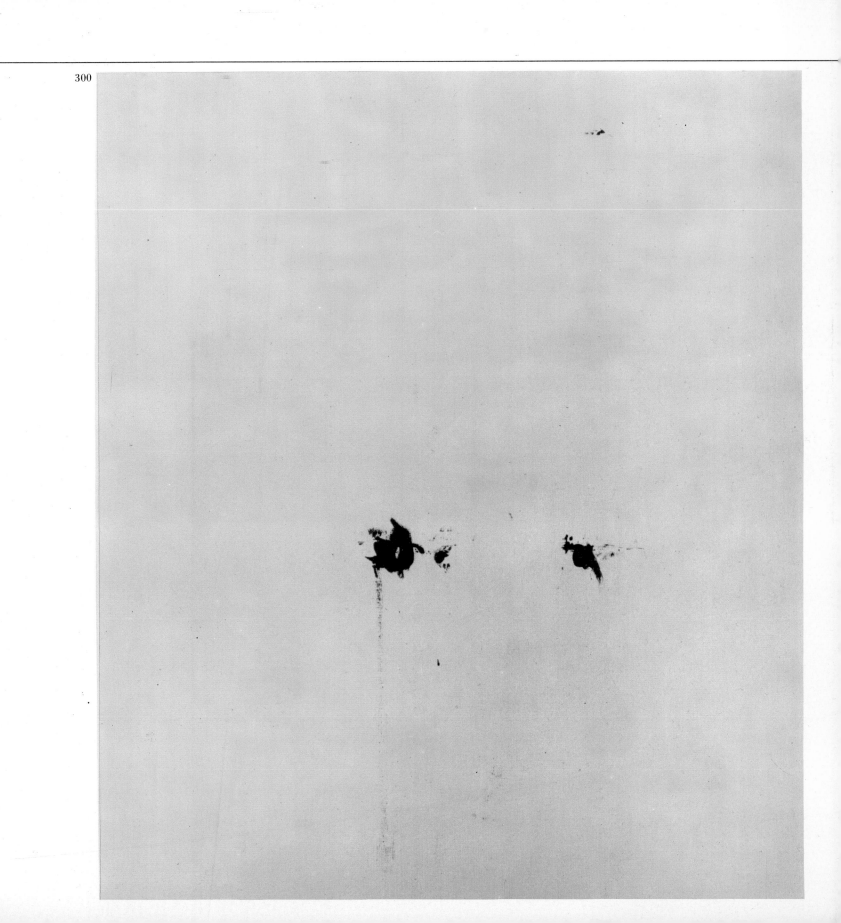

301. Heaped material. Combined process on canvas, 1968. 65 × 100 cm. Martha Jackson Gallery, New York.

302. Four fingerprints and dots. Combined process on canvas, 1968. 46 × 55 cm. Werner Rusche Collection, Cologne.

303. Material and grey collage, 1968. 162 × 130 cm. Martha Jackson Gallery, New York.

304. Blue with removals, 1968. 195 × 170 cm. Martha Jackson Gallery, New York.

301

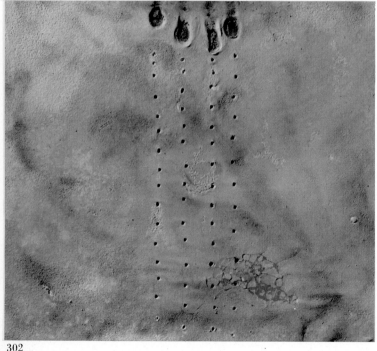

302

303

work to which the painter gives emotive form (an affirmation of the ethical character with which he endows all work on matter) **must be closely bound up with its age. It is inconcei-** *vable for a painter, unless he wants to immure himself in an ivory tower, to consider himself apart from the advances achieved by the other intellectual disciplines: philosophy, science,*

305 to 307. Screens. India ink on sewn and folded sheets, 1968. Windows of the Capuchin Monastery of Sion, Switzerland (Architect: Mirco Ravanne).

politics (an affirmation that art should be, if not committed, at least solidary). For him *the artist is alone, completely alone in front of his white canvas, and he must face the problems inherent in art, since this activity has its own laws, just as the other activities mentioned have theirs. Nobody can either help him or advise him. He can be taught and guided only by his lonely labour of experimenting, his constant struggle with the materials proper to his calling and their everyday handling* (theory is born of praxis).

His own system of preparation and work is described as follows:

Profound meditation must be an understood quality of any creative artist, since it is not for nothing that he finds himself at the head of the society (the Nietzschean selectocracy once again) *to which he belongs. But if this meditation is not accompanied by a violent struggle with his proper materials, this supposed artist... will discover that this material has not taken a single step forward, and that the years thus spent have been nothing but a sterile wandering, as is the case with any formula or theory.*

Speaking of materials, he adds:

They are in themselves inert ... the emotive capacity ... does not depend solely upon them. The artist cannot forget that the degree of efficacy of his creative work is directly related to the psychological state of the society in which the emotiveness is born (the value is always the action of the work on the conduct of the viewer); *the work will be more or less intense, and that is what gives it more or less contemporary value, according to whether the artist is more or less skilful in the development of certain forms, or —which comes to the same thing— in launching certain ideas* (form = idea) *at the most propitious moment. This comes to him through his own culture, and especially through intense awareness of his circumstance* (the idea of mosaic-culture, as it was to

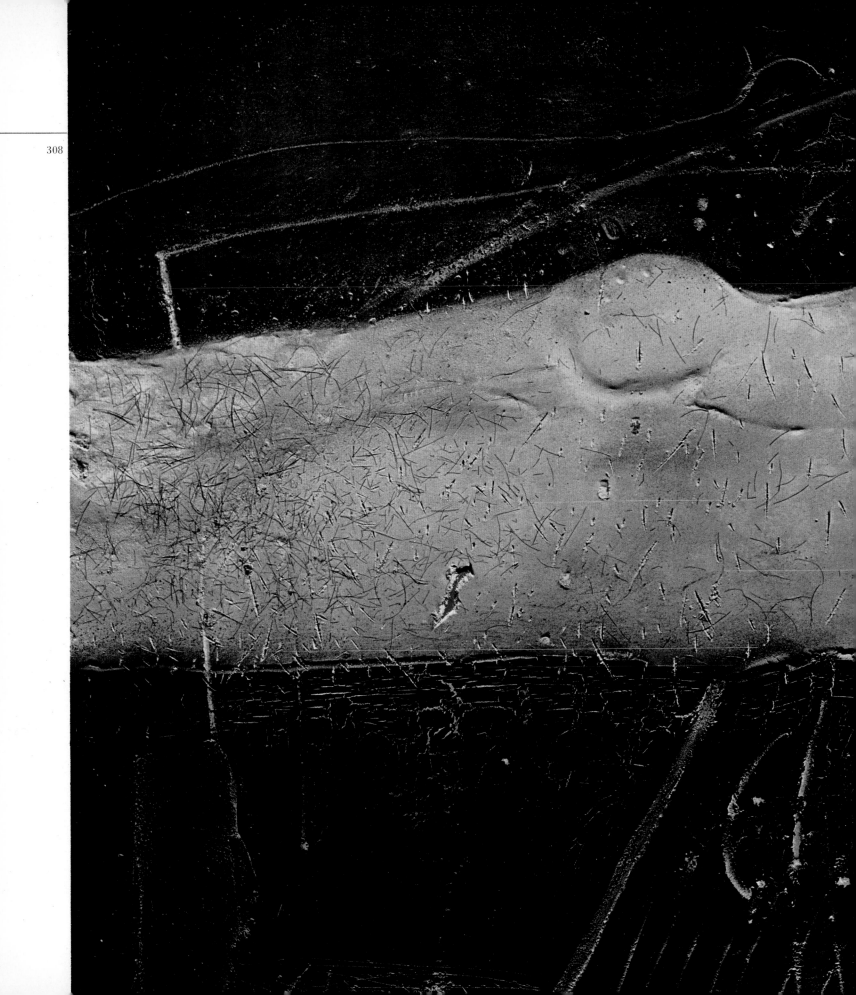

308. In the shape of a leg. Combined process on canvas, 1968. 89 × 146 cm.
Morris J. Pinto Collection, Paris.

309. Body of material and orange marks. Combined process on canvas, 1968.
162 × 130 cm. Private collection, Barcelona.

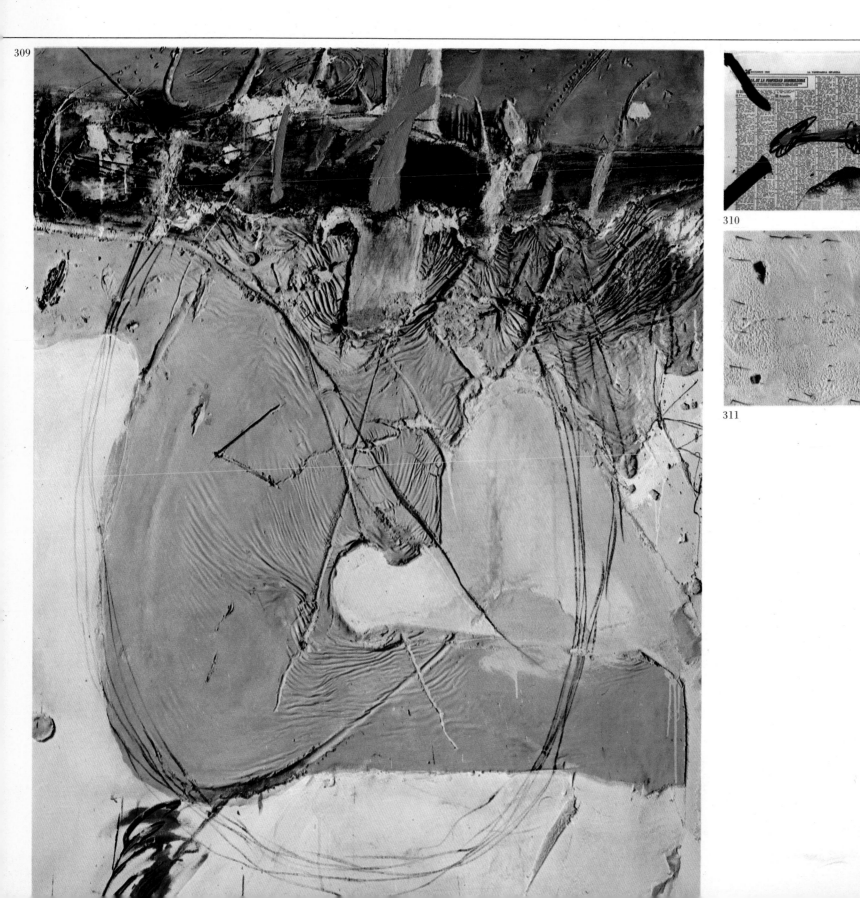

309

310

311

310. Marks on newspaper, 1968. Private collection, Barcelona.

311. Holes and nails in white. Marble-worker's sand and nails on plywood, 1968. 60 × 73 cm. Martha Jackson Gallery, New York.

312. Rag and string, 1968. 108 × 75 cm. Rudolph B. Schulhof Collection, New York.

313. Ochre material in the shape of an arch. Combined process on canvas, 1968. 195 × 130 cm. Martha Jackson Gallery, New York.

314. In the shape of a «T». Cardboard on canvas, 1968. Galerie Maeght, Paris.

312

314

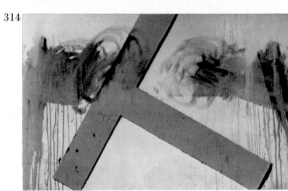

313

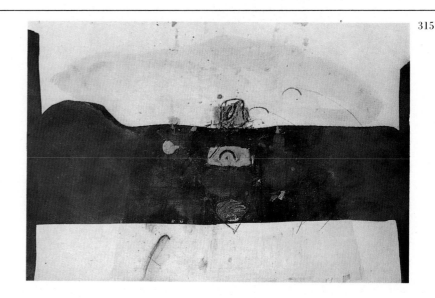

315

be defined by Moles). The real artist *is realistic in the truest sense of the word.* For him art is *a source of knowledge* based largely on the contemporary world. *Outworn forms cannot contribute contemporary ideas. If the forms are incapable of wounding the society that receives them, of irritating it, of slanting it towards meditation ... if they are not a revulsion, then they are not a genuine work of art... The viewer has to feel obliged to make an examination of conscience and to readjust his former conceptions. The artist has to make him understand that his world was too narrow, has to open up new perspectives to him. To do this is a task for the humanist.* With very clear ideas about the depreciation of forms, Tàpies adds: *When the general public finds full satisfaction in particular artistic forms, it means that these forms have lost their violence... When the artistic form is incapable of baffling the mind of the viewer or of making him change his*

ways of thinking, then it is no longer contemporary.

It should be observed that this intelligent vision of the avant-garde, the creation of forms and artistic depreciation was expressed in 1954, and that Dorfles did not publish his famous *Simbolo, communicazione, consumo* until 1962.

Speaking in Santander. One year later, in the University of Santander, Tàpies gave a very clear vision of his own viewpoint (July 1955). He declared that he did not envisage the artist as working *sub specie aeternitatis* in immutable values, nor

316

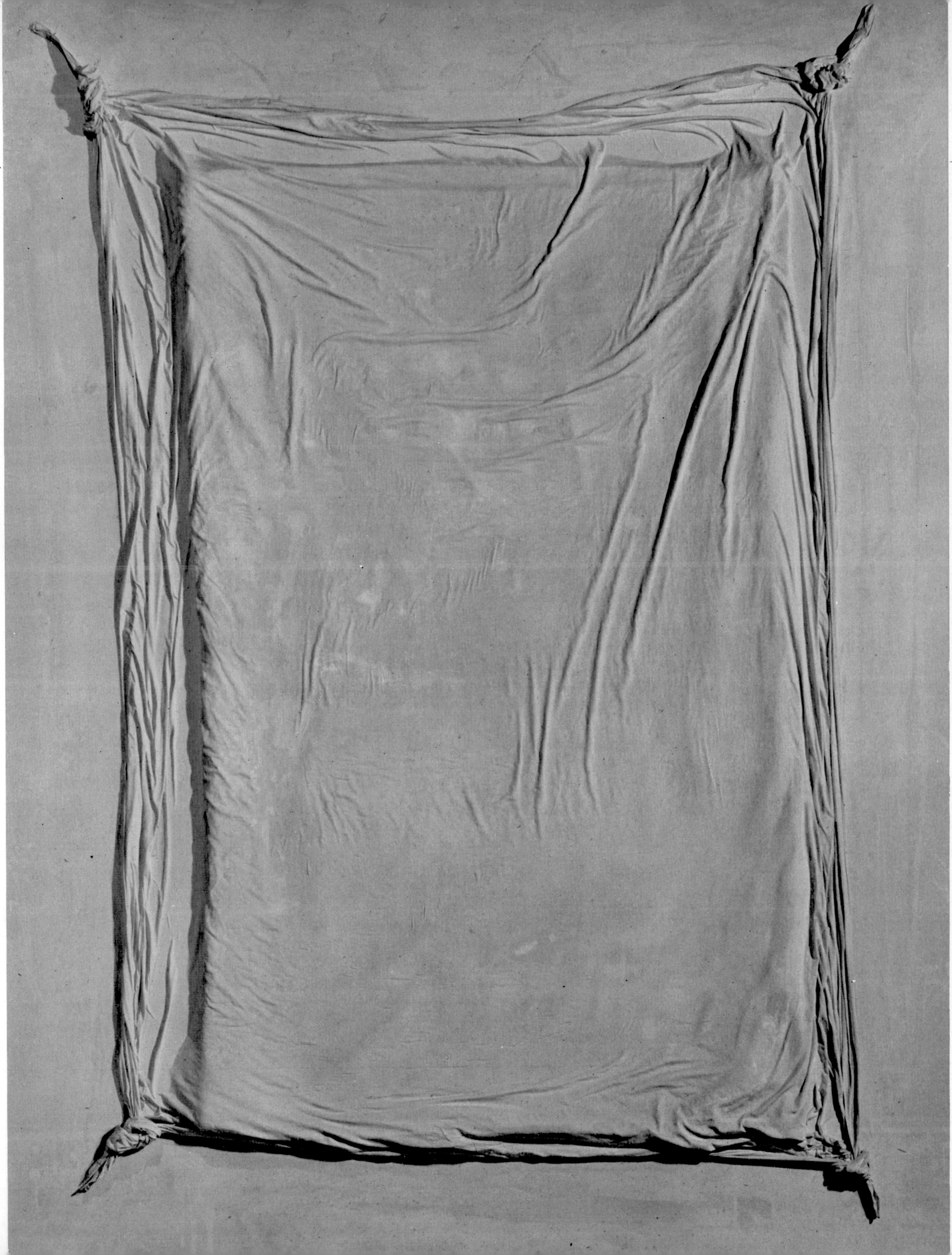

310

318. Two blankets full of straw. Combined process on canvas, 1968. 198 × 270 cm. Galerie Schmela, Düsseldorf.

319. High relief in white. Sizing on canvas, 1968. 89 × 116 cm. Galerie Schmela, Düsseldorf.

320. Fingerprints. Combined process on canvas, 1968. 81 × 100 cm. Martha Jackson Gallery, New York.

317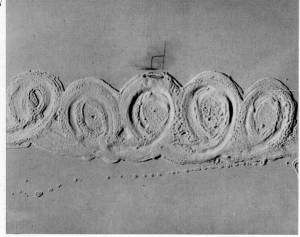

319

320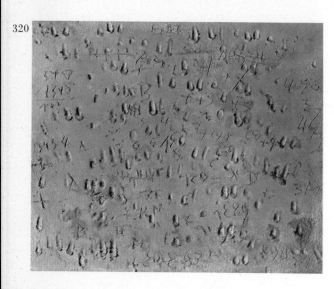

318

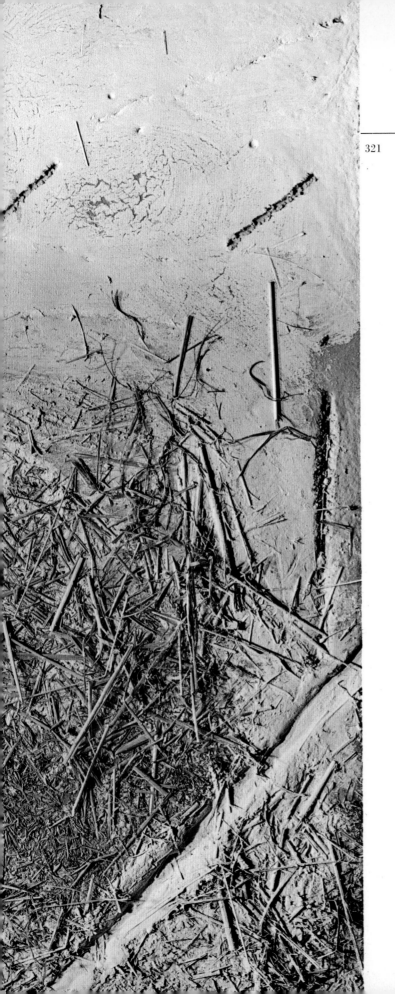

321. Blue-green and straw. Combined process with sizing on plywood, 1968. 89×116 cm. Private collection, Barcelona.

322. Straw on canvas, 1968. 65×81 cm. Galerie Maeght, Paris.

323. Painting with rice. Combined process on canvas. 1969. 89×116 cm. Sala Gaspar, Barcelona.

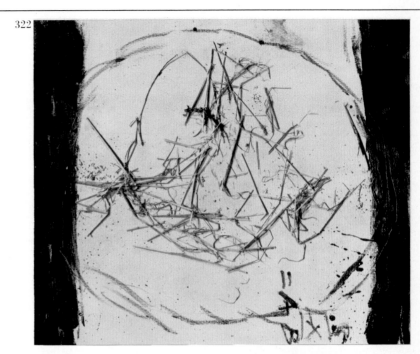

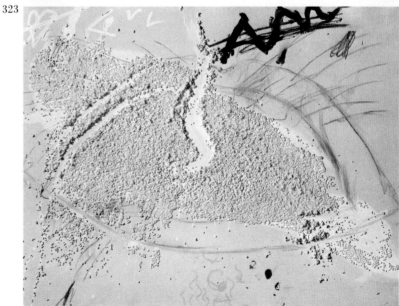

324

yet as the *slave of a programme or an ideology that are not linked to situations, to real facts that the artist is bound to discover as an autonomous thinking being... Since he is not purely receptive, he is not the reflection of an age.* Like Klee, Tàpies believes that *the artist is neither the master nor the servant of anything, but simply a spokesman for Nature.* But he adds: "*for the idea we form of Nature.*"

He does not aspire to create a personal vision of reality, but a group vision, that of a group he defines as the *group of the avant-garde intellectuals.* The philosopher, the scientist, the politician (he names them in this order) are seeking, like the artist, to give a form to what they conquer. He does this as an artist and he feels that art is *the most direct bridge between ideas and man.* The whole is born out of the lonely work of research. The artist must *hurl himself wholeheartedly into the unknown... I cannot envisage him unless he is up to his neck in the adventure in a state of transit.* But Tàpies refuses to be considered an anarchist, because he does not recognize *the act of creation as a blind dynamism or gratuitous factor... The value of a work is born only when two factors are present: on the one hand, the part that is a conquest of reality by the society that receives it; on the other hand, the fact that this conquest should be embodied in a form... At every stage in history a special state of artistic psychology is formed, what we might call the taste of an age, and upon this depends the emotional capacity of works of art. When the taste of a period is saturated ... when the means used for producing the shock are exhausted and their mechanism discovered, then the artist must find new forms that will make his work efficient ... the communicability of what is new is a fact.*

Troubadour for his people. It is interesting to see how Tàpies spoke to the public in general, through an interview with Del Arco, published in *La Vanguardia* on December 5th 1969. We may take from it a sort of résumé of his programme:

To help the public to become conscious of itself.

The artist is a specialist in profundities.

Frègoli ... a very suitable symbol for the external changes in things, which are at bottom always the same.

The absolute that is under me is exactly the same as that which is under you and under everybody else.

Illusion of progress... I think I can contribute to it.

The artist no longer serves the lords or the Church... it is possible for him to express his own ideas.

With the great social inequalities in our world, it is hardly surprising that some people cannot read me.

A great part of my work may be a provocation.

I am against the ordinary taste of the world of the rich.

To these opinions we must add some ideas contained in the catalogues of the Im Erker Gallery of St. Gallen and of the exhibition at *Notizie* in Turin, in 1963.

We live in a world that is submerged in technology, smothered by self-

325. Circle of cord. Sizing on canvas, 1969. 100×100 cm. Martha Jackson
Gallery, New York.

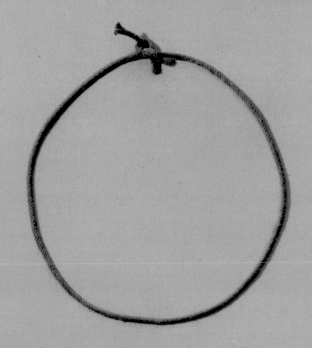

326. Material in the shape of an armpit. Combined process on plywood, 1968. 81×100 cm. Joan Miró Collection, Palma de Mallorca.

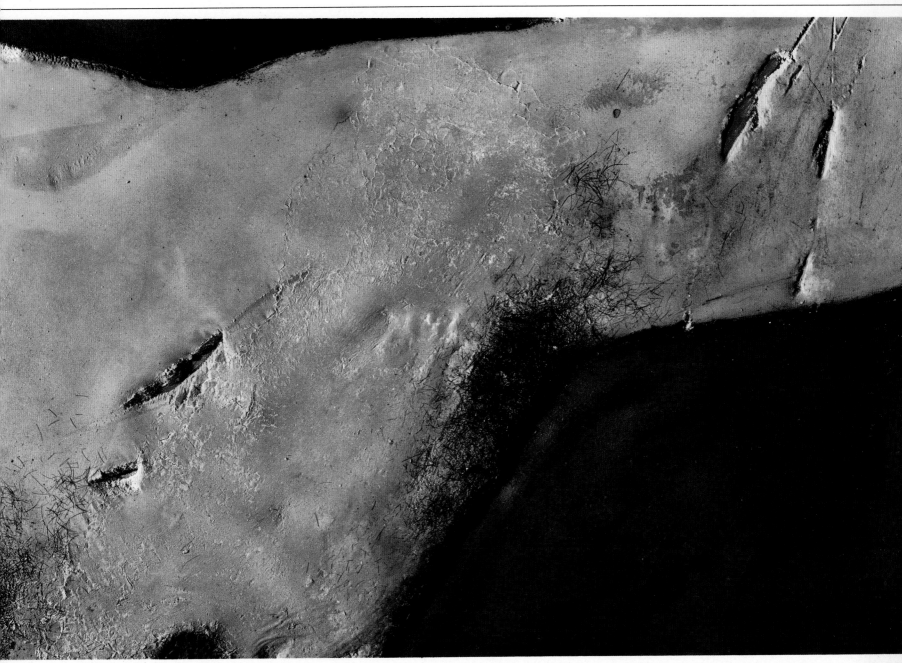

326

327. Black arch and sand. Combined process on plywood, 1968. 80×69 cm. Ardemagni Collection, Milan.

328. Big parcel of straw. Paint and sizing on canvas, 1969. 195×270 cm. Galerie Maeght, Paris.

329. White and plastic. Combined process on paper stuck to canvas, 1969. 133×118 cm. Martha Jackson Gallery, New York.

327

328

329

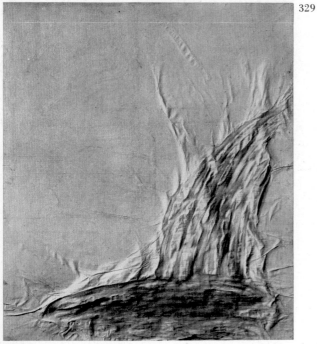

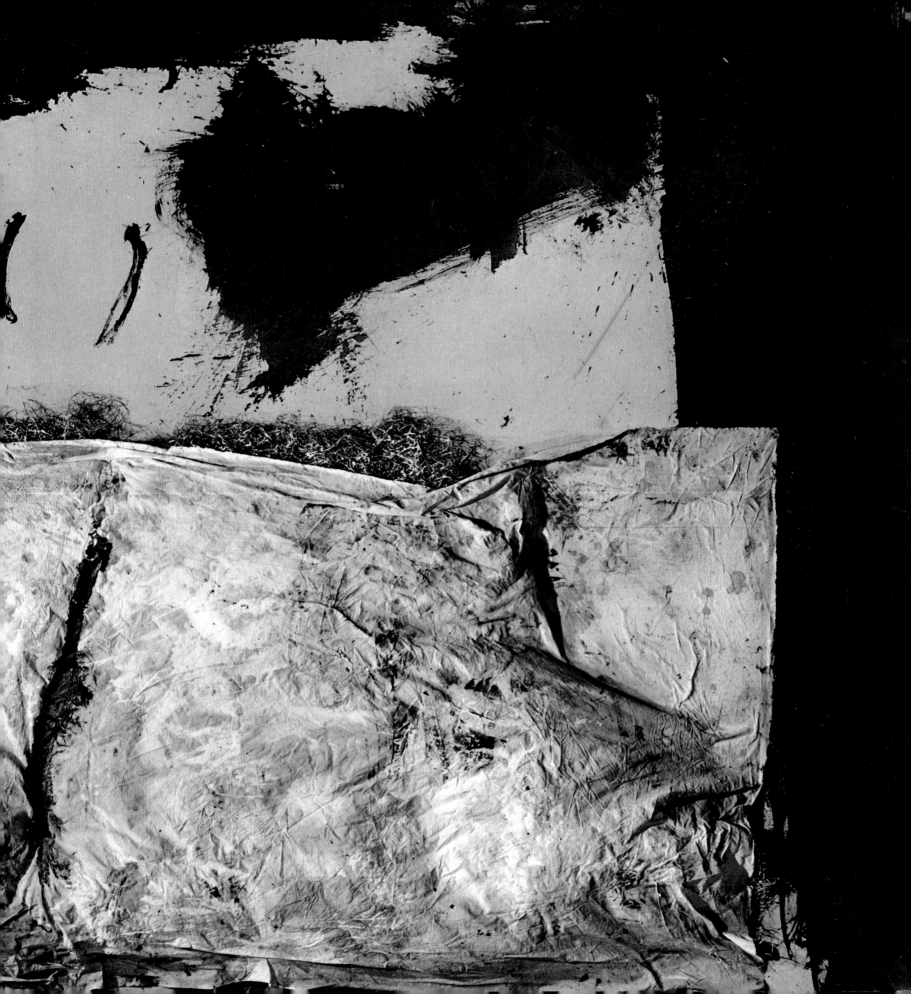

330. Pressed straw. Combined process on canvas, 1969. 195×130 cm. Martha Jackson Gallery, New York.

ish material comfort. We live in a state of constant "diversion", forgetting our most elemental roots, almost forgetting our very instincts. Everything around us is artificial and, in many aspects, false. We still cling to absurd superstitions, useless atavisms that alienate and enslave us.

To remind man of what he really is, to provide him with a subject for meditation, to give him a shock that may rouse him from the frenzy of what is not authentic, in order that he may discover himself and become conscious of his real possibilities: that is the endeavour at which my work is aimed. And not in the sense of despising technique, but in that of fighting to abolish the spiritual and material state to which we have been subjected by technique (by which I mean technique in the most general sense); from the technique necessary to make a machine work to that which is employed by rulers in leading their peoples. With my work I try to help man to overcome this state of alienation, by incorporating in his daily life objects that will put him in touch in a tangible way with the ultimate and most profound problems of our existence.

As for the means I employ in order to expound all the necessary suggestions, I try to make them as direct as possible. Instead of preaching a sermon on humility, I sometimes prefer to show people humility itself. Rather than discourse about human solidarity, it might be more worth while to indicate a heap of infinite, identical grains of sand. There are some facts that require a grave way of speaking, with an expression full of horror. There are others, however, that bring forth words of serenity and tranquillity. Here I may tell you a few words to set you meditating; there I may just as easily recite a short poem to you under the night sky as shout a warning to you at full noon... or simply give you a gentle sigh. Since I am a troubadour who sings for his people, the people of

331. Large piece of wood, 1969. 330×275 cm. Galerie Maeght, Paris.

331

332. Knot and cord. Sizing on canvas, 1969. 195×130 cm. Galerie Maeght, Paris.

332

333. Large white canvas, joined, 1969. 175×400 cm. Galerie Maeght, Paris.

333

334. Four packets of straw. Paint and sizing on canvas, 1969. 90×65 cm. Martha Jackson Gallery, New York.

334

the land I live in and of everywhere else, it is no wonder that I seek the friendship of all, men or beasts, trees or stones.

The first to notice. Participation does not only mean the attitudes and actions of Tàpies with regard to those around him, but also the attitudes and actions of his associates with regard to him. In this connection, we may observe the growth of a nucleus of people interested in his work around his own home in the district of Sant Gervasi. He lived in the Carrer de Balmes, almost at the corner of the Travessera de Gràcia. His friend Brossa lived in the street behind his, the Carrer d'Alfons XII. Pere Portabella lived almost next door, while Joan Ponç's mother had a shop further up the Carrer de Balmes, just short of the Plaça Molina. The barber at the corner of Alfons XII and Madrazo was on friendly terms with all of them. Gabino and his friends used to foregather at *La Campana* in the Carrer de Sant Eusebi, the next street parallel to Madrazo, going up Balmes. The cultural tradition of the district of Sant Gervasi was a prolongation of that of Gràcia, which had its roots among the old-time federalists and anarchists and was markedly autodidactic. Contact with the *Blaus* added the young men of the Sarrià group to those of Sant Gervasi. Puig and Tort, and afterwards J. V. Foix, were very definitely Sarrià people, with a tradition of culture and refinement. Foix, though he belonged to a family of pastry-cooks, had been a member of the literary and artistic avant-garde in the years of the Galeria Dalmau, and had played a part in the internal channelling of that world. Puig was even the son of an artist; his father was the lyrical intimist painter Puig Barella, a pupil of Torres García, and his work was half-way between the Gauguin heritage and the gentle style of Torné Esquius translated into the idiom of the twenties. Foix was the umbilical cord that was able to link the echoes of the international avant-garde and the interest of these young men who, in the rarefied world of the postwar autarchy, remained faithful to that movement. And so Prats, Miró, Gomis, Vidal de Llobatera, de Sucre and Gasch all took an interest in Tàpies, and the *Saló d'Octubre* and the *Club 49* gave him his first enthusiastic support.

The first to write. The first to publish anything about Tàpies were Sebastià Gasch (*Destino*, March 29th 1947) and Josep Maria Junoy (*El Correo Catalán*, October 17th 1948). Gasch had been the most influential critic of the Catalan avant-garde in the twenties and thirties and Junoy the first to experience the avant-garde adventure, in Paris at the time of Cubism: he had

also presented Joan Miró's first exhibition, in 1918. In 1949 Tàpies' first presentation was written, by the Brazilian Cabral de Melo, who did his best to link the painter to his socializing interests. Soon Tàpies aroused the interest of the poets, especially Joan Teixidor, and *Ariel*, the review which at that moment represented the heart of the Catalan cultural renewal, devoted some space to him in 1950, with a text by Enric Jardí.

When Brossa dedicated the *Oracle* to Tàpies, the painter's other friend, Tharrats, wrote a book entitled *Antoni Tàpies o el Dau Modern de Versalles*, which appeared in 1950; it was a poetic text, escapist and aestheticist. The same could be said of what Gordon W. Washburn wrote for Martha Jackson's catalogue, which speaks of Tàpies as a lyrical, individualist painter, melodious, free, romantic, typically adolescent, dreaming and telling himself fairy stories. When in 1963 I wrote *Tàpies o la Trans-verberació*, which was published by the *Dau al Set* in the following year, it was my endeavour to take Tàpies' painting out of this literary, poetic context, which seemed to be all they could say of him, and to place it in connection with the methodology of the history of forms. I was soon supported by Tapié.

When Michel Tapié published his *Antoni Tàpies*, also in the *Dau al Set*, in 1954, with a vision that he was later to enlarge in the book published by R. M. (1959), he clearly set forth his protest against *a school of so-called art criticism which is, in fact, the evident testimony of writers who have never loved paint-ing for itself and who want to reduce it to a supporting role, to an absolu-tely exterior illustrative symbolism.*

As Tapié could see, Tàpies was capable of leaping from illustrative aestheticism to the practice of an ethic of gesture that could give significance to matter; that is to say, a theologically moral work, based on the transformation of the somatic factor of the gesture and the contextual factor of the mate-rial into a sign capable of transmit-ting a working idea.

The Neo-Romantic vision. Now some writers, like the Spanish Neo-Romantic poet Juan Eduardo Cirlot, scion of a military family and pas-sionately interested in a symbolic esotericism, characterized by an irra-tionalism that was radical, impe-rialistic and racist, sentimental and oneirical, enamoured of darkness, cruelty and death, became fero-ciously interested in Tàpies' work. The literary, magic and nocturnal period corresponded to their ado-lescent dreams and hallucinations, while the period of the closed walls and opaque material impressed them with its radical, funereal asceticism. In it they saw the romantic values of solitude, abandonment, attrition, as well as transcendentalism. Cirlot judged the new *abstraction of textures* in the light of the ideas of Breton, seeing in it *states of mind that are transferred from the psychic world to that of space, unconsciously.* In very acute fashion he said that Tàpies was *looking for the coincidence between the textures of the materials of the outside world and the psychic impressions that correspond to them.* (Destino, No. 949, 1955.)

We have great respect for the critical work of Pierre Restany at the time of the New Realism and during the sixties, but it is curious to see how the Restany of 1958 was not so far away from the irrationalism of Cirlot. He considered Tàpies a *mystic poet* and expounded what Cirlot called the coincidence of a physical manner when he attempted to show that there are in the painter's work certain problems of "*spatiality*" through which *the internal tension and density are underlined by considerable effects of thickened matter. The paroxystic note*

of this full void is indicated to the reader by the intervention of certain elements of rupture.

Restany saw in the poetry of Tàpies *a taste for ashes and solitude, the vertigo of an immanent void brusquely ploughed up by the overwrought terror of a brutal faith.* He also saw in it —and nothing could be further from Tàpies' programme— *a longing for what is human,* which he compared with mysticism, ending with a spiritualist solo in which he supposes *that in a world that is disembodied, masochistic and avid for misery in the depths of its nature, the ardent testimony of Tàpies constitutes one of the highest justifications for the permanence of the values of spirituality and for the rejection of immanences alone.*

The lucid vision. It is enough to compare this judgment with what Tàpies himself said to his interviewer in order to measure the distance between them. Fortunately,

a) Frontispiece of *Novel·la*, in collaboration with Brossa, 1965.

b) A New Year's greeting commissioned by the students of the University of Barcelona, 1967.

c) Frontispiece for the book of poems by Jacques Dupin, *La nuit grandissante*.

d) Portrait of Carles Riba, etched by Tàpies in 1953, for the bilingual edition of *Salvatge Cor*.

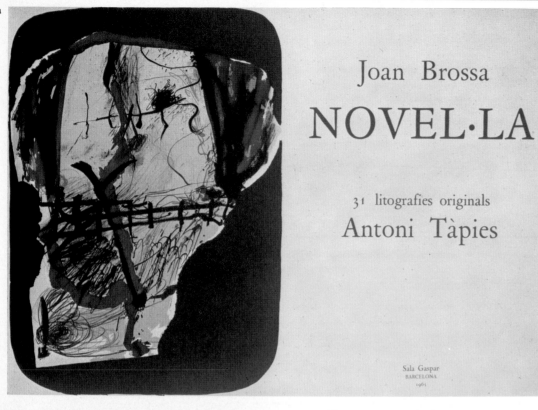

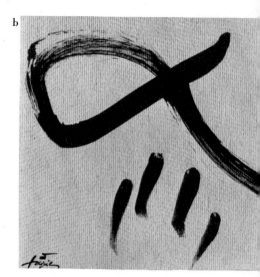

e, f) Two of the sets for Joan Brossa's *Or i Sal*, as represented at the Palau
de la Música Catalana in 1961.

g) Drawing for the frontispiece of J. V. Foix's book *Les irreals omegues*.

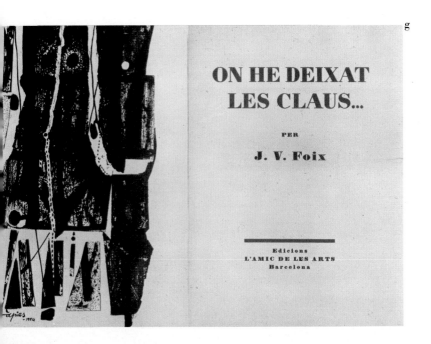

a) Cover for the only number of the review *Joc Net*, Barcelona, 1952.

b) Poster for Pere Portabella's film *No compteu amb els dits*, 1967.

however, the work of demythification that we had begun was to find continuers.

Joan Teixidor, in *Cuadernos de Arquitectura* (1959), in *Destino* (1960) and in his book *Tàpies*, published by the Sala Gaspar in 1964, has shown remarkably keen vision. He has succeeded in applying Camus' idea to Tàpies when he says that «*the men of the north flee to the Mediterranean and to the deserts of light. But where can we men of the light flee except to the invisible?*» In Teixidor's view, Tàpies finds himself in the middle of the tech-

c) & d)   Designs for posters, 1968.

nical world as if in an oasis, in a refuge for the exasperated man who finds himself alone. *Meditation through bareness and silence. Everything has a sense and the silence is a profound silence.*

Françoise Choay may perhaps have paid too much attention to Tàpies'

existential starting-point when the only definitive conclusion she came to was that his work is *the arising of something against the undifferentiated background of being.* But this viewpoint is right in indicating the opposition between *something* and *undifferentiated.* This *some-*

thing is a purely human thing for Gatt. For him the works of Tàpies are not intentionally representative but aim at being deepenings of reality, *a plunging into it to the point of becoming a part of things.* Unlike Pop art, Tàpies' paintings have no desire to be vehicles for criticism or objective reports on the consumer society. *They are beyond mass imagery; they consider it to be already dead, for they have discovered its lack of value and have seen the possibility of its developing.*

In this perspective ... he seeks a possibility of rescue, re-stating the problem of the object in all its force of abduction, recovering it from the present, making it still a responsibility and a choice for all and showing, in the face of the common figurative acceptance... what we are.

Lorenza Trucchi, in the catalogue to the exhibition at *Il Segno* in 1962, places Tàpies' painting in the framework of *painting of resistance.* She believes that *he feels nature*

as the temptation of a consolation and does not wish to grant himself these *romantic holidays.* Her Tàpies is the man sung by Neruda, *earth, vase, eyelid of mud, shape of clay.*

One of the most intelligent texts written on Tàpies was that published by Francesc Vicens in 1967; together with the *Oracle* of Brossa, it formed one of the *Fotoscops* of Gomis and Prats, entitled *Antoni Tàpies, or the Scoffer at Diamonds,* taken from the title Brossa gave to one of the pictures. For Vicens this

a

b

title fundamentally defines the artist in all that is negative in him, in the something that *forces us to say "no" to what is presented to us in conformist fashion as reality in its finished form and submerges us in the profound reality of things: evolution.* His universe is that of the profound lucidity *of those who live in their subjectivity the objective reality of this contradictory world where all the partial truths oppose and contradict one another.* Against all unilateral dogmatism, he embodies a *spirit of dialectic* based on a constant contraposition between invention and the everyday. *Those who have been touched by his vision will never again be as they were before this experience.*

Maria Lluïsa Borràs has underlined some important aspects of Tàpies' work with great lucidity. Technically, the utilization of the speeds of solidification. Conceptually, their semeiotic character. Axiologically, their polyvalence.

And so, in the admirable text published in *Taide*, in Helsinki in 1967, she spoke of each of these aspects. Of the *different qualities, according to the distinct speed at which each material, mixed with oil, becomes solid.* Of the fact that *what is fundamental, as usual, is the investigation of the primary things* and, on this basis, that *Tàpies' painting should be analyzed using as our starting-point a creative principle that expands freely within the co-ordinates of time and space.* She asserts clearly that we are dealing here with

338

a) Poster for the 1st Popular Festival of Catalan Song, 1968.

b) Cover reproducing a painting by Tàpies in the bilingual edition of *La pell de brau* by Salvador Espriu, 1963.

c) Cover for the children's magazine *Cavall Fort*, 1966.

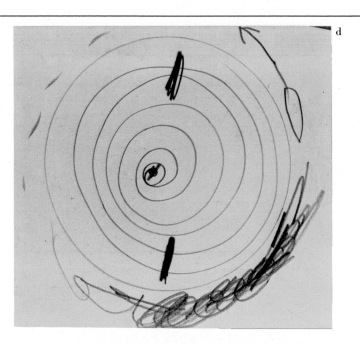

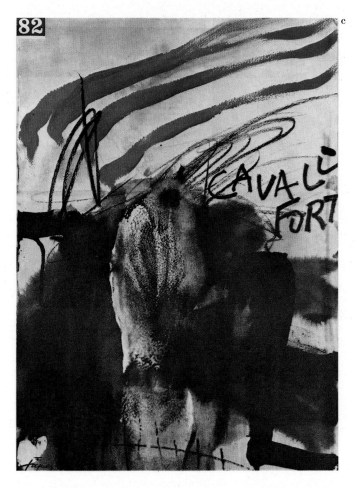

e
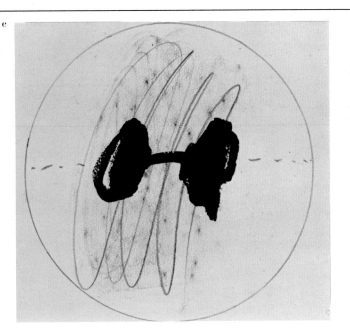

f
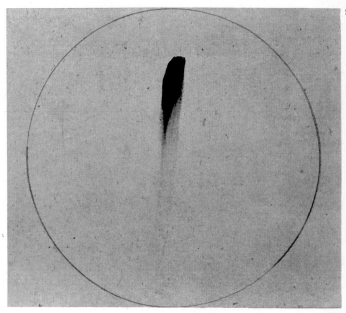

a *semeiotic aesthetic* and alludes to the ambiguous work when she increases its value by saying that *he always leaves a door open to doubt, to the dilemma of being and then being no more.*

The opaque vision. For some the "something" is a cultural fact, but an illegible one; one of these is Arnald Puig, who suffers because he refuses to accept that Tàpies means nothing, but does not know how to read him either. He states the problem of whether Tàpies does not really represent that very darkness of our personal and collective drama which does not vanish but remains rigorously closed, perhaps because we are in the thick of the battle and we hesitate as to which arms to take up. It is this confinement that is responsible for the saddest vision of Tàpies: that of those who refuse to admit he has any motivation. Among them is Argan.

Some see no more in Tàpies' painting than a physical fact. Roland Penrose has emphasized the *tactile importance* of a work that may be seen by the blind and which, for people who can see, creates a strong connection between the sight and the touch and does something for the whole body.

Beyond those who see a purely somatic painting, there are those who feel it as something cosmic.

An exaggerated viewpoint, but one which has a true side to it, is that of Lawrence Alloway when he declares his belief that Tàpies paints as if he were identifying himself with the earth, in the geographical sense, and were making the work a romantic testimony to *geocultural presence*. This may be linked to the idea of Udo Kultermann when he says that the great realism of the work comes from the fact that *there are no signs of human intervention to be seen*, or that of Herbert Read, who believes that *there is no magic other than that created by the wind and the rain*.

The cliché. For foreigners there was too easy a temptation, that of the cliché. Looking at the map, seeing the present frontiers, it was possible to identify Castile with Spain and to cast Tàpies for a role in that celebrated production known as *The Spirit of Castile*. Michel Tapié would talk of the Arab mystics, of the "nothingness" (la NADA), of Yespes, of the Baroque and of Saint John of the Cross; Restany spoke about Saint Teresa of Ávila and Saint John of the Cross, of a dialogue with God on the level of the NADA and of values of spirituality; Guy Habasque saw in Tàpies' painting the imaginary equivalent of the arid land of Spain, while Alloway said that it evoked the barren, arid, rocky, brown Peninsula.

All this threadbare subject matter is as stupid as it is elementary, for the simple facts are that the culture in which Tàpies was born and lives is not that of the mystic transcendentalisms of the Castilian tableland but, quite on the contrary, a Catalan culture composed of closeness, of the fruits of the earth,

Cover reproducing a lithograph by Tàpies, done in 1966, in Brossa's book *Poesia Rasa*.

where there is popular religious feeling without an absolute, localized in the patron saints of the villages, the trades or the mountain springs, great saints for honouring with a good meal and a dance in the square; and a city culture where the minority who practise their religion are very progressive and socializing and sing at Mass to an electric guitar, while the majority are sceptical, with some atheists on the fringes and a few little groups of Protestants, theosophists or spiritualists.

As for the landscapes, the land familiar to Tàpies, the districts where he has lived and where he has made his home, they are also the contrary of what we find in these cliché-ridden texts. They belong to the damper part of Catalonia, covered with leafy woods, where the water runs under the trees through ferns and moss, and where the mist softly blurs the blue-green darkness of the landscape, which is

JOAN BROSSA
POESIA RASA

COL.LECCIO CINC D'OROS   ARIEL

mysterious, complicated and full of little unexpected corners and filigreed curves. An intimist country, where the people are fond of sitting round a good fire, and where life is based on work, marketing and business, where everyone en-

335. Rag and collage on canvas, 1969. 90 × 65 cm. Martha Jackson Gallery, New York.

336. Black and earth. Combined process on canvas with wood, 1970. 130 × 162 cm. Galerie Maeght, Paris.

337. Homage to Richard Wagner. Paint and sizing on cardboard, 1969. Joan Brossa Collection, Barcelona.

335

336

(1970)

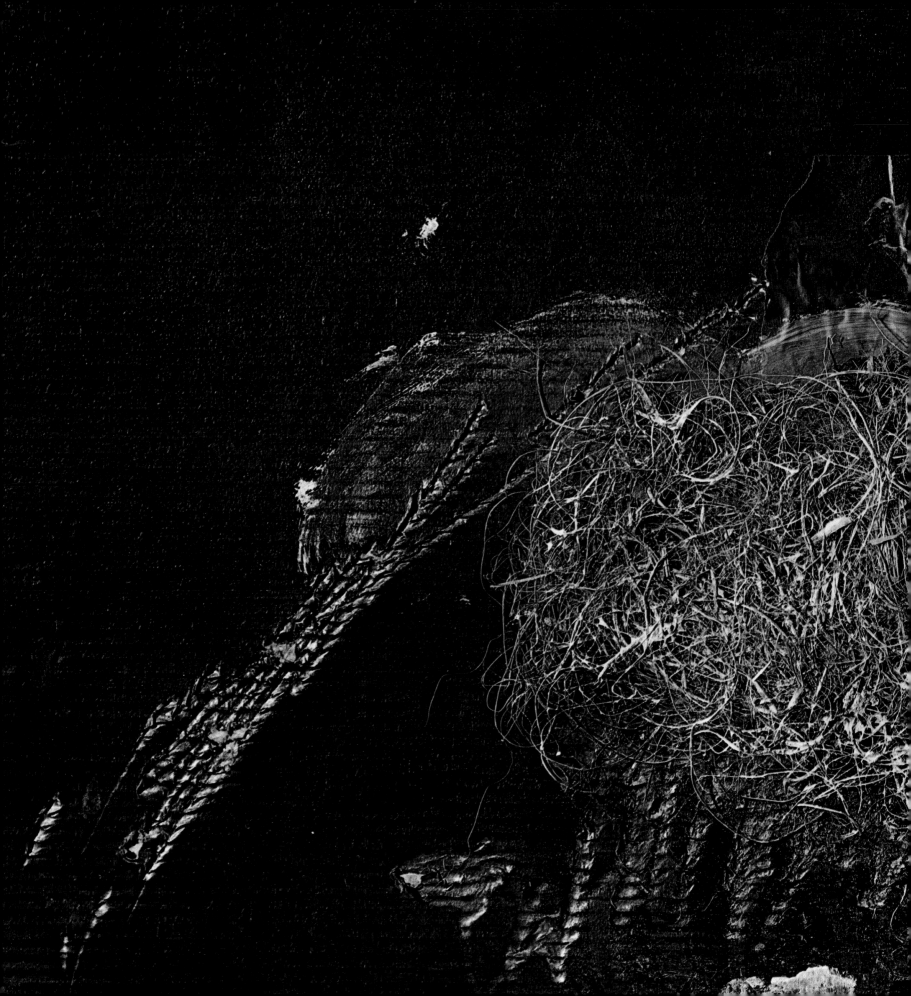

joys the pleasures of a good table and, if you'll excuse us, those of a welcoming bed. In personal and family background Tàpies is a product of this marginal culture, concerned with mystery, heterodox and individualistic, with a majority of democrats and sceptics, the very opposite of the absolutistic mysticisms of Castile. And his work reveals that very presence of the green, misty, Wagnerian region of Catalonia, equally opposed to the dryness of Castile, when he places his mystery within things rather than in an escape towards Heaven.

The fascination of death. Westerdahl says that *the natural compensations of the game of simultaneous evaluation between the cosmic and the human make Tàpies the central figure of a whole vast problem, of death or dawn.*

Possibly it is this problem of death that Aguilera Cerni sees when he observes that in Tàpies' painting the appeals to passion or to sentiment, to intuition, are instruments for knowledge, but above all that ascent in an intellectual direction he sees the wounding of matter, which suddenly reveals *the abyss of death, beyond what we know.*

There is a nothingness as an evident end, but, as Apollonio says, it is in the connection of the details that we find the formal, even statistical, aspect which makes Tàpies constructive rather than negative. Despite all this, there are many who see death in his painting; Jacques Dupin, for instance, sees in Tàpies' work the landscapes of *another world, the only one where we are expected.* Giulio Carlo Argan, in *Europa Letteraria* (1960) and in the prologue to Giuseppe Gatt's book (Capelli, Bologna, 1967), has said the most destructive things, albeit very intelligent ones, about the painting of Tàpies.

But he has not succeeded in seeing the protest or the revolt, because he has not been able to find any connection between the forms of Tàpies and his *motivated choice.* Starting with this idea of the lack of motive, to his eyes the work reveals a renunciation, a surrendering to fate that is equivalent to superstition. The signs are no longer significant symbols in it, but something motiveless, purely fatal. He does not find, therefore, the loftiness of the myth, but the presence of the amulet, the scapular, the spell. The images do not possess polyvalence, but assume a precise form. In classical art this submission was also present, but it was there with a full acceptance of the world.

For Tàpies there is no more than a negation without any possible appeal. Superstition, at the very opposite point to knowledge. Superstition, equivalent to death, which cannot be a thought, but only a fear or a desire. Total a-sociality. Bad faith, because nobody believes in the amulets. The pale madness of everyday life, the psychosis and neurosis of the *Alltagslebens,* as Freud calls it.

For Argan, Tàpies' painting cannot be explained *except as an ideological frustration, religious repression, a last, desperate moral choice; the choice of not living in a place and a time in which the place of God, exiled or imprisoned, has been usurped by the Great Inquisitor.* He believes that he feels the anguish of the absence of God, and he adds: *All that is done in an inevitable condition of bad faith is a sin, the punishment for the sin consists of not being dissolved, remaining present through a kind of invincible inertia... It is death, but an imperfect death, a death that never quite finishes living. In the recent works, where there is the evocation of the object, in Pop code, this latter is not accompanied by a futile irony but by a harsh moral reaction, of hatred for the alter which translates the desperation of the ego.*

338. Tatters. Paint with rags and strings on sized canvas over cardboard, 1970.

338

CONCLUSION

References.   It would seem that in the course of our work we have gradually found the elements for a reading of Tàpies. We are very sure that we can always see in his work the components of the historical situation, of the years of a war, of a local postwar period, of a cold war and a distension, of a revolutionary front and a neo-capitalist front.

We think we can also see in his work the components of a topological situation, of the restless districts of Sant Gervasi and Sarrià, of an avant-garde Barcelona, a universalist Catalonia and a capitalist western world.

We find it strange that an intelligent man like Argan should not have seen Tàpies' very strong roots

in a general history and in the history of his country.

Situated on the periphery of Europe, with a complex set of problems created by the nearby vision of a sharpening of political, national and social questions, haunted by the echo of symbolist culture and the suggestiveness of the avant-garde, the young Tàpies, dreaming of other worlds and angrily rejecting the one immediately surrounding him, ends by finding a way in the identification of matter with man.

Spurred on by the moment of existentialism, he conceives this identification as a statement of existence in contrast to nothingness, decidedly in favour of the claims of existence.

Up to this point his work seems to be a rapid retreading of all the steps along the way that leads from a symbolism similar to that of the youthful Klee or Ernst in narrative vein to the material painting of Dubuffet or Fautier, in an endeavour to which he brings the strength-giving, vital, inflamed force of the national tradition of Gaudí and Miró.

From this point on the references cease. Tàpies is no longer an informalist. In his later evolution Tàpies comes ever nearer to the frontier between what, for some time now, has been art and what before him was not. He approaches the borderline, reaches it and pushes it back. He agrees with McLuhan when he declares that objects and environments, in our time, very quickly cease to be of use and condemn man to the incoherence of useful things placed, as it were, in the middle of an immense rubbish bucket. The artist attacks this world of practical novelties wearing the mask of useless things. If the neo-capitalist world turns everything into pollution and scrap, art acts as a Phoenix, rising from the very rubbish dumps. The mask of the victims is the foundation of its new power, and Tàpies does not refuse it.

The prophet of poor art. By a process of special historical compression, Tàpies has felt the greatness of poor things before other artists, the greatness and the image that poverty contains of what is least alienated in man. That explains why, from the forties on, he is a true forerunner of poor art. In the year 1945 he was working with cardboard, torn papers, frayed bootlaces, without trying to make marvels of them, like Schwitters, but only endeavouring to present faithfully their bare presence.

In 1959, when he prepared a shop window for the house of *Gales*, a luxury clothes shop in the Passeig de Gràcia, and placed in it an old warehouse door in battered corrugated iron, with a dusty, broken-stringed violin in front of it, he was presenting a true manifesto of poor art, which we could interpret symbolically as an image of the imperviousness of the commercial mentality and the exile of the man outside, in the cold night, of human poetry represented by the violin.

Since then, the progressive approach of Tàpies' work to the history of protesting youth has become evident. From 1966 onwards, it was a confluence of real participation.

Suddenly, at the end of the sixties, when poor art had spread everywhere, it became evident that Tàpies had been one of its prophets.

Catherine Millet was able to give a lucid description of the fact. For her, Tàpies entered the third dimension with his non-formal thicknesses, in order to accomplish there a work of negation similar to that of Dada. *Poor art, actual art, antiform, conceptual "earthwork" or impossible, is a basically anticommercial focussing, precarious, vulgar and antiformal, which refers above all to the physical qualities of the medium and to the mutability of the materials. Its importance resides in the artists' commitment to present materials and to total reality, and in their attempt to interpret reality in a way that is subtle, cerebral, elusive, reserved and intense.*

This was the definition made of it by Germano Celant in 1967, and it should be recognized that it can be applied to all the material work of Tàpies since 1945, despite the fact that in practice the art-dealer cycle has ingeniously commercialized, quoted and sold these works. With a methodical spirit and the maximum economy of means, he attempts to operate, not to obtain aesthetic effects but with a view to direct efficacy on the viewer. Thus he inserts himself in life and does not reject the ephemeral materials that sharpen this commitment to passing time.

If in his loyalty to the tradition of monumental art he makes an effort to fix his forms, he does it in a stiff way that shows how artificial it is and, by the absurd, affirms its ephemeral character. That is why *poor art* has once more given the work of Tàpies, as Catherine Millet says, an *incontestably contemporary quality*.

We should like to add that this cardboard-stiff survival, mummified, dessicated, tinned, *figée*, of ephemeral things is the losing element in which Argan saw bad faith and superstition.

Profundity. We think that this reading on the two mental levels given by the mummified aspect and the fragility, like the reading on the two material levels of the surface and the sore or the footprint, gives the measure of what Tàpies is undoubtedly still seeking: profundity. We may recall here a poem by Nietzsche, not far removed from the ideological origins of Tàpies, which reads:

—What does the dark midnight say?
—The universe is more profound
than the day dreamt it.

—Pain says: «Pass on and die!»
But all joy desires eternity.
Deep, profound eternity.

This was the nocturnal profundity of the dreams of Tàpies' youth, beyond the familiar blue of the daytime sky.

But if we think of the Tàpies of 1970, we shall have to think of another measure of profundity. That of Marx's phrase, speaking of Utopians and realists, which says:

While the proud eagle soars in the radiant solar regions, the mole works to more purpose underground, within the decaying earth, repugnant to delicate nostrils. The eagle is the Utopian.

According to this viewpoint, Tàpies is the realist. The realist who patiently constructs the plastic testimony of a long silence.

Translated by Kenneth Lyons

BIOGRAPHICAL DATA

1923. Born in Barcelona, at number 39, Carrer de la Canuda, on December 13th. His father was a lawyer and his mother the daughter of a family of booksellers with deep roots in the life of the city.

1925. The family moves to a flat in the Gran Via.

1926. Kindergarten at the school of the Loreto nuns in Barcelona.

1927. The family moves again, this time to the Carrer d'Aragó.

1928. First schooldays at the German School of Barcelona. Complete failure to adapt. Another change of flat, this time to one in a block at number 97, Travessera de Gràcia.

1931. He is sent to another school, the Col·legi Balmes of the Piarist Fathers.

1934. He begins his secondary studies.
The family moves again, this time to number 207, Carrer de Balmes.
He shows a taste for painting and drawing from early childhood.
He has access to a vast cultural domain, thanks to his father's extensive library of books and records.
First contacts with contemporary art through certain Catalan reviews, especially the special number of *D'Ací i D'Allà* directed by J. Prats and J. L. Sert, which was one of the first anthologies of international modern art.

1936. During the Spanish Civil War he lives in Barcelona; his interest in art continues and he paints and draws autodidactically. He continues his secondary studies at the *Liceo Práctico* in the Carrer Major de Gràcia. He is deeply affected by his memories of the terrible bombardments of Barcelona and all the hardships of the war.

1938. Is employed for some months at his father's office in the Generalitat (Autonomous Government) of Catalonia.

1939. He resumes his studies at the Institut Menéndez y Pelayo.

1940. He returns to his former school, the Col·legi Balmes of the Piarist Fathers. An accident provokes a heart attack which almost kills him. A profound spiritual crisis. Later he falls seriously ill and has to spend almost two years convalescing in the mountains.

1942. Makes copies in oils of pictures by Van Gogh and Picasso. During the above-mentioned convalescence he has already done some works of an expressive kind. The fondness for music inculcated by his parents grows, especially as regards the Romantics and contemporary works. The same occurs with literature: Nietzsche, Dostoievsky, Ibsen, Unamuno...

1943. Under his father's influence, he begins to study law at the University of Barcelona, which he is to leave in 1946 to devote himself wholly to painting. He rents his first studio, in the Carrer de Jaume I.

1944. He studies for two months at an art school, the *Acadèmia Valls*, in the Carrer de Jonqueres, Barcelona.

1945. From this moment, and in the course of the two following years, he does a considerable number of works with thick impastoes and mixtures of strange materials, earth, collages, etc., in a provocative spirit akin to that of his Dadaist forerunners, anti-aesthetic, poor, ignoble, in some cases approaching street graffiti and refuse. He alternates abstraction and primitivism.

1946. He begins to take an interest in existentialist philosophy.

1947. The beginning of his friendship with the Catalan poet and playwright Joan Brossa and with the collector Joan Prats, an intimate friend of Miró. He does his first engravings.

1948. In September of this year he collaborates with a group of young writers and painters of Barcelona in founding the review *Dau al Set*, the spirit of which was maintained in its first issues by the poet Brossa, who invented its name. He exhibits for the first time, at the first *Saló d'Octubre* of Barcelona, where he shows two works done in 1947: *Pintura* (Painting) (now in the Vidal de Llobatera Collection in Barcelona) and *Collage de les creus* (Collage of the crosses) (Henry Lazard Collection, Paris). Both are the subject of much controversy. He meets Joan Miró and is encouraged by him, as also by various Catalan writers.

1949. In conjunction with other painters, he shows a considerable number of works at the French Institute of Barcelona, in an exhibition called *An aspect of Catalan painting*, sponsored by *Cobalto 49* and presented by Cabral de Melo. On the invitation of Eugeni d'Ors, he shows at the *Salón de los Once* in Madrid. He engraves his first etchings in the workshop of Enric Tormo and does a group of paintings that make manifest his relationship with Surrealism. At this time he takes a special interest in Miró, Klee, Ernst and oriental art and philosophy. He meets the poet J. V. Foix, who commissions a painting from him.

1950. First great one-man show at the Galeries Laietanes in Barcelona, organized by Josep M.ª Gudiol. Publication of *L'Oracle sobre Antoni Tàpies* by Joan Brossa and the little monograph *Tàpies, o el Dau modern de Versalles* by J. J. Tharrats (Published by *Edicions Dau al Set*). He takes an interest in Marxism.
One-man show at the Municipal Museum of Mataró. He obtains a scholarship from the French Government which permits him to live in Paris for a whole year. He stays first in the *Cité Universitaire* and later in a private residence in St. Cloud. From this moment on he makes continual journeys to Paris. He is selected by the director of the Carnegie Institute and exhibits for the first time in the International Contest of this institution in Pittsburgh.

1951. Visit to Picasso. Journey to Belgium and Holland.
Retrospective exhibition of the *Dau al Set* in the Sala Caralt of Barcelona, organized by Sánchez Poveda; dissolution of the group. Such further publications as came out under that name mainly directed by J. J. Tharrats.

1952. He is selected by Lafuente Ferrari to exhibit at the 26th Venice Biennale and is again invited by the Carnegie Institute. Another one-man show at the Galeries Laietanes of Barcelona.

A moment of reaction that causes him to flee from an excessively literary world. He does some rather geometrical works and studies of pure colour.

1953. One-man shows at the Marshall Field Art Gallery in Chicago and at the Galería Biosca in Madrid.
A period of intense creative activity. Reappearance of the thick impastoes of his first period and amplification of their earthy qualities, the scraping and tearing, the dusty, decrepit aspects, the wall and the tortures of the material, and collage.
Journey to New York on the occasion of his first one-man show in that city, at the Martha Jackson Gallery.
Presentation by Gordon B. Washburn. He signs a contract with this gallery.
Joan Ramon Masoliver induces him to participate in the São Paulo Biennale, where he obtains an Acquisition Prize.

1954. Martha Jackson makes arrangements for him to take part in numerous exhibitions in the United States: the Wadsworth Atheneum of Hartford, Connecticut, the Nebraska Art Association of Lincoln, Nebraska, the Milwaukee Art Institute of Milwaukee, *Reality and Phantasy* at the Walker Art Center, Minneapolis, etc.
He is invited to exhibit again at the Carnegie Institute.
First prize at the *Saló del Jazz* of Barcelona. Another one-man show at the Galeries Laietanes.
Publication of the monograph *Tàpies o la transverberació* by Alexandre Cirici, published by *Edicions Dau al Set*, Barcelona. In Paris he meets the writer Michel Tapié, who shows an immediate interest in his work.
He marries Teresa Barba Fàbregas and they set up house at number 28, Carrer de Sant Elias.
He participates again in the Venice Biennale.
An increase in the number of works done with earth and marble-worker's sand.

1955. Exhibition at the Sturedgalleri of Stockholm, with Tharrats and Isern, presented by Dalí.
One-man show presented by the *Club 49* in the underground rooms of the Sala Gaspar in Barcelona, in the month of March, with an introduction by Joan Teixidor. In the same month, on the invitation of E. Jaquer, he takes part in the *Phases de l'Art Contemporain* exhibition at the Galerie Creuze in Paris. Michel Tapié puts him in touch with Rodolphe Stadler, with whom he signs a contract. He gives a lecture, at the Santander Summer University, in which he defends the use of imaginative liberty and irrational impulses and the need to eschew the «accepted» academic forms, whether those of abstract, funtional rationalism or those of the so-called «socialist realism». Prize of the Republic of Colombia at the 3rd Hispano-American Biennale, held in Barcelona. His works provoke a great scandal at this exhibition and are the subject of controversy in every newspaper in the country.

1956. In February he has a one-man show at the Galerie Stadler in Paris, with works done in 1954 and 1955. Publication of the monograph *Antoni Tàpies et l'oeuvre complète* by Michel Tapié, which reproduces some of the paintings done during these two years.
Birth of his son Antoni.
He makes a deeper study of oriental techniques for achieving knowledge: Vedanta, Yoga, Tantrism, Zen Buddhism.
He shows his works at the *Club 49* in Barcelona.

1957. He wins the Lissone (Milan) first prize for young artists. One-man show at the Galerie Stadler, Paris.
One-man show at the Schmela Gallery, Düsseldorf.

1958. Journey to Venice on the occasion of his individual room at the Biennale. Wins the Unesco Prize and the prize of the David Bright Foundation of Los Angeles.
One-man show at the Galleria dell'Ariete, Milan, presented by Jacques Dupin. Begins to work on his first lithographs, published by the Sala Gaspar. First prize of the Carnegie Institute of Pittsburgh, awarded by a jury composed of J. J. Sweeney, Marcel Duchamp, Lionello Venturi, F. J. Kiesler, Raoul Ubac and Vincent Price.
One-man show at the Martha Jackson Gallery, New York.
Birth of his daughter Clara and, a few days later, death of his father.
He participates in the Osaka Festival, Japan.

1959. Publication of the monograph *Antoni Tàpies* by Michel Tapié with the selection and sequence by J. Prats Vallès, published by Edicions R. M.
Second journey to the United States. He makes the acquaintance of Franz Kline, De Kooning, Motherwell, Hans Hoffmann, etc.
One-man show at the Martha Jackson Gallery in New York and the Gres Gallery in Washington.
One-man show at the Galerie Stadler, Paris.
Three of his paintings acquired by the Town Hall of Barcelona.
He exhibits at the Kunsthalle in Berne, with Alechisky, Messagier and Mosser, and at the Van der Loo Gallery in Munich, with Antonio Saura.
He increases his production of works done with poor materials: cardboard, paper, pieces of cloth, threads, pieces of string. He shows a desire to give importance to elemental, even insignificant, things: emptiness, ashes, the ephemeral, banal, everyday things.

1960. Another one-man show at the Sala Gaspar, Barcelona.
One-man show at the Bilbao Museum of Art.
Publication of the book *Tàpies* by J. E. Cirlot, published by Ed. Omega.
Prize at the International Engraving Biennale, Tokyo.
He exhibits his lithographs at the David Anderson Gallery in New York and the Galleria dell'Ariete in Milan, with Dubuffet.
He takes part in the exhibition of *New Spanish Painting and Sculpture* at the New York Museum of Modern Art.
Takes part in the exhibition entitled *Before Picasso, After Miró* at the Solomon R. Guggenheim Museum, New York. Camilo

José Cela devotes a special number of his review *Papeles de Son Armadans* to Tàpies' work, with texts by Cela himself, Argan, Cirlot, Habasque, Read, Restany, Tapié, Teixidor, Aguilera Cerni, Bayl, Gaya Nuño, Cirici, Westerdahl, Puig, Santos, Apollonio, Dupin, Chueca, Kultermann, etc. He buys an old house in the Montseny district, where he will henceforth spend long periods. Birth of his son Miquel.

1961. He visits the United States again. One-man shows at the Martha Jackson Gallery in New York and the Gres Gallery in Washington. Publication of the catalogue of his American paintings of 1959-1960, with a text by J. J. Sweeney.
One-man show at the Rudolf Zwirner Gallery in Essen.
Exhibition, with Sam Francis, at the Otto Stangl Gallery in Munich.
One-man show at the Galerie Stadler in Paris.
One-man show at the National Museum of Buenos Aires (Instituto Di Tella), presented by Argan and Romero Brest.
One-man show at the Blanche Gallery, Stockholm.
He is one of the exhibitors at the *Arte e Contemplazione* Exhibition in the Palazzo Grassi, Venice.

1962. He visits England and Germany. In Germany Werner Schmalenbach organizes his first anthological exhibition, of work done between 1945 and 1962, at the Kestnergesellschaft in Hanover.
He does some decorations for Joan Brossa's *Or i Sal*.
He returns to New York on the occasion of his exhibition, also a retrospective one, at the Guggenheim Museum, where he shows works done between 1945 and 1962, presented by Lawrence Alloway. One-man show at the National Museum of Fine Arts in Caracas.
He visits Switzerland, where he has a one-man show at the Kunsthaus in Zurich (also works between 1945 and 1962). Another one-man show of lithographs, presented at *Il Segno* in Rome and the Pierre Gallery in Stockholm.
In September of this year he moves, with his family, to St. Gallen, in order to do the great mural painting in the Handels-Hochschule Library. Publication of *Significación de la pintura de Tàpies* by J. E. Cirlot, published by Seix i Barral, Barcelona.

1963. Prize of the Art Club of Providence, Rhode Island, U.S.A.
One-man show at the Museum of Pasadena, California.
Publication of Jacques Dupin's book for the first personal presentation of Tàpies' papers and cardboards, at the Galerie Berggruen in Paris.
One-man show at the Gallerie Notizie and the International Center of Aesthetic Research, of Turin, Italy.
He moves into the new house and studio built for him by the architect Josep-Antoni Coderch at number 57, Carrer de Saragossa, Barcelona. Publication of *El pa a la Barca* (poems by Brossa and *lithocollages* by Tàpies), published by the Sala Gaspar, Barcelona.
One-man show at the Im Erker Gallery in St. Gallen, Switzerland.

One-man show at the Martha Jackson Gallery in New York, to mark the tenth anniversary of his first presentation at this gallery.

1964. He wins one of the prizes of the Guggenheim Foundation of New York. One-man show of cardboards and papers at the Zwirner Gallery, Cologne.
Visit to Rome and the south of Italy. One-man show at the Tartaruga Gallery in Rome.
One-man show at the Galerie Stadler, Paris.
He takes part in the international exhibition *Painters and sculptors of a decade* at the Tate Gallery, London. A special room is devoted to his work at the great «*Documenta III*» *International Exhibition* of Kassel, Germany. Exhibition of a selection of the woods, papers, cardboards and *collages* done over the previous twenty years, at the Sala Gaspar, Barcelona, and publication of the book illustrated with some of these works, and with an introductory text by Joan Teixidor, published by the Sala Gaspar, Barcelona.

1965. He exhibits at the new Rudolf Zwirner Gallery in Cologne. Roland Penrose organizes a one-man show of Tàpies' work at the London Institute of Contemporary Arts.
Publication of his St. Gallen Album by the Im Erker Presse of Switzerland. Presentation of the *Novel·la*, done in collaboration with Joan Brossa, at the Sala Gaspar, Barcelona.

1966. The young writer Jordi Guardiola organizes an exhibition of Tàpies' work at the *Cercle Artístic* of Manresa, with a presentation by Alexandre Cirici. Tàpies is imprisoned and fined, along with about thirty other intellectuals, for attending an unauthorized students' meeting at the Capuchin Monastery of Sarrià, Barcelona.
Exhibition at the Galería Biosca of Madrid, presented by José M.ª Moreno Galván. One-man shows in Paris (Stadler), Stockholm (Buren Gallery), Cannes (Galerie Jacques Verrière) and Toulouse (together with Clavé and Pelayo).
He is awarded the *Grand Prix du Président de la République* at the Menton Biennale.
The «15th International Congress of Artists, Critics and Art Students» of Rimini-Verucchio-San Marino sends him a gold medal «in recognition of the moral endeavour of his artistic work».
Publication of the *9 variations on three engravings of 1947-1948*.

1967. He signs a contract with the Galerie Maeght of Paris, where he exhibits in the month of November, being presented by Tapié and Jacques Dupin.
Presentation of the «fotoscop» *Antoni Tàpies o l'escarnidor de diadèmes*, carried out by Joan Prats with photographs by Joaquim Gomis and texts by Francesc Vicens and Joan Brossa, and published by Polígrafa, Barcelona.
Grand Prize for Engraving at the Ljubljana (Yugoslavia) Biennale.
He does some lithographs for Jacques Dupin's book *La nuit grandissante*, published by the Im Erker Presse, Switzerland.

Capelli Editore, of Bologna, publishes a monograph with texts by Giuseppe Gatt, Giulio Carlo Argan, Barilli, Calvesi, Menna, Ponente and Tomassoni. Exhibition at the Kunstmuseum of St. Gallen of the complete graphic work of Tàpies, presented by E. Naegeli and R. Jaffé.
Publication of the complete catalogue, with a study by Dieter Jähning.
Ralph Wuhlin does a film on the work of Tàpies for Swedish television.

1968. Visit to Vienna on the occasion of his anthological exhibition at the 20th-Century Museum, organized and presented by Werner Hofmann.
Anthological exhibitions at the Kunstverein of Hamburg and of Cologne.
Exhibition of the book done with Dupin, and of graphic works, at the Librairie «La Hune», Paris.
Exhibition of papers and *collages* at the Galerie Maeght, Paris.
Exhibition at the Martha Jackson Gallery, New York, presented by Edward Albee.
He does some screens with pieces of sheets for the windows of the Capuchin Monastery of Sion, Switzerland.

1969. Presentation of the book *Frègoli* by Tàpies and Joan Brossa, together with three tapestries and other recent works, at the Sala Gaspar, Barcelona.
He does a series of etchings in the Arte studios, Paris.

Clovis Prevost makes a film on the work of Tàpies, commissioned by the Maeght Foundation.
He publishes some polemical articles in defense of freedom of creation, denouncing all forms of cultural «directivism», whether openly political or hiding behind a purely technological façade.
J. M. Acarín and A. Dañhel make a film called *Malír Tàpies*, commissioned by Czech television.

1970. He does a new book with Joan Brossa: *Nocturn Matinal*, published by Polígrafa, Barcelona.
He is invited to take part in the Carnegie International of Pittsburgh.
He does new *collages* and *assemblages* and, for the first time, some sculptures.
He does a new series of etchings on a large scale at the Arte studios in Paris, where André du Bouchet likewise commissions him to engrave some plates for a book of his poems. He does a poster to present the poetical works of Jacques Dupin.
Visit to Switzerland on being commissioned to do a mural for the new theatre of the town of St. Gallen.
He exhibits at the Galleria dell'Ariete in Milan, presented by Carlo Franqui.
Publication of *Tàpies, testimoni del silenci* by Alexandre Cirici, published by Polígrafa, Barcelona.
Publication of *La pràctica de l'art*, a compendium of some of his writings and declarations. Published by Ariel, Barcelona, in its *Col·lecció Cinc d'Oros*.

INDEX OF WORKS

1. Drawing on paper, 1946. Private collection, Barcelona.
2. India ink. Drawing on paper, 1945. Private collection, Barcelona.
3. Paris pencil. Drawing on paper, 1945. Private collection, Barcelona.
4. Self-portrait. Lead-pencil drawing on paper, 1945. Private collection, Barcelona.
5. Portrait. Charcoal drawing on paper, 1944. Private collection, Barcelona.
6. Cover design for the review *Dau al Set*. Drawing on paper, 1949. Private collection, Barcelona.
7. Self-portrait. Lead-pencil drawing on paper, 1947. Private collection, Barcelona.
8. Self-portrait. Lead-pencil drawing on paper, 1946. Private collection, Barcelona.
9. Lead-pencil drawing on paper, 1945. Private collection, Barcelona.
10. Lead-pencil drawing on paper, 1946. Private collection, Barcelona.
11. Design for the review *Dau al Set*. Drawing on paper, 1949. Private collection, Barcelona.
12. Lead-pencil drawing on paper, 1946. Private collection, Barcelona.
13. Lead-pencil drawing on paper. Reproduced in *Dau al Set*, 1949. Private collection, Barcelona.
14. Crayon drawing on paper, 1946. 29 × 22 cm. Private collection, Barcelona.
15. India-ink drawing on paper, 1949. Private collection, Barcelona.
16. Zoom. Paint and whiting on canvas, 1946. 92 × 73 cm. K. H. Müller Collection, Düsseldorf.
17. Scraping on cardboard, 1947. Henry Lazard Collection, Paris.
18. Personage. Paint and marble-worker's sand on canvas, 1946. 65 × 54 cm. Private collection, Barcelona.
19. Composition with figures. Paint on canvas, 1945. 61 × 50 cm. Private collection, Barcelona.
20. Collage of the rice and strings. Paint and sizing on cardboard, 1947. Henry Lazard Collection, Paris.
21. Figure on burnt wood. Paint, pastel and fire, 1947. 77 × 64 cm. Private collection, Barcelona.
22. Composition on cardboard, 1946. 42.5 × 35.5 cm. Private collection, Barcelona.
23. Figure. Paint on canvas, 1945. Josep M. Gudiol Collection, Barcelona.
24. Figure. Paint on canvas, 1945. Private collection, Barcelona.
25. Two personages on cardboard. Paint, scraping and sizing, 1947. 76 × 64.5 cm. Private collection, Barcelona.
26. Box of strings, 1946. 48 × 40 cm. Private collection, Barcelona.
27. Figure of newspaper and threads. Sizing and paint on cardboard, 1946-1947. 45 × 37 cm. Private collection, Barcelona.
28. Threads on cardboard. Sizing and paint, 1946. 39 × 47 cm. Private collection, Barcelona.
29. Composition. Paint on canvas, 1947. 38 × 46 cm. Vidal de Llobatera Collection, Barcelona.
30. Composition. Paint on canvas, 1945. 46 × 38 cm. Private collection, Barcelona.
31. Head on blue background. Paint and photograph stuck to cardboard, 1946. 39.5 × 31.5 cm. Private collection, Barcelona.
32. Collage. Paint and sizing on cardboard, 1946. 105 × 75 cm. Fragment. Private collection, Barcelona.
33. Threads and curtain ring. Paint and sizing on cardboard, 1946. 53 × 75 cm. Private collection, Barcelona.
34. Newspaper cross. Paint and sizing on cardboard, 1946-1947. 40 × 31 cm. Private collection, Barcelona.
35. Painting. Oil on canvas, 1948. 92 × 73 cm. Charles Zadok Collection, New York.
36. Triptych. Paint on canvas (central panel), 1948. 97 × 130 cm. Private collection, Barcelona.
37. Collage of the crosses. Paint and sizing on cardboard, 1947. 53 × 75 cm. Henry Lazard Collection, Paris.
38. Harlequin and cat. Paint on canvas, 1948. Enric Tormo Collection, Barcelona.
39. Greens on dark brown. Paint on canvas, 1948. 89 × 116 cm. Museum of Modern Art Collection, Barcelona.
40. Charcoal and ink. Drawing on paper, 1948. 43 × 44 cm. Private collection, Barcelona.
41. The eyes. Paint on canvas, 1948. 73 × 60 cm. Private collection, Barcelona.
42. Composition with figures. Paint on canvas, 1947-1948. 89 × 116 cm. Private collection, Barcelona.
43. Charcoal and ink. Drawing on paper, 1948. 24.5 × 31.5 cm. Private collection, Barcelona.
44. Two figures. Paint on canvas, 1947. 59 × 80 cm. Josep M. Gudiol Collection, Barcelona.
45. Drawing on paper, 1948. 32 × 48 cm. Private collection, Barcelona.
46. Oil chest. Paint on canvas, 1949. 70 × 100 cm. Joan Gaspar Collection, Barcelona.
47. Composition in reds. Paint on canvas, 1949. Private collection, Barcelona.
48. Parafaragamus. Paint on canvas, 1949. 89 × 116 cm. Private collection, Barcelona.
49. The scoffer at diamonds. Paint on canvas, 1949. 92 × 73 cm. Juan Perucho Collection, Barcelona.
50. Sofar. Paint on canvas, 1949. 50 × 61 cm. Private collection, Barcelona.
51. Hindu London. Paint on canvas, 1949.
52. Inks and paint on opaque paper, 1949. 46 × 33 cm. Galería René Métras, Barcelona.
53. Mudrc. Paint on canvas, 1949. 92 × 73 cm. Josep-Lluís Samaranch Collection, Barcelona.
54. The bouquet in eclipse. Paint on canvas, 1949. 89 × 116 cm. Sala Gaspar, Barcelona.
55. Lunar disconsolation. Paint on canvas, 1949. 81 × 100 cm. Pere Casadevall Collection, Barcelona.
56. The fire of the thorns. Paint on canvas, 1949. 89 × 116 cm. Albert Jacas Collection, Barcelona.
57. Composition. Paint on canvas, 1949. 46 × 38 cm. Santos Torroella Collection, Barcelona.
58. The eyes of the foliage. Paint on canvas, 1949. 97 × 130 cm. Güell Collection, Barcelona.
59. Dream Garden. Paint on canvas, 1949. 97 × 130 cm. Museum of Cologne Collection.
60. Pastel, 1950. Joan Obiols Collection, Barcelona.
61. Landscape of Urus. Paint on canvas, 1950. 91 × 60 cm. Josep-Lluís Samaranch Collection, Barcelona.

62. Nymphs, dryads, harpies. Paint on canvas, 1950. 97×130 cm. Joan B. Cendrós Collection. Barcelona.

63. The legerdemain of Wotan. Paint on canvas, 1950. 89×116 cm. Private collection, Barcelona.

64. Composition. Paint on canvas, 1950.

65. Arromoch, the lion. Paint on canvas, 1949. 81×100 cm. Josep-Lluís Samaranch Collection, Barcelona.

66. The constructions of Shah Abba. Paint on canvas, 1950. 97×130 cm. The Albright-Knox Art Gallery Collection, Buffalo, U.S.A.

67. The probing of the foliage. Paint on canvas, 1950. 81×100 cm. Private collection, Barcelona.

68. Composition. Paint on canvas, 1950.

69. Still life of Sirefala. Paint on canvas, 1950. 81×65 cm. Private collection, Barcelona.

70. Composition. Paint on canvas, 1950. 65×81 cm. Galería René Métras, Barcelona.

71. The barbershop of the damned and the chosen. Paint on canvas, 1950. 97×130 cm. Private collection, Barcelona.

72. The last hand. Paint on canvas, 1950. 89×116 cm. Guillem Díaz-Plaja Collection, Barcelona.

73. The letter. Paint on canvas, 1950. 89×100 cm. Josep-Lluís Samaranch Collection, Barcelona.

74. The sorrow of Brunhilda. Paint on canvas, 1950. 89×116 cm. Joan Obiols Collection, Barcelona.

75. The bird. Paint on canvas, 1951. 41×33 cm. Galería René Métras, Barcelona.

76. Homage to Federico García Lorca. Paint on canvas, 1951. 81×100 cm. Josep-Lluís Samaranch Collection, Barcelona.

77. Asia together. Paint on canvas, 1951. 81×100 cm. Sala Gaspar, Barcelona.

78. The holdup. Paint on canvas, 1951. 81×100 cm. Xavier Vilanova Collection, Barcelona.

79. Still life of a hunt. Paint on canvas, 1951. 90×90 cm. Daniel E. Schneider Collection, New York.

80. The monument. Paint on canvas, 1951. 115×110 cm. Albert Jacas Collection, Barcelona.

81. Chorale of work. Paint on canvas, 1951. 130×162 cm. Galería Biosca, Madrid.

82. Jobs. Paint on canvas, 1951. 89×116 cm. Sala Gaspar, Barcelona.

83. The cat. Paint on canvas, 1951. 65×81 cm. Cesáreo Rodríguez-Aguilera Collection, Barcelona.

84. Figure in yellows, whites and blacks. Paint on canvas, 1951. 38×46 cm. Josep-Lluís Samaranch Collection, Barcelona.

85. The collision. Paint on canvas, 1951. Alexandre Cirici-Pellicer Collection, Barcelona.

86. Crime. Paint on canvas, 1951. Galería René Métras, Barcelona.

87. Nocturne. Paint on canvas, 1952. 73×92 cm. Private collection, Barcelona.

88. Two figures. Paint on canvas, 1952. 65×80 cm. Joan Prats Collection, Barcelona.

89. Social and personal. Paint on canvas, 1951. 89×116 cm. Sala Gaspar, Barcelona.

90. Collage of the bank notes. Gouache, inks and sizing on paper, 1951. 26×31.5 cm. Private collection, Barcelona.

91. The bouquet. Paint on canvas, 1951. 100×81 cm. Museum of Modern Art Collection, Venice.

92. Prodigal night. Paint on canvas, 1951-1952. Martín Collection, Barcelona.

93. The furrows. Paint on canvas, 1952. 97×130 cm. Private collection, Barcelona.

94. Homage to Miguel Hernández. Paint on canvas, 1951. 116×73 cm. Galerie Beyeler, Basle.

95. Political archaeology. Paint on canvas, 1952. 73×92 cm. Private collection, Barcelona.

96. Composition. Paint on canvas, 1952. Museum of Figueras (Gerona).

97. The plough. Paint on canvas, 1952. 130×162 cm. Pere Portabella Collection, Barcelona.

98. Collage-composition in yellows. Paint on canvas, 1953. 89×146 cm. Private collection, Barcelona.

99. The amphora. Paint on canvas, 1952. 92×73 cm. Galería René Métras, Barcelona.

100. Composition of blues and reds. Paint on canvas, 1952. 81×100 cm. Sturedgalleri, Stockholm.

101. Composition of complementaries. Paint on canvas, 1952. Private collection, Barcelona.

102. No answer. Paint on canvas, Sturedgalleri, Stockholm.

103. The oxcart. Paint on canvas, 1952. 116×89 cm. Manuel Salsas Collection, Paris.

104. Grey ochre. Paint on canvas, 1933. 130×162 cm. Private collection, Barcelona.

105. Origin. Paint on canvas, 1953. 89×116 cm. Martha Jackson Gallery, New York.

106. Violet monotype on paper, 1953. 48×61 cm. Martha Jackson Gallery, New York.

107. Composition with red lines. Paint on canvas, 1953. Sturedgalleri, Stockholm.

108. Scraping on red. Paint on canvas, 1952. 54×63 cm. Galería René Métras, Barcelona.

109. Composition with greens. Paint on canvas, 1952. 80×80 cm. Private collection, Barcelona.

110. Screen. Paint on canvas, 1953. Josep-Lluís Samaranch Collection, S'Agaró.

111. Composition. Paint on canvas, 1953. 73×54 cm. Galería René Métras, Barcelona.

112. Epicurean meditation. Paint on canvas, 1953. 92×73 cm. Private collection, Barcelona.

113. Collage-painting. Combined process on canvas, 1954. 146×114 cm. Nippon Gallery, Tokyo.

114. Yellow and violet. Combined process on canvas, 1953. 97×130 cm. Private collection, Barcelona.

115. Painting. Paint on canvas, 1954. 97×130 cm. Private collection, London.

116. Painting on cardboard, 1953. Private collection, Paris.

117. Black with yellow mark. Paint on canvas, 1953. 100×81 cm. Sturedgalleri, Stockholm.

118. The inner fire. Combined process on canvas, 1953. 60×73 cm. Antonio de Cominges Collection, Barcelona.

119. Relief painting. Paint and varnish on canvas, 1954. 130×162 cm. Amos Kahan Collection, New York.

120. White with red marks. Combined process on canvas, 1954. 116 × 97 cm. Josep-Lluís Samaranch Collection, Barcelona.

121. Painting. Paint on canvas, 1954. 146 × 97 cm. Mutschler Collection, Ulm.

122. Grey. Paint on canvas, 1955. 65 × 81 cm. Pere Portabella Collection, Barcelona.

123. Green painting. Paint on canvas, 1954. 97 × 146 cm. Marlborough Gallery, London.

124. Grey with black marks. Combined process on canvas, 1955. 162 × 130 cm. Galerie Stadler, Paris.

125. Painting on canvas, 1955. Galerie Stadler, Paris.

126. Painting on canvas, 1955. 97 × 130 cm. Marlborough Gallery, London.

127. Large grey painting. Combined process on canvas, 1955. 195 × 170 cm. Düsseldorf Museum.

128. Painting. Combined process on canvas, 1955. 97 × 130 cm. Sala Gaspar, Barcelona.

129. Painting. Combined process on canvas, 1955. 89 × 130 cm. Museum of Contemporary Art Collection, Madrid.

130. Painting with red cross. Paint on canvas, 1954. 195 × 130 cm. Galerie Beyeler, Basle.

131. Painting. Paint on canvas, 1955. 81 × 65 cm. Galerie Stadler, Paris.

132. Black painting. Paint on canvas, 1955. 146 × 89 cm. Philippe Dotremont Collection, Uccle, Brussels.

133. Painting No. 27. Combined process on canvas, 1955. 162 × 130 cm. Piacenza Collection, Turin.

134. Collage-painting. Paint and collage on canvas, 1955. 162 × 130 cm. Kootz Gallery, New York.

135. Painting. Paint on canvas, 1955. 146 × 97 cm. Martha Jackson Gallery, New York.

136. Painting No. 2. Combined process on canvas, 1955. 146 × 97 cm. Panza di Biumo Collection, Milan.

137. Grey with graphic signs. Combined process on canvas, 1955-1956. 195 × 114 cm. Gates Lloyd Collection, Haveford, Penn., U.S.A.

138. Relief-painting. Combined process on canvas, 1956. 162 × 130 cm. Landeau Collection, Paris.

139. Three marks on grey space. Paint on canvas, 1955. 146 × 89 cm. Irving A. Glass Collection, New York.

140. Undulating grey painting. Combined process on canvas, 1956. 195 × 140 cm. Raoul Levy Collection, Paris.

141. Black and ochre painting. Combined process on canvas, 1955. 100 × 81 cm. Claude Vulliet Collection, Paris.

142. Brown. Paint on canvas, 1956. 97 × 162 cm. Museum of Hamburg Collection.

143. Painting on canvas, 1955. Galerie Stadler, Paris.

144. Winding relief. Paint on canvas, 1956. 65 × 100 cm. Rosier Collection, Lyons.

145. Crackled white. Paint on canvas, 1956. 81 × 100 cm. Holländer Collection, U.S.A.

146. Grey and black. Paint on canvas, 1956. 81 × 81 cm. Eva de Buren Collection, Stockholm.

147. Landscape-figure in grey. Paint on canvas, 1956. 146 × 114 cm. Martha Jackson Gallery, New York.

148. Untitled. Paint on canvas, 1956. 130 × 97 cm. Staatsgalerie, Stuttgart.

149. Grey with black cross. Combined process on canvas, 1955. 146 × 114 cm. Panza di Biumo Collection, Milan.

150. Large oval. Combined process on canvas, 1956. 195 × 170 cm. Paul Larvière Collection, Montreal.

151. Swirl of sand. Combined process on canvas, 1955. 81 × 100 cm. Anthony Denney Collection, London.

152. White with graphic signs. Paint on canvas, 1956. 200 × 175 cm. Washington University, St. Louis, Missouri.

153. Grey cloud effects. Paint on canvas, 1956. 50 × 61 cm. Cardazzo Collection, Milan.

154. Blackish ochre with perforations. Combined process on canvas, 1957. 146 × 114 cm. Martha Jackson Gallery, New York.

155. Graphic signs on blackish-ochre relief. Combined process on canvas, 1957. 65 × 81 cm. Streep Collection, New York.

156. Composition No. LXII. Combined process on canvas, 1957. 114 × 146 cm. Galerie Beyeler, Basle.

157. Grey painting. Paint on canvas, 1957. 81 × 100 cm. New London Gallery, London.

158. Black relief. Combined process on canvas, 1957. 81 × 65 cm. Willy and Fänn Schniewind Collection, Neviges-Rhld.

159. White, shadows and relief. Combined process on canvas, 1957. 162 × 130 cm. V. Langen Collection, Düsseldorf-Meerbusch.

160. No. VII. Combined process on canvas, 1956. 162 × 130 cm. Private collection, Milan.

161. Brown and grey. Combined process on canvas, 1957. 97 × 130 cm. Torsten Anderson Collection, Stockholm.

162. No. LXVI. Combined process on canvas, 1957. 162 × 130 cm. Franz Meyer Collection, Basle.

163. Graphic ochre. Combined process on canvas, 1960. 162 × 130 cm. Niedersächsische Landesgalerie Collection, Hanover.

164. White oval. Combined process on canvas, 1957. 100 × 81 cm. Municipal Museum of Krefeld, Germany.

165. Painting. Combined process on canvas, 1957. 146 × 97 cm. Museum of Modern Art, New York.

166. Relief with five perforations. Combined process on canvas, 1957. Galerie Stadler, Paris.

167. Black oval. Combined process on canvas, 1957. 89 × 116 cm. Anthony Denney collection, London.

168. Grey over white. Combined process on canvas, 1957. 130 × 162 cm. Panza di Biumo Collection, Milan.

169. Ochre sand. Combined process on canvas, 1957. 195 × 130 cm. Panza di Biumo Collection, Milan.

170. Calligraphy. Combined process on canvas, 1958. 195 × 130 cm. Morris Pinto Collection, New York.

171. Ochre relief on white. Combined process on canvas, 1957. Fernando Rivière Collection, Barcelona.

172. Grey relief No. VIII. Combined process on canvas, 1957. 130 × 162 cm. Jacques Dupin Collection, Paris.

173. No. XXXVII. Combined process on canvas, 1957. 130 × 162 cm. Marlborough Gallery, London.

174. Composition with white sand. Combined process on canvas, 1958. 162 × 97 cm. Sala Gaspar, Barcelona.

175. Brown relief. Combined process on canvas, 1958. 114 × 146 cm. Martha Jackson Gallery, New York.

176. Blackish-ochre reliefs. Combined process on canvas, 1958. 195×130 cm. Galleria dell'Ariete, Milan.

177. Graphic signs. Combined process on canvas, 1958-1960. 95×130 cm. Van der Loo Gallery, Munich.

178. Grey furrows. Combined process on canvas, 1956. 89×116 cm. Toni Slick, San Antonio, Texas.

179. No. XLV. Combined process on canvas, 1957. 146×97 cm. Claude Vulliet Collection, Buchillon, Switzerland.

180. The broken plate. Homage to Gaudí. Combined process with china plate stuck on canvas, 1956. 130×162 cm. Galerie Beyeler, Basle.

181. Large painting. Combined process on canvas, 1958. 200×260 cm. Guggenheim Museum, New York.

182. Reddish painting. Combined process on canvas, 1958. 114×146 cm. Panza di Biumo Collection, Milan.

183. The boot. Combined process on canvas, 1958. 195×170 cm. Galleria dell'Ariete, Milan.

184. Cards crossing on wood, 1960. 56×76 cm. Sala Gaspar, Barcelona.

185. Crossed canvas. Combined process and sizing on canvas, 1962. 170×195 cm. Martha Jackson Gallery, New York.

186. Grey canvas. Sizing on canvas, 1963. 70×100 cm. H. Richter Collection, Düsseldorf.

187. Cardboard and string, 1959. 16×48 cm. Private collection, Barcelona.

188. Pot-bellied canvas. Sizing on canvas, 1964. 65×81 cm. Joan Teixidor Collection, Barcelona.

189. Collage of comb on cardboard, 1961. Private collection, Barcelona.

190. Four corners. Sizing on paper, 1962. 65×53 cm. Private collection, Barcelona.

191. Papers and wood, 1962. R. Scharpff, Stuttgart.

192. Painting. Combined process on canvas, 1959. 55×46 cm. Galería René Métras, Barcelona.

193. Blackish brown. Combined process on canvas, 1959. Private collection, Barcelona.

194. Grey form. Paint on canvas, 1959. George Guggenheim Collection, Zurich.

195. Cardboard tied with string, 1959. 53×68 cm. Tooth Gallery, London.

196. All red. Combined process on canvas, 1959. 65×81 cm. Martha Jackson Gallery, New York.

197. Pleated cardboard, 1959. 54×71 cm. Tooth Gallery, London.

198. Blue Waves. Combined process on canvas, 1959. 60×92 cm. Galleria dell'Ariete, Milan.

199. Composition. Combined process on canvas, 1959. Fritz and Nanana Herlt, Weiden, Germany.

200. Composition. Combined process on canvas, 1959. Victoria de los Ángeles and Enric Magriñà Collection, Barcelona.

201. Blue with double oval. Combined process on canvas, 1959. 81×65 cm. Guy Dixon Collection, London.

202. Grey fragment over canvas. Combined process on canvas, 1958. 130×97 cm. Van der Loo Collection, Munich.

203. Painting. Combined process on canvas, 1958. 195×130 cm. Museum of Modern Art, Rome.

204. Brown door. Combined process on canvas, 1959. 195×130 cm. Washington University, St. Louis, Missouri.

205. Grey with two black marks. Combined process on canvas, 1959. 75×109 cm. Martha Jackson Gallery, New York.

206. Grey with two bags. Combined process on canvas, 1959. 130×130 cm. Eva de Buren Collection, Stockholm.

207. Paper cut-out in violet, 1959. 58×72 cm. J. Ferreró Collection, Barcelona.

208. Crackled white over brown. Paint on canvas, 1959. 170×195 cm. Lebworth Collection, New York.

209. Grey with oblique lines. Combined process on canvas, 1959. Museum of Modern Art, New York.

210. Grey space. Paint on canvas, 1962. 130×81 cm. Gómez Collection, Oakridge, Tennessee.

211. Marble-worker's sand with six footprints. Combined process on canvas, 1959. 265×190 cm. Panza di Biumo Collection, Milan.

212. Ochre painting. Combined process on canvas, 1959. Town Hall of Barcelona.

213. Grey corners on brown. Combined process on canvas, 1959. 195×130 cm. Town Hall of Barcelona.

214. Grey with black fringes. Paint on canvas, 1959. 162×130 cm. International Center of Aesthetic Research, Turin.

215. Black with transversal band. Combined process on canvas, 1959. 162×130 cm. Galerie Stadler, Paris.

216. Cardboard, 1959-1960. 58×107 cm. Tooth Gallery, London.

217. Torn papers on canvas, 1959. 130×97 cm. Dr. Bloom Collection, Zurich.

218. Four forms. Combined process on canvas, 1959. 60×73 cm. Galleria dell'Ariete, Milan.

219. Beige with black circle. Combined process on canvas, 1959. 81×81 cm. Galerie Berggruen, Paris.

220. Grey with a vertical cross. Combined process on canvas, 1960. 54×85 cm. H. Neuerburg, Cologne.

221. Triangle. Combined process on canvas, 1960. 89×116 cm. Martha Jackson Gallery, New York.

222. Wood on canvas, 1960. 45×99 cm. Victoria de los Ángeles and Enric Magriñà Collection, Barcelona.

223. Pink and black collage-painting. Paint and paper on canvas, 1960. 89×116 cm. Winterthur Museum.

224. Piece of paper. Victoria de los Ángeles and Enric Magriñà Collection, Barcelona.

225. Painting on wood, 1960. 51×91 cm. Private collection, Barcelona.

226. Brown space. Paint on canvas, 1960. 65×81 cm. Martha Jackson Gallery, New York.

227. Purple. Paint and sizing on canvas, 1960. 130×162 cm. William Janss Collection, Thermal, California.

228. Black matter over sack. Combined process on canvas. Victoria de los Ángeles and Enric Magriñà Collection, Barcelona.

229. Grey with black marks. Combined process on canvas, 1960. 195×170 cm. Claude Hersaint Collection, Paris.

230. Painting on wood, 1960. 51×91 cm. Private collection, Barcelona.

231. Architectural. Combined process on canvas, 1960. 265×190 cm. Instituto di Tella, Buenos Aires.

232. Two reliefs in space. Combined process on canvas, 1960. 195×170 cm. Martha Jackson Gallery, New York.

233. Sized canvas, 1961. 195×170 cm. Private collection, Barcelona.

234. Three marks on white. Combined process on canvas, 1962. Martha Jackson Gallery, New York.

235. Four cardboards, 1959. Claude Vulliet Collection, Paris.

236. Sign on cardboard, 1961. Leopold Pomés Collection, Barcelona.

237. Cardboards sewn together with strings, 1960. 46.5×69.5 cm. Sala Gaspar, Barcelona.

238. Triangular form on grey. Combined process on canvas, 1961. 195×130 cm. Galerie Stadler, Paris.

239. Grey with wavy red lines. Combined process on canvas, 1962. 162×97 cm. Luciano Pistoi Collection, Turin.

240. Dark space. Combined process on canvas, 1960. 265×380 cm. Martha Jackson Gallery, New York.

241. Cardboard box unfolded, 1960. 128×85 cm. Joan Prats Collection, Barcelona.

242. Paper on painted canvas, 1960. 100×100 cm. Tooth Gallery, London.

243. Vertical on white. Combined process on canvas, 1959. Herlt Collection, Weiden, Germany.

244. Cardboard cut diagonally, 1960. 60×44 cm. Private collection, Barcelona.

245. Large brown with graphic sign in black. Combined process on canvas, 1961. 195×260 cm. Galerie Maeght, Paris.

246. Grey with graphic signs in black. Combined process on canvas, 1962. 195×310 cm. Museum of Basle.

247. Brown bed. Combined process on canvas, 1960. 195×130 cm. Private collection, Barcelona.

248. Grey with black band. Combined process on canvas, 1962. 195×130 cm. Private collection, Turin.

249. Collage with a dish, 1962. 76×55 cm. Sala Gaspar, Barcelona.

250. Painting on pieces of cardboard, 1960. 104×75 cm. Sala Gaspar, Barcelona.

251. Blue and brown. Combined process on canvas. Eudald Serra Collection, Barcelona.

252. Flesh colour. Paint on canvas. Victoria de los Ángeles and Enric Magriñà Collection, Barcelona.

253. Graphic signs in green. Drawing on paper, 1961. Private collection, Barcelona.

254. For the victims of the Vallès floods. Combined process on canvas, 1962. Antoni de Moragas Collection, Barcelona.

255. Grey with pink stripes. Sized canvas, 1963. 148×89 cm. Galerie Stadler, Paris.

256. Ochre and black paper folded and sized, 1963. 123×91 cm. Van der Loo Gallery, Munich.

257. Stretcher-painting, 1962. 162×130 cm. Private collection, Barcelona.

258. Composition with cords. Combined process and sizing on canvas, 1963. 195×130 cm. Luciano Pistoi Collection, Turin.

259. Painting on stretcher, 1962. 130×81 cm. International Center of Aesthetic Research, Turin.

260. Brown, ochre and black. Combined process on plywood. 162×130 cm. Gustau Gili Torra Collection, Barcelona.

261. Cardboard with strings, 1962. 85×75 cm. Galerie Stadler, Paris.

262. Large grey paper with white sign. Acrylic paint over sized paper on canvas, 1965. 193×137 cm. Van der Loo Gallery, Munich.

263. Relief in grey with three small holes. Combined process, 1964. 24×41 cm. Buren Gallery, Stockholm.

264. Sized canvas, 1964. Martha Jackson Gallery, New York.

265. Grey relief in four parts. Combined process on canvas, 1963. 150×217 cm. Museum of Cologne.

266. Grey with white angle. Paint on canvas, 1963. 97×130 cm. Zwirner Gallery, Cologne.

267. Canvas and string, 1964. 80×80 cm. Martha Jackson Gallery, New York.

268. Ochre with five incisions. Combined process on canvas, 1964. 162×130 cm. Galerie Stadler, Paris.

269. Paint on isorel and white collage, 1964. 130×97 cm. Private collection, Barcelona.

270. Reddish contour. Combined process on canvas, 1963. 92×60 cm. Martha Jackson Gallery, New York.

271. Grey with three pink stripes. Combined process on canvas, 1964. 97×146 cm. Dr. Dalen Collection, Stockholm.

272. Folder covers, 1964. 41×64 cm. Dr. Krüppel Collection, Neuss.

273. Relief with cords. Sizing and paint on canvas, 1963. 162×130 cm. Private collection, Barcelona.

274. Relief in ochre and pink. Combined process on plywood, 1965. 162×114 cm. Morris Pinto Collection, Paris.

275. Paper and strings, 1964. 85×54 cm. Van der Loo Gallery, Munich.

276. Blackboard, 1965. 130×162 cm. Stedelijk Museum, Amsterdam.

277. Collage with envelope, 1966. 32.5×25 cm. Buren Gallery, Stockholm.

278. Collage with paper and string, 1965-1966. 77×57 cm. Buren Gallery, Stockholm.

279. Lacerated relief. Combined process on canvas, 1966. 116×89 cm. Martha Jackson Gallery, New York.

280. Calendar. Sizing on paper, 1966. Private collection, Barcelona.

281. Small material and collage, 1967. 32×42 cm. Martha Jackson Gallery, New York.

282. In the shape of a slate. Combined process on plywood, 1967. 81×100 cm. Private collection, Paris.

283. Newspaper with black stain, 1964. 11×13 cm. K. H. Müller Collection, Düsseldorf.

284. Landscape. Combined process on canvas, 1965. 89×116 cm. Private collection, Barcelona.

285. Line of dots. Marble-worker's sand on canvas, 1964. Sala Gaspar, Barcelona.

286. White stripes on material. Combined process on cardboard. Manuel de Muga Collection, Barcelona.

287. White on white. Marble-worker's sand on canvas, 1965. Sala Gaspar, Barcelona.

288. White arch on wood, 1967. 170×195 cm. Private collection, Barcelona.

289. Small black and red. Combined process on canvas, 1969. 33×55 cm. Eva de Buren Collection, Stockholm.

290. Painting with graphic signs. Combined process on canvas, 1969. 89×115 cm. Jacques Neubauer Collection, Paris.

291. Yellow band. Combined process on canvas, 1966. 74×117 cm. Galerie Maeght, Paris.

292. Cardboard on dark canvas, 1969. 162×130 cm. Martha Jackson Gallery, New York.

293. In the shape of a chair. Combined process on canvas, 1966. 130×97 cm. Private collection, Barcelona.

294. White with two angles. Combined process on canvas, 1964. 81×100 cm. Buren Gallery, Stockholm.

295. Grey and black sand with chain. Combined process on plywood, 1968. 130×162 cm. Martha Jackson Gallery, New York.

296. Angle on blue. Combined process on canvas, 1968. 114×116 cm. Juan March Delgado Collection, Madrid.

297. Canvas with cords, 1967. 116×89 cm. Galerie Maeght, Paris.

298. Central graphic sign, ink on Japanese paper, 1967. 93.5×64 cm. Galerie Van der Loo, Munich.

299. Material in the shape of a nut. Combined process on canvas, 1967. 195×175 cm. H. Neuerburg Collection, Cologne.

300. Two marks on white canvas, 1967. 162×130 cm. Galerie Maeght, Paris.

301. Heaped material. Combined process on canvas, 1968. 65×100 cm. Martha Jackson Gallery, New York.

302. Four fingerprints and dots. Combined process on canvas, 1968. 46×55 cm. Werner Rusche Collection, Cologne.

303. Material and grey collage, 1968. 162×130 cm. Martha Jackson Gallery, New York.

304. Blue with removals, 1968. 195×170 cm. Martha Jackson Gallery, New York.

305 to 307. Screens. India ink on sewn and folded sheets, 1968. Windows of the Capuchin Monastery of Sion, Switzerland (Architect: Mirco Ravanne).

308. In the shape of a leg. Combined process on canvas, 1968. 89×146 cm. Morris J. Pinto Collection, Paris.

309. Body of material and orange marks. Combined process on canvas, 1968. 162×130 cm. Private collection, Barcelona.

310. Marks on newspaper, 1968. Private collection, Barcelona.

311. Holes and nails in white. Marble-worker's sand and nails on plywood, 1968. 60×73 cm. Martha Jackson Gallery, New York.

312. Rag and string, 1968. 108×75 cm. Rudolph B. Schulhof Collection, New York.

313. Ochre material in the shape of an arch. Combined process on canvas, 1968. 195×130 cm. Martha Jackson Gallery, New York.

314. In the shape of a «T». Cardboard on canvas, 1968. Galerie Maeght, Paris.

315. Blue bed. Paint on canvas, 1968. 138×195 cm. Rudolph Zwirner Collection, Cologne.

316. Large sheet. Sizing on canvas, 1968. 270×195 cm. Galerie Maeght, Paris.

317. Spiral of white material. Marble-worker's sand on canvas, 1968-1969. 89×116 cm. Martha Jackson Gallery, New York.

318. Two blankets full of straw. Combined process on canvas, 1968. 198×270 cm. Galerie Schmela, Düsseldorf.

319. High relief in white. Sizing on canvas, 1968. 89×116 cm. Galerie Schmela, Düsseldorf.

320. Fingerprints. Combined process on canvas, 1968. 81×100 cm. Martha Jackson Gallery, New York.

321. Blue-green and straw. Combined process with sizing on plywood, 1968. 89×116 cm. Private collection, Barcelona.

322. Straw on canvas, 1968. 65×81 cm. Galerie Maeght, Paris.

323. Painting with rice. Combined process on canvas, 1969. 89×116 cm. Sala Gaspar, Barcelona.

324. Folded canvas. Combined process on plywood with nails, 1968. 116×89 cm. Svenska Lloyd Collection, Stockholm.

325. Circle of cord. Sizing on canvas, 1969. 100×100 cm. Martha Jackson Gallery, New York.

326. Material in the shape of an armpit. Combined process on plywood, 1968. 81×100 cm. Joan Miró Collection, Palma de Mallorca.

327. Black arch and sand. Combined process on plywood, 1968. 80×69 cm. Ardemagni Collection, Milan.

328. Big parcel of straw. Paint and sizing on canvas, 1969. 195×270 cm. Galerie Maeght, Paris.

329. White and plastic. Combined process on paper stuck to canvas, 1969. 133×118 cm. Martha Jackson Gallery, New York.

330. Pressed straw. Combined process on canvas, 1969. 195×130 cm. Martha Jackson Gallery, New York.

331. Large piece of wood, 1969. 330×275 cm. Galerie Maeght, Paris.

332. Knot and cord. Sizing on canvas, 1969. 195×130 cm. Galerie Maeght, Paris.

333. Large white canvas, joined, 1969. 175×400 cm. Galerie Maeght, Paris.

334. Four packets of straw. Paint and sizing on canvas, 1969. 90×65 cm. Martha Jackson Gallery, New York.

335. Rag and collage on canvas, 1969. 90×65 cm. Martha Jackson Gallery, New York.

336. Black and earth. Combined process on canvas with wood, 1970. 130×162 cm. Galerie Maeght, Paris.

337. Homage to Richard Wagner. Paint and sizing on cardboard, 1969. Joan Brossa Collection, Barcelona.

338. Tatters. Paint with rags and strings on sized canvas over cardboard, 1970.

BIBLIOGRAPHY

GENERAL WORKS

THARRATS, JOAN JOSEP: *Guía elemental de la Pintura Moderna*. Ed. Dau al Set. Barcelona, 1948.

CIRLOT, JUAN EDUARDO: *Magicismo Plástico*. «Diccionario de los Ismos». Barcelona, 1949.

D'ORS, EUGENIO: *Estilo y cifra*. «La Vanguardia». Barcelona, October 2nd, 1949.
Estilo y Cifra. «La Vanguardia». Barcelona, January 5th, 1950.
Estilo y Cifra. «La Vanguardia». Barcelona, May 23rd, 1950.
Novísimo Glosario. «Arriba». Madrid, May 14th, 1950.

GASCH, SEBASTIÁN: *Tres Pintores Jóvenes*. «Bisonte», No. 1. Santander, 1950.
Antología de la Escuela de Altamira. «Bisonte», No. 1, cit. 1950.
Spanish Artists. «Magazine of Art», vol. XLII-III. New York, March, 1950.
Desde Barcelona. «Ver y estimar». Buenos Aires, March, 1950.

GAYA NUÑO, JUAN ANTONIO: *Medio siglo de Movimientos Vanguardistas en nuestra Pintura*. Ed. Dau al Set. Barcelona, 1950.

SANTOS TORROELLA, RAFAEL: *Corriere di Spagna*. «Numero», No. 3 (2nd year). Florence, 1950.

SAURA, ANTONIO: *El Séptimo Salón de los Once*. «La Hora». Madrid, March 12th, 1950.

FERRÁN, JAIME: *Notas sobre la Pintura actual en Cataluña*. «Alcalá». Madrid & Barcelona, November 10th, 1952.

GAYA NUÑO, JUAN ANTONIO: *La Pintura Española del medio siglo*. Ed. Omega. Barcelona, 1952.

FARALDO, RAMÓN: *Espectáculo de la Pintura Española*. Ed. Cigüeña. Madrid, 1953.

GASCH, SEBASTIÁ: *L'expansió de l'art català al món*. Ed. Ariel. Barcelona, 1953.

SERPAN, JAROSLAV: *Premier bilan de l'Art actuel*. Ed. Soleil Noir. Paris, 1953.

PAPOVICI, C. L.: *L'Art abstrait en Espagne*. «Cimaise». Paris, October-November, 1953.

CIRICI-PELLICER, ALEXANDRE: *Pintura del siglo XX*, in Jiménez Placer, F. *Historia del Arte Español* (vol. II). Ed. Labor. Barcelona, 1955.

JÜRGEN FISCHER, KLAUS: *Zwischen dem Ungefähren und Prazisen*. «Das Kunstwerk», No. 5, Krefeld, 1956-57.

ASHTON, DORE: *Notes from Spain*. «Art and Architecture». Los Angeles, November, 1957.

CIRICI-PELLICER, ALEXANDRE: *Artes Plásticas*. «Enciclopedia Labor». Barcelona, 1957.

CIRLOT, JUAN EDUARDO: *El Arte otro*. Ed. Seix i Barral. Barcelona, 1957.

SEUPHOR, MICHEL: *Dictionnaire de la Peinture Abstraite*. Ed. Hazan. Paris, 1957.

APOLLONIO, UMBRO: *Art since 1945*. Abrams. New York, 1958.

CIRLOT, JUAN EDUARDO: *Arte contemporáneo*. Ed. Edhasa. Barcelona, 1958.

DORFLES, GILLO: *I Pittori Stranieri alla XXIX Biennale*. «Domus». Milan, September, 1958.

PALAU, JOSEP: *La Jeune École de Paris*. Ed. Le Musée de Poche. Paris, 1958.

RESTANY, PIERRE: *Peinture Espagnole*. «Cimaise». Paris, November 9th, 1958.

CIRLOT, JUAN EDUARDO: *Informalismo*. Ed. Omega. Barcelona, 1959.

CIRICI-PELLICER, ALEXANDRE: *La pintura catalana*. Ed. Moll. Palma de Mallorca, 1959.

CIRICI-PELLICER, ALEXANDRE: *Mondrian, Miró, Tobey, Tàpies*, in Brandt, *Ver y comprender el arte*. Ed. Labor. Barcelona, 1959.

CHOAY, FRANÇOIS: *L'École Espagnole*. «L'Oeil», No. 51. Paris, March, 1959.

FAHLSTROM, OYVIND: *Steget och tärningens sjunde sida*. «Paletten», No. 2. Goteborg, 1959.

HABASQUE, GUY: *Confrontation Internationale*. «L'Oeil», No. 57. Paris, September, 1959.
Au-delà de l'Informel. «L'Oeil», No. 59. Paris, 1959.

CLAIRE LEGRAND, FRANCINE: *La Peinture et la Sculpture au défi*. «Quadrum», No. 7. Brussels, 1959.

PLATSCHEK, HANS: *Neue Figurationen*. Ed. Piper & Co. Munich, 1959.

SÖDERBERG, LASSE: *Peinture et Vérité*. «Cahiers du Musée de Poche», No. 2. Paris, June, 1959.

TAPIÉ, MICHEL: *Esthétique en devenir*. Ed. Dau al Set. Barcelona, 1959.

WESCHER, HERTA: *La participation espagnole à la XXIXème Biennale de Venise*. «Quadrum», No. 6. Brussels, 1959.

BAYL, F.: *Bilder unserer Tage*. Dumont. Cologne, 1960.

MARCHOORI, GIUSEPPE: *La Pittura Straniera nelle Collezioni Italiene*. Ed. Fratelli Pozo. Turin, 1960.

MORENO GALVÁN, JOSÉ MARÍA: *Introducción a la Pintura Española*. Ed. Publicaciones Españolas. Madrid, 1960.

O'HARA, FRANK: *New Spanish Painting and Sculpture*. The Museum of Modern Art. New York, 1960.

PONENTE, NELLO: *Tendances Contemporaines*. Ed. Skira. Geneva, 1960.

READ, HERBERT: *A Short History of Modern Art*. Thames & Hudson. London, 1960.

RESTANY, PIERRE: *Lyrisme et Abstraction*. Ed. Apollinaire. Milan, 1960.

VICENS, FRANCESC: *Prolegomènes à une esthétique autre de Michel Tapié*. International Center of Aesthetic Research. Turin, 1960.

AREAN, CARLOS A.: *La Escuela Pictórica Barcelonesa*. Ed. Publicaciones Españolas. Madrid, 1961.
Veinte Años de Pintura de Vanguardia en España. Ed. Nacional. Madrid, 1961.

CIRLOT, JUAN EDUARDO: *Pintura Catalana Contemporánea*. Ed. Omega. Barcelona, 1961.

DORFLES, GILLO: *Ultime tendenze nell'Arte d'oggi*. Ed. Feltrinelli. Milan. 1961.

HAFTMAN, WERNER: *Malerei im 20 Jahrhundert*. Prestel. Munich, 1962.

RAGON, MICHEL: *Naissance d'un Art Nouveau*. Ed. Albin Michel. Paris, 1962.

CLAUS, JÜRGEN: *Theorien zeitgenössischer Malerei*. Rowohlt. Hamburg, 1963.

ROH, FRANZ: *Junge spanische Malerei*. «Das Kunstwerk», No. 7, Baden-Baden, 1963.

RODRÍGUEZ AGUILERA, CESÁREO: *Antología Española de Arte Contemporáneo*. Ed. Barña. Barcelona, 1965.

YOSHIAKI, TONO: *After Pollock*. Bitjutsu Shuppan Sha. Tokyo, 1965.

CIRICI-PELLICER, ALEXANDRE: *Die Entwiklung der Kunst Spaniens bis zu Gegen wart*, in *Kunst Unserer Zeit*. Ed. Du Mont. Cologne, 1966. English translation, *The Art of Spain from 1945 to 1965*, in *Art of our time*. Thames & Hudson. London, 1966.

AGUILERA-CERNI, VICENTE: *Panorama del Nuevo Arte Español*. Ed. Guadarrama. Madrid, 1966.

FRANÇA, JOSÉ AUGUSTO & SANTOS TORROELLA, RAFAEL: *Espagne*. «Aujourd' hui», No. 52. Paris, February, 1966.

GROHMAN, WILL et al.: *Art of our time*. Thames & Hudson. London, 1966.

PÁNIKER, SALVADOR: *Conversaciones en Cataluña*. Ed. Kairós. Barcelona, 1966.

CIRICI-PELLICER, ALEXANDRE: *Artes Plásticas*. «El Arte Universal», Ed. Danae. Barcelona, 1967.

CLAUS, JÜRGEN: *Theorien zeitgenössischer Malerei*, Italian translation Il Saggiatore. Milan, 1967.

DORFLES, GILLO: *Ultime tendenze nell'Arte d'oggi*, Spanish translation Ed. Labor. Barcelona, 1967.

HANN, OTTO: *Art objectif.* Catalogue of the exhibition in Galerie Stadler. Paris, 1967.

LAMBERT, JEAN-CLARENCE: *La Peinture Abstraite.* Ed. Rencontre. Lausanne, 1967.

VALLIÈRE, DORA: *L'Art Abstrait.* Le Livre de Poche. Paris, 1967.

DIENST, ROLF-GUNSTER: *Positionen.* Dumont Aktuell. Cologne, 1968.

MORENO GALVÁN, JOSÉ M.ª: *La última Vanguardia.* Ed. Magius. Madrid, 1969.

BIHALJI-MERIN, OTTO: *Adventure of Modern Art.* Henry N. Abrams, Inc. New York, 1969.

HAFTMANN, WERNER; SANDLER, IRVING; RAGON, MICHEL; LEGRAND, FRANCINE; DORFLES, GILLO; JAFFÉ, HANS L. C.; APOLLONIO, UMBRO; LIPPARD, LUCY; BIHALJI-MERIN, OTTO: *Depuis 45, l'art de notre temps.* La Connaissance, S.A. Brussels, 1969.

HERRMANNS, RALPH: *Världens vackraste tavla.* Bonniers. Stockholm, 1970.

WORKS PARTICULARLY CONCERNING TÀPIES

GASCH, SEBASTIÁN: *Unos dibujos de Antoni Tàpies.* «Destino». Barcelona, March 29th, 1947.

JUNOY, JOSÉ M.ª: *De espaldas a la realidad.* «Correo Catalán». Barcelona, October 17th, 1948.

BROSSA, JOAN: *Tres aiguaforts.* Ed. Enric Tormo. Barcelona, 1949.

DE MELO, CABRAL: Presentation in the catalogue of the exhibition at the French Institute. «Cobalto», No. 3. Barcelona, 1949.

PUIG, ARNALDO: *La encrucijada del arte.* «Dau al Set». Barcelona, October-November-December, 1949.

D'ORS, EUGENIO: *Tres en los Once.* «Arriba». Madrid, March 14th, 1950.

TEIXIDOR, JOAN: *Los nocturnos de Tàpies.* «Destino». Barcelona, November 4th, 1950.

FERRÁN, JAIME: *La obra de Tàpies.* «Estilo». Barcelona, November, 1950.

BROSSA, JOAN: *Oracle sobre Antoni Tàpies.* «Dau al Set». Barcelona, November, 1950.

THARRATS, JOAN JOSEP: *Antoni Tàpies o el Dau modern de Versalles.* «Dau al Set». Barcelona, 1950.

SANTOS TORROELLA, RAFAEL: *Un pintor y un poeta.* «Correo Literario». Madrid, December 15th, 1950.

JARDÍ, ENRIC: *Antoni Tàpies.* «Ariel». Barcelona, 1950.

RODRÍGUEZ AGUILERA, CESÁREO: *Antoni Tàpies.* «Revista». Barcelona, May 15th, 1952.

WASHBURN, GORDON B.: Presentation in the catalogue of the exhibition at the Martha Jackson Gallery. New York, 1953.

BURG, COPELAND C.: *Spaniard's painting at Field's.* «Chicago American». Chicago, April 6th, 1953.

VIVANCO, LUIS FELIPE: *Comentando la exposición de Tàpies.* «Revista». Barcelona, May 7th, 1953.

SÁNCHEZ, CAMARGO: *El realismo mágico y la abstracción en el pintor Tàpies.* «Foco». Madrid, May, 1953.

FERRÁN, JAIME: *La pintura de Antoni Tàpies.* «Cuadernos Hispano-Americanos». Madrid, June, 1953.

THARRATS, JOAN JOSEP: *Tàpies en Nueva York.* «Revista». Barcelona, November, 1953.

CIRICI-PELLICER, ALEXANDRE: *Tàpies o la transverberació.* Ed. Dau al Set. Barcelona, 1954.

TAPIÉ, MICHEL: *Antoni Tàpies.* Ed. Dau al Set. Barcelona, 1955.

CIRLOT, JUAN EDUARDO: *Explicación de las pinturas de Tàpies.* «Destino», No. 949. Barcelona, 1955.

GASCH, SEBASTIÁN: *Con Tàpies, En el taller de los artistas* «Destino». Barcelona, June 11th, 1955.

VALVERDE, JOSÉ M.ª: *Unos cuadros de Tàpies.* «Revista». Barcelona, February 2nd, 1956.

ALVARD, JULIEN: *Tàpies.* «Cimaise», No. 6 (ser. IV). Paris, 1957.

TEIXIDOR, JOAN: *Entre les lletres i les arts.* Ed. Horta. Barcelona, 1957.

DUPIN, JACQUES: Presentation in the catalogue of the exhibition at the Galleria dell'Ariete, Milan, 1958.

VALSECCHI, MARCO: *Antoni Tàpies.* «Il Giorno». Milan, May 27th, 1958.

DORFLES, GILLO: *Due casi limite: Fontana e Tàpies.* «Letteratura», Nos. 33-34. Milan, 1958.

RESTANY, PIERRE: *Tàpies.* «Cimaise». Paris, October-November, 1958.

DEL ARCO, MANUEL: *Mano a mano-Antoni Tàpies.* «La Vanguardia Española». Barcelona, December 5th, 1958.

Black Prince. «Time», No. 11 (vol. 7). New York, March 16th, 1959.

CHOAY, FRANÇOIS: *Tàpies, mystique du presque rien.* «France observateur». Paris, April 30th, 1959.

MEYER, FRANZ: *Tàpies, Alechinsky, Messagier, Moser.* Presentation in the catalogue of the exhibition at the Kunsthalle, Berne, September-October, 1959.

CIRLOT, JUAN EDUARDO: *Tàpies y la escuela española actual.* «Destino», No. 1157. Barcelona, October 10th, 1959.

TAPIÉ, MICHEL: *Antoni Tàpies.* Ed. R.M. Barcelona, 1959.

TEIXIDOR, JOAN: *Antoni Tàpies.* «Cuadernos de Arquitectura», No. 38. Barcelona, 1959.

CHOAY, FRANÇOIS: *Antoni Tàpies.* «Museum Journal», No. 6 (ser. 5). Otterloo, December, 1959.

CASTILLO, ALBERTO DEL: *La sinceridad de Antoni Tàpies.* «Diario de Barcelona», February 14th, 1960.

CIRLOT, JUAN EDUARDO: *Tàpies.* Ed. Omega. Barcelona, 1960.

ARGAN, GIULIO CARLO: *La superstizione di Tàpies.* «L'Europa Letteraria», Rome, 1960.

PLA, JOSÉ: *La rueda del tiempo.* «El Correo Catalán». Barcelona, May 3rd, 1960.

CIRICI-PELLICER, ALEXANDRE: *Tàpies o el conocimiento.* «Revista», No. 409. Barcelona, 1960.

MARSÀ, ANGEL: *Antoni Tàpies.* «El Correo Catalán». Barcelona, December 13th, 1960.

CELA, CAMILO JOSÉ: *La imagen de la seriedad.* «Papeles de Son Armadans», No. 57. Madrid & Palma de Mallorca, December, 1960.

TEIXIDOR, JOAN: *Los argumentos de Tàpies.* «Papeles de Son Armadans», No. 57 cit. 1960.

BAYL, FRIEDRICH: *Tàpies o el silencio.* «Papeles de Son Armadans». No. 57 cit., 1960.

GAYA NUÑO, JUAN ANTONIO: *La pintura oclusiva de Antoni Tàpies.* «Papeles de Son Armadans», No. 57 cit., 1960.

HABASQUE, GUY: *Situación de Antoni Tàpies.* «Papeles de Son Armadans», No. 57 cit., 1960.

CIRICI-PELLICER, ALEXANDRE: *Tàpies realista.* «Papeles de Son Armadans», No. 57 cit., 1960.

WESTERDAHL, EDUARDO: *Tàpies: significación intemporal del muro.* «Papeles de Son Armadans», No. 57 cit., 1960.

AGUILERA CERNI, VICENTE: *Para una definición de Antoni Tàpies.* «Papeles de Son Armadans», No. 57 cit., 1960

PUIG, ARNALDO: *Primera aproximación a la pintura de Antoni Tàpies.* «Papeles de Son Armadans», No. 57 cit., 1960.

MIRÓ, JOAN: *L'obra d'Antoni Tàpies*. «Papeles de Son Armadans», No. 57 cit., 1960.

PRATS VALLÈS, JOAN: *Carta a J. E. C.* «Papeles de Son Armadans», No. 57 cit., 1960.

BROSSA, JOAN: *Enumeració en sospirar*. «Papeles de Son Armadans», No. 57 cit., 1960.

CRESPO, ÁNGEL: *Planeta à Tàpies*. «Papeles de Son Armadans», No. 57 cit., 1960.

FERREIRO, CELSO EMILIO: *Tàpies, pintor de hoxe*. «Papeles de Son Armadans», No. 57 cit., 1960.

KERRIGAN, ANTHONY: *A Draught for the Painter*. «Papeles de Son Armadans», No. 57 cit., 1960.

MOYÀ GILABERT, LLORENÇ: *El solc*. «Papeles de Son Armadans», No. 57 cit., 1960.

SANTOS TORROELLA, RAFAEL: *Antoni Tàpies*. «Papeles de Son Armadans», No. 57 cit., 1960.

BONET, BLAI: *Carta a Antoni Tàpies*. «Papeles de Son Armadans», No. 57 cit., 1960.

TAPIÉ, MICHEL: *Una profundidad cualitativa*. «Papeles de Son Armadans», No. 57 cit., 1960.

CIRLOT, JUAN EDUARDO: *Metafísica de Tàpies*. «Papeles de Son Armadans», No. 57 cit., 1960.

APOLLONIO, UMBRO: *Arte de Tàpies*. «Papeles de Son Armadans», No. 57 cit., 1960.

DUPIN, JACQUES: *Nota sobre Tàpies*. «Papeles de Son Armadans», No. 57 cit., 1960.

CHUECA GOITIA, FERNANDO: *Tàpies, pintor del devenir*. «Papeles de Son Armadans», No. 57 cit., 1960.

KULTERMANN, UDO: *Antoni Tàpies*. «Papeles de Son Armadans», No. 57 cit., 1960.

RESTANY, PIERRE: *Tàpies o la vida total*. «Papeles de Son Armadans», No. 57 cit., 1960.

READ, HERBERT: *Antoni Tàpies, su arte*. «Papeles de Son Armadans», No. 57 cit., 1960.

CIRLOT, JUAN EDUARDO: *Der spanische Maler Antoni Tàpies*. «Die Kunst». Munich, January, 1961.

SWEENEY, JAMES JOHNSON: *Tàpies: A catalogue of painting in America 1959-1960*. Gres Gallery & Martha Jackson Gallery. Washington and New York, 1961.

PERUCHO, JOAN: *Antoni Tàpies o el hervor de lo inerte*. «Destino». Barcelona, March 25th, 1961.

DE SAGARRA, JOSÉ M.: *Polémica y Bizantinismo*. «La Vanguardia Española». Barcelona, May 14th, 1961.

CIRLOT, JUAN EDUARDO: *La peinture de Tàpies*. «Quadrum», No. 12. Brussels, 1961.

TAKIGUCHI, SHUZO: *Poetic tribute to Tàpies*. «Mizue», No. 677. Tokyo, 1961.

TONO YOSHIAKI: *Antoni Tàpies*. «Mizue», No. 677. Tokyo, 1961.

KANKI, KEIZO: *Catalonia and Tàpies*. «Mizue», No. 677 cit., 1961.

KULTERMANN, UDO: *Antoni Tàpies*. «Das Kunstwerk», No. 12-14. Baden-Baden, June, 1961.

ASHTON, DORE: *Antoni Tàpies*. «Art International», No. 5-6 (vol. 5). Zurich, June-August, 1961.

BADOSA, ENRIQUE: *Más allá de una polémica*. «El Noticiero Universal». Barcelona, 1961.

GALE, JOHN: *Don't show my paintings*. «The Observer». London, January 14th, 1962.

VOLPI, MARISA: *Testimonianza umana di Tàpies*. «Il Verri», No. 1. Milan, February, 1962.

CIRLOT, JUAN EDUARDO: *Significación de la pintura de Tàpies*. Ed. Seix i Barral. Barcelona, 1962.

TRUCCHI, LORENZA: Prologue to the catalogue of the exhibition at the «Il Segno» gallery, Rome, 1962.

PRESTON, STUART: *Fifty paintings by Antoni Tàpies*. «The New York Times». New York, March 22nd, 1962.

KOZLOFR, MAX: *Tàpies. Exhibition Guggenheim Museum*. «Art International», No. 4-5. Zurich, 1962.

DALÍ, SALVADOR: *Tàpies, Tàpies, classic, classic!* «Art News». New York, May, 1962.

SCHMALENBACH, WERNER: *Tàpies*. «Kestner Gesellschaft». Hanover, 1962. *Antoni Tàpies*. «Werk». Winterthur, June, 1962.

ALLOWAY, LAWRENCE: *Antoni Tàpies*. The Solomon Guggenheim Museum. New York, 1962.

HÜTTINGER, EDUARD: *Antoni Tàpies*. Kunsthaus. Zurich, 1962.

BONNEFOY, Y.: *Dualité de l'Art d'Aujourd'hui*. «Art de France» No. II, Paris, 1962.

AREAN, CARLOS A.: *Tàpies*. «Cuadernos Hispano-Americanos», No. 156. Madrid, October, 1962.

RAMÍREZ DE LUCAS, JOSÉ: *Antoni Tàpies o el sentido del fragmento misterioso*. «Arquitectura», No. 54. Madrid, June, 1963.

CORREDOR MATHEOS, J.: *Antoni Tàpies*. «La Prensa». Barcelona, November 12th, 1963.

JACKSON, MARTHA: Prologue to the catalogue of the exhibition at the Martha Jackson Gallery. New York, December, 1963.

PLATSCHEL, HANS: Prologue to the catalogue of the exhibition at the Im Erker Gallery, St. Gallen, 1963.

DUPIN, JACQUES: *Antoni Tàpies, papiers et cartons*. Ed. Berggruen. Paris, 1963.

LÓPEZ SANCHO, LORENZO: *La pintura de Tàpies*. «La Vanguardia Española». Barcelona, May 13th, 1964.

TAILLANDIER, YVON: *Rencontre avec Tàpies en quête de l'homme pur*. «XXème Siècle», No. 24. Paris, 1964.

TEIXIDOR, JOAN: *Antoni Tàpies. Fustes, papers, cartons i collages*. Ed. Sala Gaspar. Barcelona, 1964.

MARCHIS, GIORGIO DE: Review of the exhibition at the Galleria La Tartaruga in Rome. «Art International». Lugano, April, 1964.

BONET, BLAI: *Tàpies*. Ed. Polígrafa. Barcelona, 1964.

CIRICI-PELLICER, ALEXANDRE: *Tàpies (1954-1964)*. Ed. Gustavo Gili, Barcelona, 1964.

(English edition: The Little Library of Art. Methuen, London, 1965).

OLIVER, JOAN: *Tros de Paper*. «Serra d'Or». Montserrat, January, 1965.

PELLSJÖ, OWE: *Antoni Tàpies och verklighten*. «NT-ÖD», Norrköping, December 29th, 1965.

PENROSE, ROLAND: Prologue to the catalogue of the exhibition at the Institute of Contemporary Arts. London, 1965.

GROHMANN, WILL: *Das Album St. Gallen von Antoni Tàpies*. «Frankfurter Allgemeine Zeitung». Frankfurt-am-Main, January 8th, 1966.

GAYA NUÑO, JUAN ANTONIO: *Tàpies al cabo de los años*. «Blanco y Negro». Madrid, March 12th, 1966.

PLUCHART, FRANÇOIS: *Tàpies, peintre aux dix mille suiveurs*. «Combat». Paris, June 7th, 1966.

GATELLIER, GILBERT: *Tàpies-Riopelle*. «Arts», No. 15. Paris, June 21st, 1966.

HAHN, OTTO: *Tàpies, laboureur du marbre*. «L'Express». Paris, June 20th-26th, 1966.

PLUCHART, FRANÇOIS: Prologue to the catalogue of the exhibition at the Galerie Jacques Verrié. Cannes, 1966.

WALDO SCHWARTZ, PAUL: *Tàpies: art finds poetic testament.* «The New York Times». New York, June 14th, 1966.

THE H. W. WILSON COMPANY: «Current Biography», No. 7, vol. 27. New York, July, 1966.

MORENO GALVÁN, JOSÉ MARÍA: *La pintura de Tàpies: nota para empezar a escribir.* Catalogue of the exhibition at the Galería Biosca. Madrid, 1966.

TAPIÉ, MICHEL: Prologue to the catalogue of the exhibition at the Galerie Stadler. Paris, 1966.

TAILLANDIER, YVON: *Tàpies ou le mur de la méditation.* «Connaissance des Arts». Paris, June, 1966.
Tàpies ou le mur qui rêve. «XXème siècle». Paris, December, 1966.

VILLAGÓMEZ: *Plásticos y Plastas: Tàpies.* «La Codorniz», No. 1,268. Madrid-Barcelona, 1966.

TEIXIDOR, JOAN: *Antoni Tàpies.* «Destino». Barcelona, February 4th, 1967.

PORCEL, BALTASAR: *Antoni Tàpies, testimoni de la sordidesa.* «Serra d'Or». Montserrat, February, 1967.

HERRMANNS, RALPH: *Antoni Tàpies det nya Spaniens målare.* «Svenska Dagbladet». Stockholm, March 19th, 1967.

EVANS, DAN: Prologue to the catalogue of the exhibition at the Martha Jackson Gallery. New York, April, 1967.

CIRLOT, JUAN EDUARDO: *El problema de Tàpies.* «La Vanguardia Española». Barcelona, May 6th, 1967.

GARCÍA-SOLER, JORDI: *Antoni Tàpies entrevistat.* «Tele-Estel», May 18th, 1967.

BORRÀS, MARIA LLUÏSA: *Antoni Tàpies.* «Taide». Helsinki, October, 1967.

BROSSA, JOAN & VICENS, FRANCESC: *Tàpies o l'escarnidor de diademes.* Fotoscop Gomis-Prat. Ed. Polígrafa. Barcelona, 1967.

TAPIÉ, MICHEL: *Avec Antoni Tàpies-Derrière le miroir.* Galerie Maeght. Paris, November, 1967.

DUPIN, JACQUES: *Devant Tàpies-Derrière le miroir.* Galerie Maeght. Paris, November, 1967.

MOULIN, RAOUL-JEAN: *Tàpies, présence de l'homme et du temps.* «Les Lettres Françaises», No. 1,208. Paris, 1967.

MICHEL, JACQUES: *Le réalisme d'Antoni Tàpies.* «Le Monde». Paris, November 10th, 1967.

COGNIAT, RAYMOND: *Du chevalet au mur.* «Le Figaro». Paris, November 16th, 1967.

DUPARC, CHRISTIANE: *Le dos au mur.* «Le Nouvel Observateur», No. 159, 1967

ARGAN, GIULIO CARLO: Prologue to the book *Antoni Tàpies.* Ed. Cappelli. Bologna, 1967.

GATT, GIUSEPPE: *Antoni Tàpies.* Ed. Cappelli. Bologna, 1967.

BARILLI, RENATO: *Antoni Tàpies.* Ed. Cappelli. Bologna, 1967.

CALVESI, MAURIZIO: *Antoni Tàpies.* Ed. Cappelli. Bologna, 1967.

MENNA, FILIBERTO: *Antoni Tàpies.* Ed. Cappelli. Bologna, 1967.

PONENTE, NELLO: *Antoni Tàpies.* Ed. Cappelli. Bologna, 1967.

TOMASSONI, ITALO: *Antoni Tàpies.* Ed. Cappelli. Bologna, 1967.

SEMPRONIO (ANDREU AVELÍ ARTÍS): *Tàpies en «Fotoscop».* «Tele-Exprés». Barcelona, November 28th, 1967.

JÄHNIG, DIETER: Prologue to the catalogue of the exhibition at the Museum of St. Gallen. St. Gallen, 1967.

RIBALTA, EUGENI: *Antoni Tàpies, un testimoni de solidaritat.* «Presència», No. 133. Gerona, 1968.

HOFMANN, WERNER: Prologue to the exhibition at the Museum des 20 Jahrhundert. Vienna, 1968.

SOTRIFFER, KRISTIAN: *Fragment als neue Dimension.* «Die Presse». Vienna, March 16th-17th, 1968.

GASSIOT-TALABOT, GERALD: *Paris II.* «OPUS», No. 5. Paris, 1968.

ALBEE, EDWARD: Prologue to the catalogue of the exhibition at the Martha Jackson Gallery. New York, 1968.

VALDOUBT, PIERRE: *Derrière le miroir.* Ed. Maeght. Paris, 1968.

ZÚÑIGA, ÁNGEL: *Tàpies.* «La Vanguardia Española». Barcelona, December 17th, 1968.

PLATTE, HANS: Prologue to the catalogue of the exhibition at the Hamburg and Cologne Museums.
Tàpies, un silence criant. «L'Art Vivant», No. 1. Paris, November, 1968.

FOSHEE, RUFUS: *Kline and Tàpies works.* «Greenwich Village». New York, November 28th, 1968.

RODRÍGUEZ AGUILERA, CESÁREO: *Antoni Tàpies o l'escarnidor de diademes.* «Papeles de Son Armadans», No. 148. Palma de Mallorca, June, 1968.

CASTILLEJO, JOSÉ: Catalogue of the exhibition at the Schmela Gallery, Düsseldorf, April-May, 1968.

CARDOSO, RAFAEL: *Das estructuras físicas e da renovação de materia na obra de Tàpies.* «Jornal do Comércio». Lisbon, 1968.

BOUDAILLE, GEORGES: *Antoni Tàpies.* «Cimaise». Paris, 1968.

MILLET, CATHERINE: *Tàpies, l'art pauvre en question.* «Les Lettres Françaises». Paris, October 29th, 1969.

LEVEQUE, J. J.: *Tàpies et l'art pauvre.* «Le Journal Nouveau». Paris, October 18th, 1969.

CONIL LACOSTE, MICHÈLE: *Antoni Tàpies: d'une gravité à l'autre.* «Le Monde». Paris, October 30th, 1969.

ABADIE, DANIEL: *Tàpies, les icônes du silence.* Idées «Galeries des Arts». Paris, October, 1969.

CIRICI-PELLICER, ALEXANDRE: *Tàpies, talp.* «Serra d'Or». Montserrat, December, 1969.

SUBOTIC, IRINA: *Umetnost materije Antonia Tàpiesa.* Catalogue of the exhibition at the Museum of Modern Art. Belgrade, 1969.

BORRÀS, MARIA LLUÏSA: *Antoni Tàpies, veinte años de camino.* «Destino», No. 1,638. Barcelona, February 22nd, 1969.

CIRLOT, J. E.: *Explicación de las pinturas de Tàpies.* «La Vanguardia Española». Barcelona, December 27th, 1969.

SAGARRA, JUAN DE: *El pintor.* «Tele-Exprés». Barcelona, July 7th, 1969.

SÁNCHEZ, LOLITA: *Un paseo con Tàpies por el Putxet.* «Tele-Exprés». Barcelona, July 5th, 1969.

GICH, JUAN: *Tàpies, Noviembre 1969.* «La Vanguardia Española». Barcelona, November 5th, 1969.

VALLÈS ROVIRA, JOSÉ: *Tàpies, de la tragedia a la felicidad.* «Tele-Exprés». Barcelona, November 14th, 1969.

BORRÀS, MARIA LLUÏSA: *Frègoli evocado por Brossa y Tàpies.* «Destino». Barcelona, November 15th, 1969.

MARSÀ, ÁNGEL: *Tàpies y la incomunicación.* «El Correo Catalán». Barcelona, November 15th, 1969.

CASTILLO, ALBERTO DEL: *Las exposiciones.* «Diario de Barcelona». Barcelona, November, 1969.

SANTOS TORROELLA, RAFAEL: *Tàpies o el muro infranqueable.* «El Noticiero Universal». Barcelona, November 12th, 1969.

DEL ARCO, MANUEL: *Mano a mano: Tàpies.* «La Vanguardia Española». Barcelona, November 20th, 1969.

MOLLOY, DOROTHY: *Catalan artist utilises basic matter as art.* «Irish Independent». Dublin, December 16th, 1969.

SINISGALLI, LEONARDO: *Lacrime e lutti nel Sud di Tàpies.* «Tempo». Milan, August 23rd, 1969.

TAPIÉ, MICHEL: *Antoni Tàpies.* Grandi Monografie Pittori e Scultori d'oggi, Fratelli Fabbri, Editori. Milan, 1969.

JIM: *Tàpies.* Revista «Vallès». Granollers (Barcelona), December 13th, 1969.

FRANQUI, CARLO: *Antoni Tàpies.* Prologue to the catalogue of the exhibition at the Galleria dell'Ariete. Milan, 1970.

CIRLOT, JUAN EDUARDO: *La obra actual de Tàpies*. «Goya», No. 94. Madrid, 1970.

CORREDOR MATHEOS, JOSÉ: *Las transformaciones de Frègoli*. «Bellas Artes 70», No. 4. Madrid, 1970.
Antoni Tàpies a Barcelona. «Le Arti», Year XX, No. 3. Milan, March, 1970.

CIRICI-PELLICER, ALEXANDRE: *Antoni Tàpies, testimoni del silenci*. Ed. Polígrafa. Barcelona, 1970.

GARCÍA-SOLER, JORDI: *El testimoni de Antoni Tàpies*. «La Vanguardia Española», Barcelona. January 14th, 1971.

WRITINGS AND DECLARATIONS OF ANTONI TÀPIES

En el taller de los artistas, statements made to Sebastià Gasch and printed in «Destino», June 11th, 1955.

Yo he venido... lecture given at the «Universidad Internacional Menéndez y Pelayo», Santander, 1955. Published in «Cuadernos Hispano-Americanos», No. 70, Madrid, October, 1955. (German translation in «Blätter und Bilder», No. 6, Vienna, January-February, 1960; published again in *Theorien zeitgenössischer Malerei* by J. Claus, published by Rotwot, Hamburg, 1963 (Italian edition: Il Saggiatore, Milan, 1967).

Mano a mano, statements made to Del Arco in an interview for «La Vanguardia Española», Barcelona, December, 5th, 1958.
Replies to a questionnaire compiled by J. R. Menéndez in «Universidad», No. 4 (year II), Barcelona, 1959.

Visto y oído, statements made to Del Arco in an interview for «Destino», Barcelona, February 13th, 1960.

Conversaciones sobre el arte actual, replies in an interview by R. Santos Torroella for «El Noticiero Universal», Barcelona, April 5th, 1961.
Text for the catalogue «Paintings in America 1959-60», Gres Gallery and Martha Jackson Gallery, Washington and New York, 1961.
Replies to a questionnaire (The *Cuestionario Marcel Proust*) by L. Permanyer, in «Destino», Barcelona, December 29th, 1962.

Über mein Schaffen, catalogue for the exhibition at the Im Erker Gallery, St. Gallen, July, 1963.

Mosaico parisiense, statements made to L. López Sancho in an interview for «La Vanguardia Española», Barcelona, May 31st, 1964.

Rencontre avec Tàpies en quête de l'homme pur, statements made to Yvon Taillandier in an interview for «XXème Siècle», Paris, December, 1964.

Arp, catalogue for the Hans Arp exhibition at the Im Erker Gallery, St. Gallen, October, 1966.

El joc de saber mirar, for the children's magazine «Cavall Fort», published by the Catechistic Secretariats of Vich, Solsona and Gerona, January, 1967.

Antoni Tàpies, testimoni, replies to a questionnaire by B. Porcel in «Serra d'Or», Montserrat, February, 1967.

Arte y funcionarios, «Destino», Barcelona, November 2nd, 1968. A résumé of this text was published in «La Quinzaine», Paris, December, 1968, under the title *Sommes-nous tous des monstres?*, as well as in the review «Studio International», London, March, 1970.

Antoni Tàpies, autobiográfico, statements made to B. Porcel and printed in «Destino», Barcelona.

La academia de lo social y lo implicado, «Destino», No. 1652, Barcelona, May 31st, 1969.

Un paseo con Tàpies por el Putxet, statements made to Lolita Sánchez and printed in «Tele-Exprés», Barcelona, July 5th, 1969.

Intranscendencia estética y conformismo, «Destino», No. 1684, Barcelona, January 10th, 1970.

Cultura per al poble, «Serra d'Or», Montserrat, February, 1970.

La pràctica de l'art, in the collection «Cinc d'Oros» of Edicions Ariel, Barcelona, 1970. It contains the following works: *Art-idea, La vocació i la forma, Declaracions, La tradició i els seus enemics en l'art actual, Visita a Picasso, Recordant Jean Arp, La innocència de Miró, El joc de saber mirar, Art i funcionaris, Un art per als rics?, Comunicació sobre el mur, L'acedèmia del social i de l'implicat, Intranscendència estètica i conformisme, Estafes culturals, Sobre uns textos de Marcuse, Res no és mesquí*.

FILMS ABOUT TÀPIES

Antoni Tàpies, a film by Rolph Wohlin produced for Swedish Television. Stockholm, 1967.

Antoni Tàpies, a film by Clovis Prevost, with advice from Joan Brossa and music by Carlos Santos. Produced by the Maeght Foundation. Paris, 1968.

El pintor Antoni Tàpies, a film by J. A. Acarín produced for Czech Television. Prague, 1969.

EXHIBITIONS

INDIVIDUAL EXHIBITIONS

Galeries Laietanes. Catalogue published in an issue of «Dau al Set», together with the *Oracle sobre Antoni Tàpies* by Joan Brossa. Short monograph: *Tàpies o el Dau modern de Versalles* by J. J. Tharrats (with reproductions). Barcelona, October 28th-November 10th, 1950.

Galeries Laietanes, Barcelona, May 3rd-23rd, 1952.

Marshall Field Art Gallery, Chicago, April 4th-May 1st, 1953.

Galería Biosca, Madrid, April 21st-May 5th, 1953.

Martha Jackson Gallery. Catalogue with presentation by Gordon B. Washburn. New York, October 28th-November 14th, 1953.

Galeries Laietanes. Publication of an issue of «Dau al Set»: *Tàpies o la transverberació*, by A. Cirici-Pellicer. Illustrated catalogue. Barcelona, May 1st-15th, 1954.

Club 49. Underground rooms of the Sala Gaspar. Barcelona, May, 1955.

Galerie Stadler. Catalogue with a prologue by Michel Tapié. Publications of *Tàpies et l'œuvre complète* by Michel Tapié (with reproductions). Paris, February, 1956.

Club 49. Sala Gaspar. Barcelona, November, 1956.

Galerie Stadler. Catalogue with a prologue by Michel Tapié. Paris, June 14th-July 13th, 1957.

Schmela Gallery. Düsseldorf, 1957.

Martha Jackson Gallery. Illustrated catalogue. New York, February 21st-March 14th, 1957.

Galleria dell'Ariete. Catalogue with a text by Jacques Dupin. Milan, May-June 1958.

Individual room in the pavilion at the 29th International Biennale of Art. Venice, 1958.

Martha Jackson Gallery. New York, February 24th-March 21st, 1959.

Gres Gallery. Washington, 1959.

Galerie Stadler. Paris, April-May, 1959.

Kunsthalle (with Alechinsky, Messagier, Moser). Illustrated catalogue with prologue by Franz Mayer. Berne, September 26th-October 25th, 1959.

Van der Loo Gallery (with Antonio Saura). Catalogue with reproductions. Munich, 1959.

Sala Gaspar. Barcelona, February 7th-27th, 1960.

Museo de Arte. Bilbao, April, 1960.

Martha Jackson Gallery. Lithographs. New York, March 22nd-April 7th, 1960.

Galleria dell'Ariete. Lithographs (with Dubuffet). Milan, March, 1960.

Martha Jackson Gallery. Catalogue illustrated with pictures by Tàpies collected in America between 1959 and 1960. Text by Antoni Tàpies. Prologue by James Johnson Sweeney. New York, 1961.

Gres Gallery (the same exhibition as at the Martha Jackson Gallery). Washington, 1961.

Galerie Stadler. Catalogue with reproductions. Paris, June 20th-July 20th, 1961.

Museo Nacional. Instituto Torcuato Di Tella. Illustrated catalogue with presentation by Giulio Carlo Argan: *La superstizione di Tàpies*. Buenos Aires, August, 1961.

Blanche Gallery. Stockholm, 1961.

Otto Stangl Gallery (with Sam Francis). Munich, 1961.

Rudolf Zwirner Gallery. Essen, April, 1961.

Kestner-Gesellschaft. Anthological exhibition. Illustrated catalogue with a prologue by Werner Schmalenbach. Hanover, 1962.

Guggenheim Museum. Anthological exhibition of works done between 1945 and 1961. Illustrated catalogue with a prologue by Lawrence Alloway, bibliography and list of exhibitions. New York, March-April, 1962.

Kunsthaus. Illustrated catalogue with a prologue by Eduard Hüttinger. Zurich, April 28th-June 3rd, 1962.

Museo Nacional de Bellas Artes. Illustrated catalogue with a presentation in Spanish by Joan Teixidor and one in English by Lawrence Alloway. Caracas, 1962.

Galleria Il Segno. Lithographs. Catalogue with a text by Lorenza Trucchi. Rome, 1962.

Galerie Pierre. Stockholm, 1962.

Art Museum. Pasadena, 1963.

Galerie Berggruen. *Papiers et cartons*. Illustrated catalogue with a text by Jacques Dupin. Paris, 1963.

Im Erker Gallery. Illustrated catalogue with texts by Hans Platchek and Antoni Tàpies. Biographical note and list of exhibitions. St. Gallen, 1963.

International Center of Aesthetic Research. 23 lithographs. Turin, November, 1963.

Gallerie Notizie. Catalogue with a text by Tàpies and a biographical note. Turin, November 5th-December 15th, 1963.

Martha Jackson Gallery. Catalogue with a text by Martha Jackson and an original lithograph by the artist. New York, 1963.

Galleria La Tartaruga. Catalogue with a text by Antoni Tàpies: biographical note, list of exhibitions and bibliography. Rome, February, 1964.

Rudolf Zwirner Gallery. *Cartons et collages*. Cologne, January 10th-February 10th, 1964.

Galerie Stadler. Paris, May 12th-June 9th, 1964.

Buren Gallery. Catalogue with a text by Lasse Söderberg. Stockholm, October-November, 1964.

Moss Gallery. Toronto, October 17th-31st, 1964.

Galerie Agnes Lefort. Montreal, November 18th-December 1st, 1964.

Sala Gaspar. *Papers, cartons, fustes i collages de 1946 a 1964*. Publication of the book with text by Joan Teixidor. Barcelona, November 7th-27th, 1964.

Galerie Bernard. Paintings and lithographs. Solothurn, February 19th-March 23rd, 1965.

Van der Loo Gallery. Gouaches, drawings and collages. Illustrated catalogue, with a text by Antoni Tàpies. Munich, April, 1965.

Rudolf Zwirner Gallery. Paintings from 1948 to 1964. Cologne, April, 1965.

Institute of Contemporary Arts. Catalogue with an introduction by R. Penrose. London, June 3rd-July 3rd, 1965.

Im Erker Gallery. St. Gallen Album (10 lithographs). St. Gallen, June 26th-July 10th, 1965.

Sala Gaspar. *Novel·la* by Joan Brossa. Gouaches and drawings. Barcelona, November 20th-December 14th, 1965.

Cercle Artístic. 12 lithographs. Catalogue with a text by A. Cirici-Pellicer. Manresa, January 15th-30th, 1966.

Galería Biosca. Illustrated catalogue with a text by José M.ª Moreno Galván. Madrid, February 1st-28th, 1966.

Galerie Stadler. Illustrated catalogue with a text by Michel Tapié. Paris, June 7th-July 9th, 1966.

Centre Culturel (with Clavé and Pelayo). Toulouse, June-July, 1966.

Galerie Jacques Verrière. Catalogue with a text by François Pluchart. Cannes, September, 1966.

Buren Gallery. 25 gouaches and collages. Stockholm, October, 1966.

Martha Jackson Gallery. Recent paintings. Catalogue with a text by Dan Evans. New York, April, 1967.

Kunstmuseum. *Das gesamte graphische Werk*. Catalogue with a text by Dieter Jähnig. St. Gallen, June-July, 1967.

Galerie Maeght. Catalogue with texts by Michel Tapié and Jacques Dupin. Paris, November, 1967.

Sala Gaspar. Gouaches for the presentation of the book *Antoni Tàpies o l'escarnidor de diademes*. Barcelona, December, 1967.

Museum des 20 Jahrhunderts. Anthological exhibition organized by Werner Hofmann. Illustrated catalogue with a prologue by Hofmann himself and Tàpies. Vienna, March 16th-April 21st, 1968.

Im Erker Gallery. Presentation of the book *La nuit grandissante*, poems by Jacques Dupin, lithographs by Tàpies. St. Gallen, March, 1968.

Librairie La Hune. Presentation of the book *La nuit grandissante* and graphic works. Paris, April, 1968.

Kunstverein. Anthological exhibition presented by Hans Platte. Hamburg, May-June, 1968.

Kunstverein. Anthological exhibition. The same catalogue. Cologne, July-August, 1968.

Martha Jackson Gallery. Illustrated catalogue with a text by Edward Albee. New York, November, 1968.

Galerie Maeght. *Papiers et collages*. Illustrated catalogue with a text by Pierre Valboudt. Paris, December, 1968.

Schmela Gallery. Paintings and gouaches. Düsseldorf, 1968.

Galerie Maeght. Recent paintings and collages. Illustrated catalogue with a poem by Joan Brossa. Paris, October, 1969.

Sala Gaspar. Paintings, tapestries, collages and lithographs of the book *Frègoli*, carried out with Joan Brossa. Barcelona, November, 1969.

Galerie Stadler. Paintings previous to 1966. Paris, May-June, 1969.

Special room at the Engraving Biennale. Liubiana, 1969.

Museum of Modern Art. Graphic work. Illustrated catalogue *Antoni Tàpies-Jasper Johns*. Belgrade, September, 1969.

Kunstverein. The complete graphic work from the *Dr. Friedrich and M. Pilar Herlt* Collection. Kassel, February-March, 1969.

Národní Galerie. 28 graphic works (with Hartung, Johns and Hozo). Prague, 1969.

Galleria dell'Ariete. Recent paintings and collages. Catalogue with a prologue by Carlo Franqui. Milan, June-July, 1970.

Galerie Bleue, Gouaches and collages. Stockholm, October-November, 1970.

Martha Jackson Gallery. New York, November, 1970.

Galerie Maeght. Paintings and objects. Zurich, March-April, 1971.

Galerie Hachette. Lithographs. London, February-March, 1971.

COLLECTIVE EXHIBITIONS

Saló d'Octubre. Barcelona, 1948.

Un aspecte de la pintura catalana. French Institute of Barcelona, 1949.
Salón de los Once. Madrid. 1949.
Saló d'Octubre. Barcelona, 1949.
Galería Sapi. Palma de Mallorca, 1949.

French Institute of Barcelona, 1950.
Las once mejores obras de arte del año. Madrid, 1950.
The Pittsburgh International Exhibition of Contemporary Painting. Department of Fine Arts, Carnegie Institute. Pittsburgh, 1950.

«Dau al Set» retrospective exhibition, Sala Caralt. Barcelona, 1951.
1st Hispano-American Biennale of Art. Madrid, 1951.
Saló d'Octubre. Barcelona, 1951.
Salón de los Once. Madrid, 1951.

26th Esposizione Biennale Internazionale d'Arte. Venice, 1952.

Salón de los Once. Madrid, 1952.
Galería Sur, Santander, 1952.
The Pittsburgh International Exhibition of Contemporary Painting. Department of Fine Arts, Carnegie Institute. Pittsburgh, 1952.

2nd Biennale of the Museum of Modern Art. Sao Paulo, 1953.
Museo Nacional. Bogotá, 1953.
2nd Hispano-American Biennale of Art. Havana, 1953.
University of Panama. Panama, 1953.
Pintores Españoles. Santiago de Chile, 1953.
Salón de los Once. Madrid, 1953.
Las once mejores obras de arte del año. Academia Breve, Madrid, 1953.
La pintura catalana actual. Barcelona, 1953.

27th Esposizione Biennale Internazionale d'Arte. Venice, 1954.
Saló del Jazz. Barcelona, 1954.
Reality and Fantasy 1900-1954. Walker Art Center. Minneapolis, 1954.
Nebraska Art Association, «64th Annual Exhibition». Lincoln, 1954.
Milwaukee Art Institute. Milwaukee, 1954.
Wadsworth Atheneum. Hartford, 1954.

Phases de l'Art Contemporain, Galerie Creuze, Paris, 1955.
Galerie du Dragon. Paris, 1955.
Galerie Stadler. Paris, 1955.
3rd Hispano-American Biennale of Art. Barcelona, 1955.
The Pittsburgh International Exhibition of Contemporary Painting, Department of Fine Arts, Carnegie Institute. Pittsburgh, 1955.

Expressions et Structures, Galerie Stadler. Paris, 1956.
The Arts Council of Great Britain. London, 1956.
Whitworth Art Gallery. Manchester, 1956.
28th Esposizione Biennale Internazionale d'Arte. Venice, 1956.

4th Biennale of the Museum of Modern Art. São Paulo, 1957.
50 ans d'art abstrait, Galerie Creuze. Paris, 1957.
Salon de Mai. Paris, 1957.
Galerie Stadler. Paris, 1957.
The Exploration of Form, Arthur Tooth and Sons Ltd. London, 1957.
Martha Jackson Gallery. New York, 1957.
Rome-New York, Art Foundation. Rome, 1957.
Exposición del Arte Otro. Barcelona and Madrid, 1957.
Premio Lissone. Milan, 1957.

Some paintings from the E. J. Power Collection, The Institute of Contemporary Arts. London, 1958.
Galerie Stadler. Paris, 1958.
Osaka Festival. Osaka, 1958.
The Exploration of Form, Arthur Tooth and Sons Ltd. London, 1958.
29th Esposizione Biennale Internazionale d'Arte (individual room). Venice, 1958.
Salon de Mai. Paris, 1958.
Martha Jackson Gallery. New York, 1958.
The Pittsburgh International Exhibition of Contemporary Painting and Sculpture, Department of Fine Arts, Carnegie Institute. Pittsburgh, 1958.
L'art du XXème siècle, Palais des Expositions. Charleroi, 1958.
Neue Malerei in Frankreich, Städt, Kunstsammlungen (Rathaus). Soest, 1958.

Documenta II. Kassel, 1959.
Premio Lissone. Milan, 1959.
Arte Nuova, International Exhibitions of Painting and Sculpture, Circolo degli Artisti, Palazzo Graneri, Turin, 1959.
County Museum, Los Angeles (in 1960: The Baltimore Museum of Art), 1959.
Antoni Tàpies & Alberto Burri, Galerie Beyeler. Basle, 1959.
Salon de Mai. Paris, 1959.

Tàpies & Saura, Van der Loo Gallery. Munich, 1959.
4 Maler, Kunsthalle. Berne, 1959.
European Art Today, Institute of Arts. Minneapolis, 1959.
Festival de Torino. Turin, 1959.
Museum of Art, San Francisco; National Gallery of Canada, Ottawa; French and Co., New York, 1959.
Recent Acquisitions, The Museum of Modern Art. New York, 1961.
North Carolina Museum of Art. Raleigh, 1959.
15 Maler in Paris, Kölnischer Kunstverein. Cologne, 1959.
Inaugural, Guggenheim. New York, 1959.
Antagonismes, Musée des Arts Décoratifs. Paris, 1960.
Stadtisches Museum. Leverkusen, 1960.
Four Internationals, Moss Gallery. Toronto, 1960.
La nueva pintura de España, Arthur Tooth and Sons Ltd. London, 1960.
Galerie Stadler. Paris, 1960.
Tàpies et Dubuffet, Galleria dell'Ariete. Milan, 1960.
Before Picasso-After Miró, The Solomon R. Guggenheim Museum. New York, 1960.
New Spanish Painting and Sculpture, The Museum of Modern Art. New York, 1960.
The Pursuit and Measure of Excellence, 1960 Art Festival, Weatherspoon Art Gallery, The Woman's College of the University of North Carolina. Greensboro, 1960.
Martha Jackson Gallery. New York, 1960.
New Forms-New Media, Martha Jackson Gallery. New York, 1960.
Jonge Kunst uit de Collection Dotremont, Stedelijk van Abbe Museum, Eindhoven, 1960.
Salon de Mai. Paris, 1960.
Neue Malerei, Städtische Galerie. Munich, 1960.
Picasso, Miró, Tàpies, Saura, Chillida, Ingelheim/R., 1960.
Exhibition at the Instituto Torcuato di Tella, Museo Nacional de Bellas Artes. Buenos Aires, 1961.
International Exhibition of Graphic Art. Tokyo, 1961.
Antoni Tàpies & Sam Francis, Otto Stangl Gallery. Munich, 1961.
New Europeans, Contemporary Arts Museum. Houston, 1961.
Recent Acquisitions, The Museum of Modern Art. New York, 1961.
The Pittsburgh International Exhibition of Contemporary Painting and Sculpture, Department of Fine Arts, Carnegie Institute. Pittsburgh, 1961.
Arte e Contemplazione, Palazzo Grassi. Venice, 1961.
Salon de Mai. Paris, 1961.
One Hundred Paintings from the G. David Thompson Collection, Guggenheim Museum. New York, 1961.
Kompas, Stedelijk van Abbe Museum. Eindhoven, 1961.
Modern Spanish Painting, The Arts Council of Great Britain, The Tate Gallery. London, 1962.
Contemporary Spanish Painting and Sculpture, Marlborough Fine Arts, Ltd. London, 1962.
Salon de Mai. Paris, 1962.
The 30th Exhibition of the Japan Print Association. Tokyo, 1962.
L'incontro di Torino, Palazzo della Promotrice al Valentino. Turin, 1962.
Salon de Mai. Paris, 1963.
I Salon de Galeries Pilote. Lausanne, 1963.
Forum. Ghent, 1963.
The Dunn International. The Beaverbrook Art Gallery, Fredericktown and The Tate Gallery, London, 1963.

Opere Scelte, Galleria Notizie. Turin, 1963.
Galerie Stadler. Paris, 1963.
Guggenheim International Award, Guggenheim Museum. New York, 1964.
Documenta III. Kassel, 1964.
Painting and Sculpture of a Decade, Calouste Gulbenkian Foundation, The Tate Gallery. London, 1964.
Métaphysique de la Matière. Galerie Stadler. Paris, 1964.
The Pittsburgh International Exhibition, Carnegie Institute. Pittsburgh, 1964.
España Libre, Rimini, Florence, Reggio, Emilia, Venice, Ferrara, 1964.
Salon de Mai, Paris, 1964.
Salon de Mai. Paris, 1965.
4 Internationals - Burri, Nevelson, Tàpies, Van Leyden, Martha Jackson Gallery. New York, 1965.
Les oeuvres d'art integrées dans l'architecture, Alice Pauli Gallery, London, 1965.
International 65, The J. L. Hudson Gallery. Detroit, 1965.
40 Key Artists of the Mid-20th Century, Institute of Art. Detroit, 1965.
Weiss-Weiss, Schmela Gallery. Düsseldorf, 1965.
Contemporary Spanish Artists, The Bundy Art Gallery. Waitsfield (Vermont), 1965.
Galerie Stadler. Paris, 1965.
Salon de Mai. Paris, 1966.
Métaphysique de la Matière, Palais des Beaux Arts. Charleroi, 1966.
Spazio, forma e colore all'Università di San Gallo, Palazzo Ducale. Venice, 1966.
6th Biennale of Menton, 1966.
Homage to Antonio Machado, The Spanish Refugee Aid, Inc. New York, 1966.
Architektur und Kunst, Kunstverein. Biel, 1966.
Salon de Mai. Paris, 1967.
Salon des Réalités Nouvelles. Paris, 1967.
Dix ans d'art vivant, 1955-1965, Maeght Foundation. St. Paul de Vence, 1967.
Pittsburgh International. U.S.A., 1967.
7th International Engraving Exhibition. Liubiana (Yugoslavia), 1967.
Exposició Homenatge a Picasso, Hospital of the Holy Cross. Barcelona, 1967.
Salón de Mayo, Havana, 1967.
Rosc 1967, *The poetry of vision*. Dublin, 1967.
Spanische Kunst der Gegenwart, Kunsthalle. Nuremberg, 1967.
Vom Bauhaus bis zur Gegenwart, Kunstverein. Hamburg, 1967.
Kent State University, 2nd Invitational Exhibition of Contemporary Painting and Sculpture, 1968.
Spansk Kunst i dag, Louisiana Museum. Humlebaek (Denmark), 1968.
Salon de Mai. Paris, 1968.
L'art vivant, 1965-1968, Maeght Foundation. St Paul de Vence, 1968.
Peintres européens d'aujourd'hui, Musée des Arts Décoratifs. Paris, 1968.
Documenta IV. Kassel, 1968.
Menschenbilder, Kunsthalle. Darmstadt, 1968.
Artistes espagnols: Gris, Picasso, Miró, Tàpies, Chillida, Galeria Beyeler. Basle, 1969.
Salon de Mai. Paris, 1969.
Miró otro, Architectural Association. Barcelona, 1969.
Art espagnol d'aujourd'hui, Musée Rath. Geneva, 1969.
Sammlung Sprengel II, 1965-1969, Kestner-Museum. Hanover, 1969.
Al voltant de Jacques Dupin, Wünsche Gallery. Bonn, 1970.
Carnegie International. Pittsburgh, 1970.
Selections from the Guggenheim Museum. New York, 1900-1970.

MUSEUMS AND INSTITUTIONS OPEN TO THE PUBLIC WHICH CONTAIN WORKS BY TÀPIES

AMSTERDAM:	Stedelijk Museum.
BALTIMORE:	Museum of Art.
BARCELONA:	Museum of Modern Art.
	Bar and Lounge of the Town Hall.
BASLE:	Kunstmuseum.
BERLIN:	Kunstmuseum.
BOGOTÁ:	Museo Nacional.
BOLOGNA:	Museo d'Arte Moderna.
BONN:	Kunstmuseum.
BOSTON:	Museum of Modern Art.
BUENOS AIRES:	Instituto di Tella.
BUFFALO:	The Albright-Knox Art Gallery.
COLOGNE:	Kunstmuseum.
CUENCA:	Museo de Arte Abstracto.
DÜSSELDORF:	Kunstsammlung Nordrhein-Westfalen.
EINDHOVEN:	Stedelijk van Abbe Museum.
GÖTEBORG:	Konstmuseum.
HAMBURG:	Kunsthalle.
HANOVER:	Niedersächsische Landesgalerie.
HOUSTON (TEXAS):	Museum of Fine Arts.
ITHACA:	White Memorial Gallery.
LONDON:	The Tate Gallery.
MADRID:	Museo de Arte Contemporáneo.
MILAN:	Museo Lissone.
MONTREAL:	Museum of Contemporary Art.
NEW YORK:	The Museum of Modern Art.
	The Solomon R. Guggenheim Museum.
PARIS:	Centre National d'Art Contemporain.
PITTSBURGH:	Carnegie Institute.
ROME:	Galleria Nazionale d'Arte Moderna.
ROTTERDAM:	Museum Boymans-van Beuningen.
SÃO PAULO:	Museo de Arte Moderno.
SION:	Capuchin Monastery.
ST. GALLEN:	Kunsthaus.
	Handels Hochschule.
ST. LOUIS (MISSOURI):	The Washington University.
ST. PAUL DE VENCE:	Fondation Maeght.
STOCKHOLM:	Museum of Modern Art.
TURIN:	International Center of Aesthetic Research.
VENICE:	Museo d'Arte Moderna.
VIENNA:	Museum des 20 Jahrhunderts.
WINTERTHUR:	Kunsthaus.
ZURICH:	Kunsthaus.